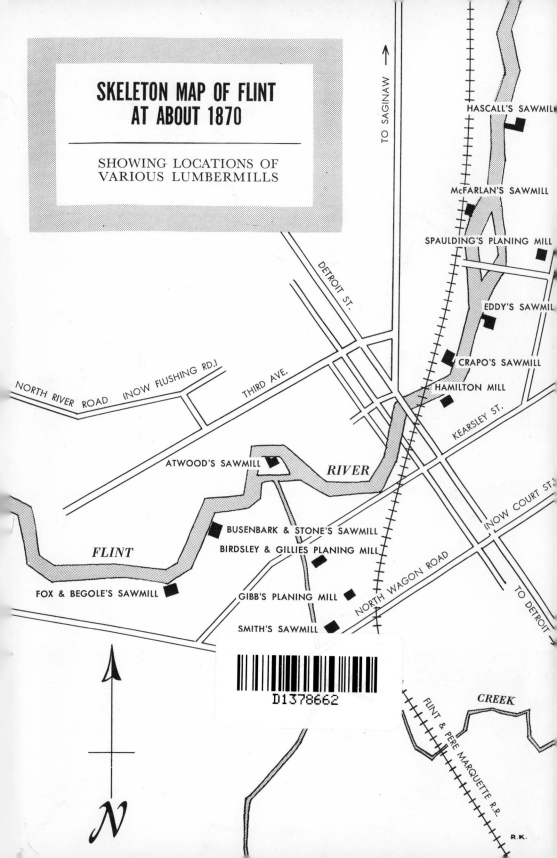

SKELETON MAP OF FLINT AT ABOUT 1870

SHOWING LOCATIONS OF
VARIOUS LUMBERMILLS

TO SAGINAW →

HASCALL'S SAWMILL

McFARLAN'S SAWMILL

SPAULDING'S PLANING MILL

DETROIT ST.

EDDY'S SAWMILL

CRAPO'S SAWMILL

HAMILTON MILL

KEARSLEY ST.

NORTH RIVER ROAD (NOW FLUSHING RD.)

THIRD AVE.

ATWOOD'S SAWMILL

RIVER

(NOW COURT ST.)

BUSENBARK & STONE'S SAWMILL

BIRDSLEY & GILLIES PLANING MILL

FLINT

FOX & BEGOLE'S SAWMILL

GIBB'S PLANING MILL

NORTH WAGON ROAD

TO DETROIT

SMITH'S SAWMILL

D1378662

CREEK

FLINT & PERE MARQUETTE R.R.

𝒩

R.K.

LUMBERMAN FROM FLINT

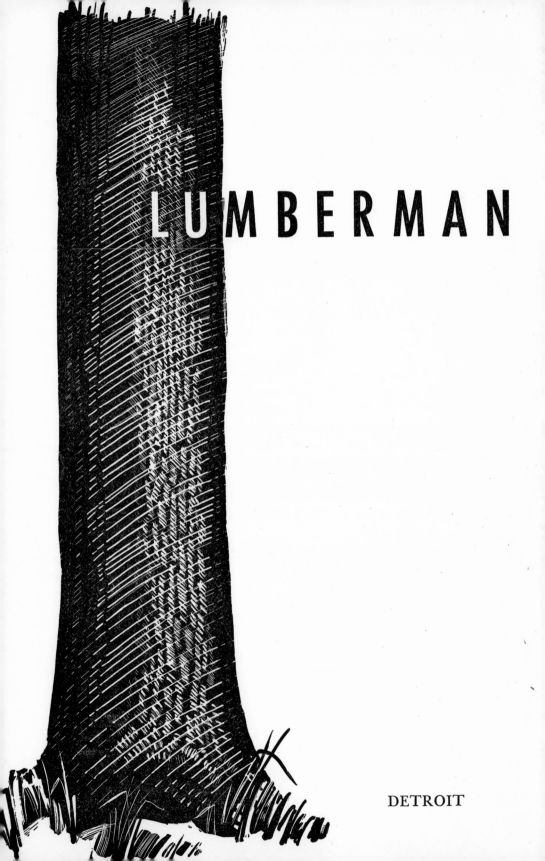

LUMBERMAN

DETROIT

FROM FLINT

THE MICHIGAN CAREER OF
HENRY H. CRAPO
1855 - 1869

MARTIN DEMING LEWIS
Assistant Professor of History
Baldwin-Wallace College

WAYNE STATE UNIVERSITY PRESS   1958

Library of Congress Catalog Card Number: 57-13065
Copyright, 1958, Wayne State University Press, Detroit 2

PREFACE

The basic theme of this book is the surging development of the American economy in the middle years of the nineteenth century, a process which we see here reflected in the life story of one man. The particular focus of the book arises from the fact that it was conceived and executed primarily as a study in business history, an approach to economic history concerned not so much with the aggregate results of economic development as with the process by which some of these results were achieved in an individual business concern. Here we can see the problems of business enterprise in detail, as they were actually worked out in real life.

In tracing the career of Henry Crapo as a lumberman in Michigan, we see something of the dramatic growth of that state's economy, a growth which was shared by other states of the Old Northwest and which played no small part in determining the outcome of the Civil War. We can also find in his career much that throws light on the development of the lumber industry itself.

Paradoxically, although Michigan was the leading lumber producer of the nation from the Civil War to the end of the nineteenth century, no adequate history of that industry in the state has yet been written. I hope that this study will help stimulate interest in that story and prove of some value for a general history of Michigan lumbering.

Finally, since we are dealing with the life of a particular individual, we cannot overlook the fact that he had interests and influence extending beyond the limits of his business affairs. Crapo's role in Michigan politics is a fascinating one; a virtual newcomer to the state, he was drafted by his party to serve in positions of ever-greater leadership in the political affairs of Michigan.

I should like to express my appreciation for the generous cooperation of Dr. L. G. Vander Velde and Dr. F. Clever Bald and their staff at the Michigan Historical Collections in making the Crapo Manuscripts available for research. The staff of the Burton Historical Collection at the Detroit Public Library was also most helpful. My manuscript has been read both by Dr. Vander Velde and by Henry D. Brown, Director of the Detroit Historical Museum, and I am grateful for their valuable comments.

Certainly I should be remiss if I failed to speak of my great obligation to the history faculty of the University of Chicago, at whose hands I received my initiation into the historian's craft. I am deeply indebted to Professor William T. Hutchinson, both for his sponsorship of this work in its original form as a doctoral dissertation at the university, and for the inspiration during many pleasant classroom hours of his precise scholarship and his keenly analytical approach to historical problems. The untimely death of Professor R. Richard Wohl has made it impossible for me to acknowledge as I should have wished the generous interest which he took in the progress of this book. His friendly advice and criticism did much to improve my manuscript, and indeed, to make this volume possible. These few lines can do little to express my obligation to him.

Mr. William W. Crapo of Detroit and Mrs. Catherine Crapo Bullard of New Bedford, great-grandchildren of the subject of this book, have given valuable assistance in many ways, especially in locating illustrations. In these acknowledgments, another member of the Crapo family deserves recognition as well. The late Henry H. Crapo of New Bedford, who bore the same name as his distinguished grandfather, was responsible for the deposit of the Crapo Manuscripts in the Michigan Historical Collections without restriction on their use for scholarly research. In thus opening to students of economic history a large body of confidential business and personal records, Mr. Crapo set an enviable example which it is hoped many others will follow.

Needless to say, I alone am responsible for the manner in which the story has been presented.

M. D. L.

CONTENTS

ILLUSTRATIONS

INTRODUCTION

I

By the 1850's, Henry Howland Crapo might quite properly have felt that he had already made his mark in life. To all outward appearances he was at the zenith of his career. He was but four years younger than the nineteenth century itself and was solidly established as one of the more substantial citizens of New Bedford, Massachusetts, the New England whaling town that had been his home for most of his adult life. He was not rich, even by the standards of the time, but he was comfortably well-to-do, and he held the respect and confidence of the business community of New Bedford.

His own role in the business life of that thriving port had many and varied aspects. He was secretary (and *de facto* manager) of the Commercial Mutual Marine Insurance Company, a concern whose activities were of vital importance to the town's leading industry. His Wasemequia Nurseries was a flourishing commercial enterprise, an outgrowth of his hobby of fruit-tree culture. More important from a business standpoint, he was deeply engaged in real estate operations in New Bedford and in the Middle West, both on his own account and as agent for eastern capitalists with surplus funds to invest. Finally, he took an active interest in the whaling industry itself, to the extent of part ownership in a number of whaling vessels. One of these even bore his name, the bark *Henry H. Crapo.*

In the year 1855 he was fifty-one years of age, and seemingly the time was fast approaching when he would step back from the active pursuit of business affairs and relax into a comfortable retirement. Appearances, however, would in his case have been most deceiving. In the closing months of that year Crapo stood on the threshold of an entirely new and different career which would prove to be his life's great adventure.

This drastic upset of his established way of life was precipitated by his purchase of 12,000 acres of timber land out west in Michigan. His plan was simple. As the owner of a large tract of pine, he intended to proceed at once with the conversion of the trees into lumber. The end result, he confidently expected, would be a substantial profit. Business ventures were nothing new to Crapo, and there is no reason to suspect that he thought of this one as anything but prudent. Yet it was fraught with consequences of which he had not the slightest expectation.

His first few years in Michigan caused him bitter anxiety and disappointment, and brought him perilously close to bankruptcy. Time and again he reproached himself for ever getting involved in the lumber business. Only after years of the most intense struggle did his efforts begin to pay off. But before events had run their course he had won wealth and prestige as one of Michigan's foremost lumbermen—and his brief but spectacular Michigan career was capped by two terms as chief executive of his adopted state.

The last fourteen years of Crapo's life were dramatic indeed. The very fact that he could embark on such an adventure when already past middle age, and carry it through so successfully, suggests that he was an unusual individual. He was. Of all the words which might be chosen to epitomize his personality, one stands out sharply: *drive*. He was a man of energy, purpose, and determination. His one great ambition was to satisfy himself that he had done a good job.

In forsaking the staid environment of New Bedford for a new life in Michigan, Henry Crapo was joining the vast migration that spread westward across the American continent in the middle years of the nineteenth century. All sorts of men were part of this movement. The great majority were farmers, leaving behind worn-out acres in the East for the fertile virgin farmlands of the Mississippi Valley. Others were professional men—doctors, lawyers, preachers, teachers—seeking to build their careers in the young and growing communities of the Middle West. And then there were the businessmen, bringing with them capital and skill in economic organization and applying these resources for their own profit and for the development of the riches of the new region. All shared in the drama of one of the greatest mass movements of population known to history. Each had in its own sphere a special kind of drama as well.

In the businessman's career, the dusty categories of economic theory came to life. The entrepreneurial decision, the investment of capital, the planning of production, the search for markets—these were not mere words, but the flesh and bones of a very human struggle to get something done.

The businessman, of course, was far from being the only participant in the process of production. It would be absurd, for example, to ignore the labors of the workers who manned his enterprises, and equally so to forget how many Americans in the mid-nineteenth century were neither employees nor employers, but rather worked for themselves on farms or in their own workshops. But it was the businessman who was the active factor in economic development. His was the critically important role of organizing and directing the tremendous expansion of productive activities that was changing the face of the American continent.

Henry Crapo would have scoffed at the notion that he was an agent of progress. He was in business to make a profit. Yet the forces which have created modern America were set in motion by the activity of countless men who, like Crapo, were striving to further their own fortunes by establishing and developing new economic enterprises.

This process has not received the attention it deserves from historians. We know far too little of how businessmen secured their capital, how they organized their production, how they found markets for the goods they produced. When we know more of these matters, we will have a better understanding of our economic development as a nation. Much of the early history of business in America still lies locked in the untold stories of enterprises long gone and forgotten. In this book we will be bringing one such story to life. Henry Crapo's venture in the pine timber country of Michigan was, of course, the unique experience of a particular individual, but it nevertheless typifies a vital part of our national experience.

The great handicap facing the business historian is the scarcity of material from which the life history of a business can be reconstructed. Businessmen did not make speeches about the way they ran their firms. Many of their decisions and actions were carried out through personal contact and never embodied in a written record. Of the records they did make, few have been preserved and fewer still have been opened to the eyes of historians. In Crapo's case we are fortunate in both respects. A host of letters, penned a century ago in his vigorous hand to his son back East in New Bedford, give in intimate detail a running account of his progress as a lumberman. The relationship between father and son was one of the closest confidence and trust, and in these letters we find Crapo revealing his thoughts almost as if he were speaking aloud to himself. They permit us to relive with him the drama of his years in Michigan.*

II

In our twentieth-century era of steel and concrete, we are inclined to forget the dominating importance of wood to the Americans of earlier times. Among the many things that set America apart from the Old World was our widespread use of wood as a building material. The practice was in keeping with our national passion for getting things done in a hurry. Structures of stone might meet the needs of an old and stable civilization, but were manifestly impractical in a country where new communities were springing up overnight. So when Americans built their houses, barns, stores, workshops, and factories, they turned to the material that was cheap, easy to transport, and easy to use—wood.

As a natural result, the lumber industry held a most important place in the economy of nineteenth-century America. As late as 1870, lumber manufacture was the virtual equal of the iron industry in both capital employed and value of product. According to the census of that year, these two industries led all others in capitalization, while flour milling alone displayed a larger gross product. The manufacture of cotton goods, which a decade earlier had held first place in capital invested and second in value of product,

* The Crapo Manuscripts are described in Appendix B. Unless otherwise noted, letters and other manuscript materials cited are from this collection.

had slipped by 1870 to fourth and fifth rank respectively in these two basic measures of economic importance.*

The lumber industry had its beginnings in the establishment of small and usually crude sawmills scattered throughout the countryside, converting logs into lumber for the people of the immediate vicinity. Even during the Colonial period, however, a sizable manufacture of lumber on a truly commercial basis had developed in northern New England, and to a lesser extent in the Hudson River Valley and parts of the South. Sawed lumber from these centers went not only to supply the needs of towns and settled agricultural districts but was an important part of our export trade as well. As the nation expanded in the nineteenth century, the lumber industry kept pace.

In 1840, the first year for which we have any adequate statistics, more than one-fourth of the lumber output of the nation was produced in New York state. Maine, which probably had led in earlier years, now ranked second, and Pennsylvania, third in importance. As the center of both lumbering and economic activity generally moved westward, the relative importance of these older states declined steadily even though for a time their production continued to increase. Briefly, Pennsylvania supplanted New York at the head of the list. The most striking phenomenon of the century, however, was the meteoric rise of the industry in Michigan.

Michigan first achieved notice as a lumber state when the census of 1850 showed it in fifth place. Ten years later it had risen to third, surpassing both Maine and Ohio in importance. By 1870 it led the list, and it continued to hold top place for the rest of the century. Neither Wisconsin nor

* See Appendix A, Table 1, The Six Most Important Manufacturing Industries, 1860 and 1870.

Minnesota ever came close to matching the output of Michigan's peak years; when the former displaced it in the top-ranking spot in 1900, it was only because Michigan's production had dropped sharply with the exhaustion of its timber resources. Indeed, the Wolverine state's record output of nearly five and a half billion board feet of lumber in 1890 was unsurpassed anywhere until the year 1920, when production in the state of Washington went slightly over this mark.*

Crapo's years as a lumberman in Michigan, 1855 to 1869, paralleled closely the period in which the industry in that state mushroomed to leadership in the nation. In his early struggles for economic survival and in the great expansion of his lumber production which came in later years, Crapo's story was a part of the story of his new state.

When he came to Michigan in 1855, the state had been a member of the Union for but eighteen years. The states to the south—Ohio, Indiana, and Illinois—had been settled early in the nineteenth century, and had won statehood in 1803, 1816, and 1818, respectively. At first, however, few immigrants ventured northward into the great peninsula between Lake Erie and Lake Michigan. In the decade of the 'thirties this pattern changed rapidly. The Erie Canal was opened across New York state in 1825, and a new migration from the old Northeast began streaming into the region bordering on the lakes and into Michigan as well. Between 1820 and 1830 Michigan's population jumped from 8,896 to

---

* See Appendix A, Table 2, Relative Importance of Lumber-Producing States, 1840–1900.

The standard measure of lumber was the board foot, that is, a board one foot long, one foot wide, and one inch thick, or its equivalent in other dimensions. This same system of measurement was applied to the logs themselves before they were sawed into lumber. Thus "one thousand feet of logs" meant that quantity of logs which would yield one thousand board feet at the sawmill.

31,639, but the real settlement of the peninsula came in the boom years of the following decade. By 1837 statehood was achieved. That same year was marked by a nation-wide panic and economic crisis. Nevertheless, when the census of 1840 was taken the new state claimed 212,267 inhabitants. In ten years the population had increased almost seven fold! The Wolverine state was here to stay. During each of the next two decades the population nearly doubled again, reaching 397,654 in 1850 and 749,113 in 1860.

This burgeoning population was one factor in the rise of the state's lumber industry, but the most important cause of its growth was pointed to by an anonymous Michigan pamphleteer writing in 1856:

> Iowa, with an area of 51,000 square miles of prairie, has not a pine tree within her borders, and hardly timber enough for fire wood. She is filling up with a hardy, enterprising and industrious farming population, more rapidly than any other western State. . . .
>
> The vast plains and prairies of Illinois will always create a demand which can be supplied by this State more advantageously to both parties than by any other lumber region. . . . Northwestern Ohio depends upon Michigan almost exclusively for her Pine, and the valleys of the Ohio and Mississippi Rivers are already beginning to make large demands upon us. Albany and New York must look to us mainly for their "clear" lumber, for no other region in the whole country can produce so fine a quality, so great a quantity, or at rates so reasonable.[1]

The demand for Michigan lumber attracted men and capital from the depleted lumber regions of the East, along with others who like Crapo knew nothing of the business but could recognize an opportunity when they saw one. Small local sawmills serving the needs of the early settlers in the state had been in existence for some time. Now they came to be joined by others established for the purpose of tapping this broader market.

Virtually the entire northern half of Michigan's Lower Peninsula was covered with forests of magnificent white pine, the species of tree valued above all others for lumber. It grew straight and tall, with some specimens towering to heights of 150 feet and more, with a diameter at times approaching 10 feet. Its wood was light and easily worked, yet strong enough for all ordinary uses. A large part of this timber lay within easy reach of streams which found their way either to Lakes Huron and St. Clair on the east or Lake Michigan on the west. In 1857 it was estimated that 814,600,-000 feet of lumber were sawed in the state, 446,000,000 feet coming from mills on the eastern slope and 338,600,000 feet from the western slope, with perhaps 30,000,000 feet being manufactured in the Upper Peninsula where the industry was just beginning to take root.[2]

The Saginaw Valley, where the Cass, the Flint, the Shiawassee, and the Tittabawassee came together to form the broad Saginaw River, was the major lumber region on the eastern side of the Lower Peninsula. In 1847 the first shipment of Saginaw pine had reached the Albany market, and from this time on the Saginaw Valley grew steadily in importance as a supplier of lumber to Michigan and the rest of the nation.

In Michigan as elsewhere, the industry followed a basic seasonal cycle which was dictated by the nature of the lumbering process. Winter meant snow and frozen ground in the woods, making it possible for oxen or horses to haul the heavy logs to the river banks after they had been cut. Spring, with its melting snows and freshets, was the time when logs could best be run downstream to the mills. Throughout the summer the buzz of sawmills sounded as the logs were fished out of booms in the river and converted into piles of green lumber and mountains of fresh sawdust. Autumn often found the mills still running until ice in the river should "lock up" the logs for another year, while at the same time the work began of hauling supplies into the woods and building a camp for the next season's logging.

This dependence on climatic conditions stamped the lumber industry with its own peculiar character and added to the difficulties of the lumberman who already faced the uncertainties of market conditions common to all businesses. An open winter with little snow might facilitate the cutting of trees, but at the same time it would drastically reduce the number of logs which could be successfully banked in preparation for the spring drive down river. The drive, too, was at the mercy of the weather, for its success depended on high water lasting long enough to carry all the logs safely into the booms at the mills. Though most Michigan sawmills used steam instead of water power to run the saws, an excessively dry summer might leave logs stranded on mud flats and force the saws to halt for want of raw material. Late floods, on the other hand, might submerge the mill yards in their low-lying position on the banks of rivers and thus cause suspension of operations for the opposite reason.

These physical problems of the lumberman had their counterparts on the business side of the industry. The lumber operator had to base his plans on a long-term forecast of demand, since it was inherent in the lumbering process that close to a year would elapse before standing timber could be converted into pine boards ready for sale. Even then, still more delay might be required before a market could be found for the lumber. All this meant that the lumberman's capital was tied up over a long period of time. It also put a severe limitation on his ability to adjust production to current market conditions. He could not readily expand his output to take advantage of rising prices, and, equally important, he could not escape commitments made many months before if the market should suddenly drop. This inflexibility was aggravated by the unpredictable influence of weather conditions, which might affect marketing as well as production.

All in all, lumbering was a hard business, and certainly no place for a novice. Yet that is just what Crapo was when he undertook his Michigan venture in 1855. At the time he saw only dimly or not at all the difficulties that would beset him. His ultimate success in the face of great obstacles came only because he was able to draw on unusual resources of energy and determination, a native quickness to learn, and a lifetime of experience in the affairs of men.

one

NEW BEDFORD

I

Henry Howland Crapo was born in the year 1804 in the small rural community of Dartmouth, Massachusetts. It may help us to visualize something of the world he was entering if we recall that this was but the twenty-eighth year of American independence from Great Britain. Thomas Jefferson was President of the United States under a Constitution adopted only fifteen years before. As yet only three new states had been added to the original thirteen. These three—Kentucky, Tennessee, and Ohio—were the forerunners of a vast trans-Appalachian migration; but in the year of Crapo's birth most of the American people still lived in a relatively narrow area stretching north and south along the Atlantic coast.

Crapo's origins were humble, yet typical of the vast majority of the Americans of his day. His father was a farmer, and his early years were marked by the chores and drudgery that formed an inescapable part of rural life. Denied the opportunity for formal schooling by the demands of work on the farm, he was nevertheless spurred on by a restless and inquiring mind to seek such education as he could win by his own efforts. It is a measure both of the rude standards of the time and of his driving ambition for learning that he found his first employment, at the age of seventeen, as village schoolmaster.[1]

Teaching was an ill-paid vocation, but Crapo remained at it for close to ten years. More than a mere income, it meant to him an opportunity to continue his own education and thus to surmount the limitations of the narrow environment in which he had grown up. In the process of this self-directed learning he acquired a knowledge of the principles of surveying and was soon able to turn this new skill to good account in supplementing his meagre compensation as a teacher.

Despite his limited ability to support a family, he married at the age of twenty-one, and in the course of the next five years two children were born. There can be no doubt that this increased responsibility weighed heavily on him, and the year after his father's death he resolved to put his hard-won education to use in a broader field. Quite naturally, his decision was to move to nearby New Bedford, an up-and-coming whaling port of some seven or eight thousand inhabitants. It was to be his home for the next twenty-three years. He was then twenty-eight years old.

He found his surveyor's skill in steady demand. Gradually he branched out into other activities of service to the businessmen of the town—gauger, accountant, land agent, auction and commission merchant. While he had no capital of his own, his friends and acquaintances soon came to include many who did have surplus funds, and his reputation for probity and business acumen led them to entrust him with considerable sums for investment as he saw fit. In a privately-published biography, his grandson has written that

> it can hardly be said he borrowed [the money], since it was literally thrust upon him. At that time there were few opportunities for people of moderate means to make safe investments yielding a fixed income. . . . So when a man, not himself actually engaged in business, or a part owner in a whale ship, had put his money in the New Bedford Institution for Savings to

the permissible limit, he sought to lend his surplus to some trustworthy and capable individual and took his note therefor.

Crapo was quick to seize the opportunities offered in this way. His real estate dealings in and around New Bedford increased steadily, at first with the funds of others and later with his own as well. Several times he bought up tracts of land and laid them out in streets and lots. After enough lots had been sold to cover the original investment, he would hold the balance for the inevitable increase in value as the land was built up. Speculative purchases of merchandise provided another source of income. As his experience broadened, "he became the adviser to many men and women in their affairs" and served in various quasi-legal capacities in probate and bankruptcy proceedings. It is noteworthy, however, that he did not specialize in any one particular line of endeavor. It would be difficult indeed to identify his occupation by any single term. One is tempted to call him "servant-at-large to the business community of New Bedford." Active though he was as agent, intermediary, and even promoter, his limited resources precluded any extensive enterprise solely on his own account.

No doubt the responsibility of supporting a growing family made most welcome his election in 1835 as town clerk, treasurer and collector of taxes, at an annual stipend of $800.* For fifteen years (during which time the salary was gradually increased to $1,500) this office provided Crapo with a financial anchor while he continued to participate in other more or less remunerative business ventures. Between 1836 and 1845 he compiled and published five edi-

* When New Bedford was incorporated as a city in 1847, he was continued in office as city treasurer and collector of taxes.

tions of a *New Bedford Directory,* an enterprise which he regretfully abandoned when he discovered that it could not be made to pay its way. The year 1842 found him acting as sales agent for what was probably America's largest commercial nursery, the Linnaean Botanist Gardens and Nurseries of Flushing, New York. Horticulture was then a fashionable pastime for retired sea captains and merchants with time on their hands, and Crapo discovered that helping them stock their gardens could be profitable. He was himself deeply interested in horticulture, and by 1847 found it possible to mix business and pleasure with the establishment of his Wasemequia Nurseries, offering for sale to the public "Fruit and Ornamental Trees and Plants." All the while, of course, he continued to pursue his varied activities as agent and broker in purely commercial transactions.

His regular income as a public official, however, remained of great importance to him, a fact which is underlined by his dismay, in 1849, when a turn in local politics endangered his tenure as city treasurer. He wrote gloomily to his son, then in his first year at Yale, that

> for presuming to question the infallibility of his "Honor," and for the crime of having faithfully and independently discharged the obnoxious duties of "Tax Gatherer" for fourteen years, and for the crime of being in some other person's way, for each and all of these crimes and misdemeanors, I am to be decapitated, in other words, *politically* to have my head cut off.[2]

The loss of the position might not have troubled him greatly had it not been that times were bad and business prostrated, and his family responsibilities heavy (he now had one son and nine daughters). Under any circumstances finding an entirely new way of making a living was bound to be a difficult task for a man of forty-four. Looking to the future, he was confident that "bye and bye" his nursery business would prove sufficiently profitable to enable him to maintain his family by it, and to free him "from those prejudices and unreasonable censures that are always entertained towards public men . . . and especially tax gatherers." At the time, however, it was not. His situation was complicated by the fact that he was in debt, no doubt as a result of land purchases and other speculations in which he had been engaged. Were it not for this, he felt that he might safely devote his full time to building up the Wasemequia Nurseries. As it was, prudence dictated that he should seek some other employment from which he could count on a steady income.

It was shortly after this time that he secured the position which he was to hold for the remainder of his New Bedford career, that of secretary of the Bedford Commercial Insurance Company (later known as the Commercial Mutual Marine Insurance Company). It goes without saying that his selection for this post was due in large measure to the contacts he had made with and the respect he had won from the wealthy and influential merchants of the town. Undertaking the management of the affairs of the company, he came into ever closer contact with these men, whose habit it was to congregate in the insurance office much as they would in a private club.*

II

With the steady income from his new appointment, and with his closer relationship with the monied men of New

---

* Crapo's salaries from this post and from another of less importance, that of president of the Bristol County Mutual Fire Insurance Company, gave him $3,000 a year.—*Detroit Advertiser & Tribune,* July 22, 1864.

Bedford, Crapo soon was able to expand his speculative dealings in real estate, turning more and more towards lands in the Middle West. His first purchase of western land had been made in 1836, when he bought two lots of government land in Illinois for $200, paying $25 to an agent to make the entry. About the same time his brother David migrated to Ohio, carrying with him authorization to take up certain public lands on Crapo's account. Those early ventures led him to make his first western trip in 1838 to examine his lands and learn more about the possibilities of the region. Though on a small scale, he continued to make investments in land in Ohio and other western states throughout the years which followed both on his own account and as agent for others.

Early in the 1850's, however, he began to engage in such ventures on a greatly increased scale. Some fifteen years earlier there had been a Michigan land fever in New Bedford, in the course of which many of the local merchants and investors had made speculative purchases of large tracts of wild land. The Panic of 1837 and the prolonged depression which followed had put the damper on any rapid realization of profit from these lands, and many of the New Bedford men were becoming tired of paying taxes each year with little prospect of any return. With the passage of years, Michigan had grown rapidly, and around 1850 Crapo conceived the plan of buying out the original purchasers and then making a concerted and organized effort to sell the lands to the settlers who by then were coming into the state in large numbers. The largest single transaction was for the Howland tract of 16,000 acres, which he bought together with Joseph Grinnell, at the time "distinctly the leading citizen of New Bedford." The manner of financing is interesting. The purchase terms called for $4,500 in cash and the balance in three annual payments of the same amount. The down payment was obtained on a joint note given by the two men to the Marine Bank of New Bedford (of which Grinnell was president). Before a year had passed Crapo had sold enough of the land to cover the original note, and he apparently was able to continue in this way until the entire purchase had been paid for without Grinnell ever putting up a single dollar and with his own contribution being limited to his expenses incurred in promoting the sale of the land, for which he was compensated by a 12 per cent commission. Ultimately, when the account was closed in 1865, the enterprise showed a net profit of more than $24,000, which was divided equally between the two men.[3]

These gratifying results were of course not achieved immediately, nor without much sustained effort on Crapo's part. He was obliged to make frequent trips to Michigan, sometimes lasting two or three months, during which he traveled over the lands, engaged local agents, and personally sought out prospective buyers.

On one of these visits he made the acquaintance of William S. Driggs, a land agent of Detroit, who was interested in selling some of his own holdings. Writing Driggs early in 1854 to accept his offer on certain lands, Crapo explained that the tracts would be bought jointly by himself and James Arnold, "one of my neighbors, who furnishes all the means." He described Arnold as "one of our richest men—a heavy capitalist," but pointed out that "the whole business is however in my hands, Mr. Arnold giving himself very little trouble or consideration in reference to the purchase."[4]

Apparently impressed with Crapo's acquaintanceship with men of means in New England, towards the end of that same year Driggs came to him with a new proposition. This time he sought to secure Crapo's aid in arranging for a loan of $50,000. As security he offered a large tract of pine lands located in Lapeer County, Michigan, totaling some 12,000 acres. At first Crapo's efforts seemed doomed to failure, for times were bad and money scarce. New Bedford men heard the proposition for the loan "with manifest astonishment," and Crapo soon found himself at the point of writing Driggs to say that nothing could be done to raise the money on any terms. At this juncture, however, he received another letter from Driggs offering him a commission of $2,000 if he could negotiate the loan, together with traveling expenses to Michigan for inspecting the land should that prove necessary. Thus stimulated, Crapo made another effort and this time was successful in finding the money to be lent to Driggs for five years at 10 per cent interest per annum.[5]

Under Crapo's urging, James Arnold had agreed to make the loan. Arnold, the same wealthy retired businessman who had been Crapo's backer in the earlier purchase from Driggs, was as always the very picture of caution in his financial affairs. Despite the very profitable terms on which the loan was to be made, he remained skeptical as to the sufficiency of the security offered, and insisted as a condition for making the loan that Crapo himself verify to his own satisfaction the value of the lands to be mortgaged. Even after giving his initial consent to the proposition, Arnold continued to worry Crapo, daily expressing his qualms as to the wisdom of the venture. As it became clear to Crapo that far greater time and effort would be required to carry through the deal than he had anticipated, he wrote Driggs saying that he would require $2,500 commission rather than the $2,000 previously offered.[6] Since other business made it impossible for Crapo himself to go to Michigan, his son William was sent instead to examine the lands in the company of Emory Truefont, a Michigan "viewer" or appraiser of timber lands with whom Crapo had dealt in the past and whose opinions he trusted implicitly.[7] The results of the inspection and title verification proved quite satisfactory, and the loan was consummated on December 27, 1854.

III

In the mid-1850's, Michigan pine was gradually becoming more attractive for actual lumbering operations than for mere speculative holding, and a year after Arnold had taken the mortgage on the Driggs tract, a man named Edson turned up in New Bedford with a new proposition. Driggs had apparently decided to try to sell the land, possibly because he required more ready cash in addition to the $50,000 he had borrowed, or perhaps simply because he was finding onerous the prospect of paying the 10 per cent interest on the loan. This would, after all, amount to $25,000 over five years' time for the use of $50,000. Edson had talked with him about purchasing his pine land and working off the timber and had come East seeking capital to aid him in the venture. His reception in New Bedford was discouraging. Arnold was naturally quite unwilling to permit lumber to be taken off the land while he held the mortgage on it. He was equally unwilling to accept payment of the loan before maturity without a large bonus, in view of the satisfactory security he held and the high rate of interest he was receiving on his money. Other men in conservative New Bedford business circles were likewise uninterested in investing money with a complete stranger from the West for such an enterprise, and Edson left, apparently abandoning the scheme.[8]

The incident had aroused Crapo's own interest in the land, however, particularly since he was familiar with it from his negotiations with Driggs in the fall of 1854 and from his son's personal inspection of the tract. In the preceding fifteen months, he had entered some 8,000 acres of Michigan pine land in various parts of the state, with the idea that he might at some later time turn to lumbering on it.* Drigg's land was better suited to immediate exploitation, however, because of its location, and the knowledge that Driggs might sell the land apparently set Crapo to thinking more actively about a venture in the lumber business. Lumbering was a business about which he knew nothing, but he felt confident of his ability to learn and saw in the Driggs tract a chance for a sizable and rapid profit.

With this in mind, shortly after Edson left New Bedford Crapo wrote to Driggs inquiring the best terms on which the land could be purchased. He made it clear to Driggs that he would himself be seeking funds from others in New Bedford to make the purchase, though he intended to keep the actual management of the business in his own hands.[9] Driggs replied with an offer to sell for $150,000, and shortly thereafter came to New Bedford himself to promote the deal. Within two weeks of his initial inquiry, Crapo was able to write Driggs accepting the offer.[10]

The venture was well beyond Crapo's own means. According to his son's recollection, Crapo's entire property at the time was worth little more than $50,000, and the bulk of

* In a letter to his brother, David, at Odessa, Mich., Nov. 7, 1855, Crapo had elaborated on this idea, saying that it was "very probable that in the course of a year or two, I may . . . go into the Lumber and some other business in the vicinity of or at Ionia. . . . By spending at different times, some 3 months there in the year, I might carry on the lumbering business so as to make money. If I had a couple of good steam mills there now, I suppose they might be run by the thousand, and logs cut and drawn by the thousand, and lumber sold at the Mills or hauled by the thousand, so as to pay well. But I should not think of doing anything about this until the Rail Road reaches Ionia." In using the expression "by the thousand" Crapo presumably meant that his intention would be to operate as a lumberman by contracting with others to perform the various functions involved, at so much per thousand feet of lumber.—Crapo Manuscripts, Letter Press Book 4.

it was in real estate and other non-liquid investments. He had succeeded, however, in communicating his enthusiasm for lumbering on the Driggs tract to both James Arnold and a mutual acquaintance in New Bedford, Oliver Prescott. How successful he was may be measured by Arnold's considerable skepticism just twelve months before at accepting the very same lands as security for a loan one-third the sum for which they were now to be purchased. To justify the price of slightly more than $12 an acre, Crapo had prepared elaborate calculations from which it appeared that the venture would be lucrative indeed. Net profits from lumbering, he figured, would be $30,000 per year after expenses, thus repaying the entire original investment within five years. At the end of that time, he calculated, the lumber still remaining on the land, together with the value of the land itself exclusive of timber, should be worth the tidy sum of $1,310,535. No wonder the proposition appealed to even the hyper-cautious Arnold! *

And Arnold was the man who had to be convinced. Although the venture was planned as a partnership, with each of the three men holding an equal one-third interest, neither Crapo nor Prescott was in a position to pay in their share at the start. It was finally agreed that Arnold would advance the necessary sums to the other two partners, taking their notes.[11] Until their shares should be paid in, the title to the lands was to remain solely in Arnold's name. Crapo, as the active partner, was to receive a salary of $3,000 a year, plus a commission of 6 per cent on all sales of timber, lumber, or the lands themselves. The entire management of the business was to be in his hands: getting in the logs from the land, having them sawed and getting them to market, selling

* "Summary by H. H. Crapo of Probable Receipts and Expenditures and of the Final Profits." The entire document is given in Appendix B.

the lumber, and collecting payment. Receipts were to be credited first to his salary and commission, and to the current expenses of the business, after which they would go towards meeting payments due Driggs on the purchase. Any remaining income would then be divided equally among the three partners.

Driggs was to be paid $25,000 in cash on January 1, 1856 as the first installment towards the purchase. The balance was to be paid off over three years, with interest at 7 per cent, payable semi-annually. Sixteen thousand dollars was due April 7, 1856; $9,000 on January 1, 1857; $25,000 on January 1, 1858; and finally, $19,000 on January 1, 1859. The balance remaining of the $150,000 purchase price was to be made up by the partnership's assumption of the $50,000 loan made earlier by Arnold, together with $6,000 allowed by Driggs on account of interest.*

Sitting comfortably in New Bedford, Crapo and his associates laid plans to begin lumbering that very winter. Driggs had told them that despite their late start, they should have no difficulty in getting off 5 million feet of lumber in their first season. It was on this figure, and on their expectations of 10 million feet annually in succeeding years, that Crapo's calculation of prospective profit was based. Many settlers had recently come into the region where the land was located and were eager to find winter work in lumbering. Older residents had available for sale the various

* Partnership agreement between Arnold, Prescott, and Crapo, dated Dec. 22, 1855, Crapo Manuscripts, Box 15. An interesting sidelight on the purchase was that Driggs received no security for the payment of the installments other than the personal notes of the partners. Though this was contrary to "the rule of my business life," he wrote Crapo, "in this case the high reputation for wealth and honor of the gentlemen whose paper you propose to give carries with it the assurance that the payments will be promptly and fairly met."—William S. Driggs, Detroit, to H. H. Crapo, New Bedford, Dec. 15, 1855.

provisions which would be required for the logging camps. The lands in the Driggs tract lay on or near the Flint River, and Driggs had assured the New Bedford men that it would be entirely practical to run the logs down the river to Saginaw, already an active center for the shipment of lumber to both Chicago and the eastern markets, via the Great Lakes.

So eager were the partners to get started in their new venture that on December 26, 1855—exactly one month after his initial overture to Driggs—Crapo departed for Michigan, planning to spend the entire winter there in getting things under way.

IV

On December 28, he arrived in Detroit. Several days were taken up in making final arrangements with Driggs for the transfer of the land and in consulting as to the best course to follow in commencing lumbering operations. While Crapo was still in New Bedford, Driggs had advised him that the best way to get in the logs would be to contract with some experienced local man to handle the whole affair, hiring men and teams, securing provisions, and so on. The Detroit man had even volunteered his services in locating someone to undertake the task.[12] Now that Crapo was in Michigan, however, he found that all such people had long since engaged themselves for the winter. Though men and teams could easily be hired by the day, this hardly seemed a very practical way for him to begin, in view of his utter lack of experience in the business. In what was to prove the first of a long series of disappointments, he decided he would be lucky indeed if by incessant labor he could succeed in cutting and getting to the river half the amount of logs on which he had planned. He determined to reserve judgment, however, until he could get to Lapeer to look the situation over for himself.[13]

On December 31 he set out from Detroit to see for the first time the acres of magnificent pine which had lured him from his comfortable New Bedford life. The discomfort of the fifty-eight mile trip in an open sleigh was prophetic of what the future held in store for him. Arriving cold and tired at Lapeer, he found all who were in any way connected with lumbering "disposed to frighten me, and if possible to deter my doing anything now I am here." [14] At first he was inclined to discount such discouraging talk as being motivated by self-interest and fear of competition. He felt the experience to be gained by making some kind of start, no matter how small, would counterbalance the serious disadvantage under which he would have to work. But after three more arduous days in the woods, he was forced to conclude that it would be in the best interests of the business to postpone any attempt at logging until the following winter, meanwhile doing everything possible to insure adequate preparation. He decided to make a brief trip to the nearby towns of Flint and Saginaw to gather more information, and then to return to New Bedford where he faced the task of explaining to his partners, and particularly to the apprehensive Arnold, the necessity for the delay of an additional year in realizing any income from their purchase.[15]

His growing disillusionment was unmistakable, nevertheless. From Flint he wrote his son: "It is certainly a great concern, and from its magnitude I almost regret ever engaging in it." Such words, however, were not for the ears of Messrs. Arnold and Prescott, and he sought to reassure them by providing William with calculations to show that the absolute minimum their purchase could be worth would be $488,000, taking the lowest possible estimate of the quantity of timber on the land. "It is decidedly the most valuable tract of Pine Timber, owned together, in all this region," he wrote.*

Whether these words were penned solely to bolster confidence back home, it is hard to say. Whatever the case may be, by the time Crapo reached Saginaw the following day he was even more discouraged, and he sat down to vent his feelings in a bitter letter to Driggs:

> I must say that I am heartily sick of the enterprise, and would give no small sum to be put back again where I stood before the purchase was made. I do not mean to charge upon you, or any one, anything wrong in this matter; but I have certainly permitted myself to be deceived very foolishly by placing too much confidence in the highly colored and overwrought statements of others. We have paid too much for the property by $50,000 at least; and as the thing has got into the papers I have an opportunity every hour of hearing the opinion of others on the subject, without their suspecting that I am the purchaser. It is regarded everywhere as a very foolish purchase, and by men who know the land.

The thing that bothered him most was his discovery that running the logs down the Flint River to Saginaw would be a risky proposition at best. In several places below Flint the stream was broken by dangerous rapids. To rely on it as his sole outlet to market seemed to Crapo to be foolhardy in the extreme, from all he had been able to learn. He had also become quite skeptical of Driggs's estimate of the quantity of timber on the land—fearful, indeed, that there was less than one-quarter the

* The calculation was based on a figure of 150 million feet of lumber at $3.00 a thousand feet "on the stump" together with the land itself at $3.00 an acre.—Letter to William Crapo, Jan. 4, 1856.

amount Driggs had claimed. He had visions of being able to make no more from the tract than would be required to meet interest and taxes, "which would make a perfect slave of myself and use up the lumber without ever restoring the capital." Not the least of his disappointment lay in having left his family and a good situation. All in all, he wrote, "I am certainly in a bad fix."

After reciting his woes at length, Crapo concluded his letter by an appeal to Driggs to allow him an agent's commission on the sale, particularly since the latter had "made a fortune" by selling the land at the agreed price. The other two partners would not suffer no matter how the venture turned out, but, he wrote, "upon me the whole labor, risk of health, fatigue, constant anxiety, care and responsibility falls." Appealing to Driggs's sense of "liberality," rather than "by way of claim or right," Crapo asked that he be allowed as commission the $7,000 note which would fall due January 1, 1858. In making this request, Crapo acted with something less than candor so far as his New Bedford associates were concerned, suggesting to Driggs that the matter remain strictly confidential between the two men, "as no benefit can result to me by letting anyone know that I consider the purchase anything but a good one." [16]

As might be expected, Driggs was hardly agreeable to the suggestion, and in his reply implied that Crapo had been imposed upon by men who sought to deceive him for their own purposes. Recognizing the difficulties that Crapo had faced on this, his first trip to the lands, he assured him that with more time to examine the purchase, he would revise his opinion and decide that he had indeed acquired a most valuable property.[17]

Perhaps Crapo had expected no more; in any case, he was committed to the enterprise, and had to do the best he could under the circumstances. After leaving Saginaw he returned to examine more of the lands, "wallowing through the snow and creeping over logs 4 or 5 ft. high, covered with one foot of snow at least." The Michigan winter was in full swing, and "there was never a better time than the present for logging," he wrote William, reiterating his disappointment at being unable to do anything until the following year. Commenting on the bitter weather—twenty-two degrees below zero—he noted nevertheless that

> I am very well, and have endured the cold and exposure far better than I anticipated. . . . If I were 15 or 20 years younger, and could have my family with me, I should enjoy myself far better than being shut up in a hot room with more calls upon me than I could possibly meet. As it is, however, my mind and thoughts dwell constantly upon home and its enjoyments and comforts.[18]

After several more days in the woods, he set out for New Bedford, arriving home January 19, 1856, after an absence of less than a month.

two

THE PROBLEMS OF A LUMBERMAN: I
(1856 - 1857)

I

Back in New Bedford, Crapo had little leisure time as he sought to disengage himself from his other affairs and to prepare for his new responsibilities. One of his first steps was to resign his position as secretary of the Marine Insurance Company, his place being taken by his son, who had been assistant secretary and had carried on his duties during his earlier absences. As he went about his business, the lumber enterprise was never far from his mind. A steady series of appeals went out to his land agents in the West urging prompt collections and remittances, as he sought to gather funds for working capital.[1]

Hard pressed for cash though Crapo was, his enthusiasm for the prospects in lumbering operations led him to plunge even deeper into the purchase of Michigan pine lands. Within a few months after the acquisition of the Driggs land by the three New Bedford partners, he had also bought for his personal account a total of 3,717 acres of timber land located in the same general area. The tracts which he purchased for himself were not so conveniently located as was the Driggs land, but at $3.00 and $4.00 per acre he felt that these acquisitions would to some degree offset what he was rapidly coming to consider the extravagant price paid to Driggs. Interestingly, Driggs himself was the intermediary through whom one of these new purchases was made. After reminding Driggs once again that he felt the partners had paid half again more than Driggs's own land was worth, Crapo added that

> although I have been "down in my feelings" and views in regard to the purchase of your Pine Lands and have been what some would term "sick of my bargain" "nigh unto death," yet you see I have sufficient courage and confidence to go on and buy more Pine Lands.

The measure of Crapo's confidence can be seen in the fact that with these purchases he obligated himself for the immediate payment of $2,888 and an ultimate total of more than $11,500. This, despite the fact that he had been unable to pay in his share of the original purchase![2] "I am in for it," Crapo wrote Driggs, "and see no way now but to devote myself to the work."

> This will be *the* great undertaking of my life, and whatever my feelings may be in the matter I shall take hold of the work with all the energy and determination which I am capable of; yet, a man who has spent 52 years of his life and 35 yrs. of that time in almost unremitted toil, cannot enter into an enterprise of this magnitude without some misgiving. I am however prepared for the work, and hope yet to succeed.[3]

II

Forced to accept the necessity of a season's delay in commencing operations, Crapo busied himself during the spring and summer of 1856 laying plans for the conduct of the new enterprise. There was much that had to be decided. In plunging into the pine land venture, he had only the most sketchy idea of how he would proceed. His glowing estimate of profits drawn up before the purchase merely took an assumed value per acre of the standing timber "on the stump" and by simple multiplication transformed this figure into the proceeds to be expected from the investment. Obviously he could not expect to realize this value automatically. Nevertheless, there is no suggestion in his notes or correspondence that he had any idea of becoming personally involved in the actual operations of either logging camp or sawmill. Apparently he anticipated no more active role for himself than making contracts, checking from time to time on their fulfillment, and arranging for the sale of logs or lumber in wholesale lots.

After arriving in Michigan, however, he soon realized that the successful prosecution of the venture would in all probability require a far greater involvement than he had envisioned. He spent many hours talking with lumbermen, merchants, public officials, and other local citizens, learning much about the lumber business and receiving an abundance of advice on the course he should follow. Although he found little agreement among the various opinions offered, out of these conversations he at least gained a good picture of the possible alternatives facing him in planning his business.[4]

His objective in the enterprise was simple enough—"to work [the lands] off into cash," as he wrote in one letter to his son. The problem was to find the best way to this goal. The simplest method, of course, would be to sell "stumpage rights" (permission to cut the standing timber and take off the logs). This procedure would relieve Crapo of any concern for the physical problems of lumbering. It would offer, however, but little opportunity for profit, and would be at best a slow way to turn the pine land purchase back into money. If, on the other hand, the trees were felled and the logs hauled to the nearest river bank, the logs could either be sold there or be run downriver for sale at a sawmill town. At the time of Crapo's entry into the business, most owners of pine lands probably limited themselves to one or the other of these methods of disposing of their timber.

Going one step beyond the latter alternative, the firm could itself undertake the sawing of the logs into lumber. If this were done, the marketing of the lumber would also have to be considered. It might be sold to lumber merchants at the mill, or the firm could undertake the marketing function as well, shipping the lumber directly to Chicago, Buffalo, or Albany and seeking out purchasers there. Crapo and his associates faced the problem of deciding how many of these steps their firm should attempt, in order best to serve their objective of converting the Driggs tract into cash and profit.

They also had to determine the means to be employed in carrying out these steps. Men and teams could be hired directly to do the logging, or the work could be contracted for at so much per thousand feet of logs. Similarly, if the logs were not to be sold outright but were to be converted into lumber as part of the operations of the firm, the sawing might either be done on contract or by the firm's undertaking to operate a mill of its own.*

* These alternatives applied generally wherever lumbering operations were being carried on. See "The Lumber Business in the State of Maine," *Hunt's Merchants Magazine*, XXXV (Sept., 1856), 317, for an account of the various modes of operation prevailing in that state, and Richard N. Current, *Pine Logs and Politics: A Life of Philetus Sawyer, 1816–1900* (Madison, 1950), p. 104, for a discussion of the industry in Wisconsin. In the latter case, the "several distinct operations" which before the Civil War "had usually been in the hands of different groups of men" came to be consolidated between 1863 and 1872 as "sawmill owners in search of ever larger profits increased the size of their plants and reached out to control every stage in the lumbering process."

A decision on these alternatives had to be reached before anything could be done. Crapo's freedom of action in setting his course, however, was considerably limited by the specific conditions of his own particular situation. One of the most important of these influences was a fact of geography which he had failed to appreciate in making the purchase.

His plan, so far as he had had any when he first embarked on the enterprise, was to run his logs down the Flint River to Saginaw. That town was already a sawmill center of some importance, its lumber finding ready access to markets by way of the Great Lakes. It had ample facilities for having logs sawed on contract, and a good market for the logs themselves should outright sale be preferred.* The hidden difficulty in Crapo's original plan lay in the fact that at several places between Flint and Saginaw, the Flint River was broken by dangerous rapids which would make the running of logs along this course both risky and unreliable. At least one Saginaw man with whom Crapo talked was inclined to discount this difficulty, and told him that the Michigan rivers were far better than those in Maine, but Crapo remained skeptical.[5] His fear that he would be unable to get his logs safely down to Saginaw led him to give consideration instead to making Flint his base of operations.

Flint, the county seat of Genesee County, was a town of slightly more than two thousand inhabitants. It was located

---

*Estimates of the number of mills in the vicinity of Saginaw vary. An East Saginaw man, writing in reply to a series of questions put to him by Crapo, said there were forty steam mills within twenty-five miles of the place along the Saginaw River. "Perhaps half" of these were stocked from lands belonging to the owners, but he assured Crapo that the facilities of the others would be quite adequate for even the large quantity of logs—10 million feet annually—which Crapo anticipated putting in.—HHC, NB to C. T. Disbrow, East Saginaw, Dec. 5, 1855, in LPB 4; Disbrow to HHC, Dec. 21, 1855. For explanation of the abbreviations used here and in subsequent notes, see "Notes," p. 269.

some thirty miles upriver from Saginaw, in the midst of a prosperous farming area which had been settled somewhat earlier than most of the Saginaw Valley region and was growing rapidly in population. In 1850 the town boasted two sawmills. By 1854, as plank roads came to link Flint with neighboring communities and provide a wider (though still local) market, the number of mills had increased to seven.[6]

From the standpoint of Crapo's lumber operations, it had the advantage of being much closer than Saginaw to the Driggs tract, while at the same time it was more sizable and important than the villages of Lapeer and Marathon in Lapeer County, where the pine land itself was located. On his first trip to Michigan in the role of lumberman, several of the town's businessmen had urged on Crapo the advantages of making his headquarters there.[7] The one obvious difficulty in such a move was the fact that the sawmills of Flint, an inland town, lacked access to outside markets by water transportation, the usual means of shipping lumber.

There were compensating factors, however. For one thing, Flint's local market for lumber was more substantial than that of Saginaw, whose lumber industry depended almost entirely on distant markets. Even more important to a man with an eye for the future, a railroad was planned which would connect Flint with Port Huron at the east and, ultimately, with Lake Michigan at the west. This so-called "Northern Railroad" had first been projected by the state in 1837, but the plans for a publicly-owned rail system in Michigan had broken down in the wake of that year's panic. After railroad building had passed into private hands, several attempts had been made to revive the project, and several times construction had actually been started. Now, in the summer of 1856, the company had been reorganized with British capital, and it appeared certain that work would be resumed and this time rapidly brought to completion. Crapo's faith in the building of this road, and in the outlet it would afford for lumber sawed at Flint, proved decisive in his choice of that point as headquarters for his new enterprise.[8]

To base his operations there instead of at Saginaw meant that Crapo would be forced to acquire his own sawmill facilities, for the mills at Flint could offer neither a dependable market for the sale of logs nor adequate surplus capacity for having logs sawed on contract. Sawmill operation had not been part of Crapo's original conception of the enterprise. Once word of his pine land purchase had gotten out, however, the owners of several mills in different locations had approached him with offers to sell. No doubt this circumstance, if nothing else, had led him to wonder whether such facilities might not be a valuable aid in producing a profit from the Driggs pine tract. In April, 1856, declining the offer of a mill at East Saginaw, he wrote that "the time may come when I should be desirous of making just such a purchase," but that he had not yet decided "as to the particular mode of operations by which I shall endeavor to convert my Pine Timber into Lumber." [9]

Still undecided on the course to follow, he set out early in May from New Bedford on a second trip to Michigan. Staying the better part of two months, he visited Lansing, Grand Rapids, Kalamazoo and other parts of the state, besides spending considerable time in Flint, Saginaw, and Lapeer County. While there he studied the lumber business from all angles, paying particular attention to sawmill operations which were in full swing during the summer months. In Flint he employed a local millwright to examine several of the mills in the vicinity which were for sale. One of these was the Walkley mill. It was located in the center of the town, and was one of the four main mills at Flint. The preceding year its steam-driven saws had turned out only 1½ million feet of lumber, out of a total of nearly 9 million feet sawed at Flint, but it had a capacity of nearly twice that amount.[10] The property seemed well suited to the plan of operations which was gradually evolving in Crapo's mind. Before returning home he made arrangements with William M. Fenton, a prominent Flint citizen and former lieutenant-governor, to negotiate for its purchase should the idea be approved by the other partners.

Back in New Bedford, he presented his estimate of the situation to Arnold and Prescott. They in turn left the question to Crapo's own judgment and discretion, and he at once authorized Fenton to buy the property for a maximum of $10,500. He offered full payment in cash as an inducement to secure a better price, and the deal was finally made for $10,000. A large booming privilege on the Flint River went along with the mill, as well as eleven acres of land so situated as to provide an excellent site for erecting another mill later on, should that prove desirable.[11] Once again he wrote his Michigan land agents urging them to make collections and remit all funds due him as rapidly as possible. "Money is very scarce here and I am in great want of every dollar I can raise." [12]

With the decision to operate his own mill at Flint, Crapo had gone far towards determining the future course of his Michigan enterprise. The increased responsibilities entailed by this step made him all the more conscious of his limited knowledge of the lumber business, however, and soon after concluding the mill purchase he made a quick trip to Maine to study lumbering operations along the Penobscot and the Kennebec Rivers.[13]

Meanwhile, he had begun to make plans for his first season of logging. On his trip to Michigan the previous winter he had arranged for the construction of a store building in the village of Marathon which would serve as a supply point for logging crews in the woods. During the summer he took steps to locate potential logging contractors, having handbills circulated in Michigan and engaging in frequent correspondence on the subject. With enough applicants lined up in advance to assure an active winter of logging, Crapo left New Bedford for Michigan in September to make final arrangements. There he made contracts with three different jobbers to get in a total of 5 million feet of logs, planning to stock the Flint mill with 2½ to 3 million feet, and to attempt running the rest down the river to Saginaw.[14]

In hiring contractors to do his logging, he was following the advice of both Driggs and others with whom he had talked in Michigan. He could see many advantages, however, in hiring and running his own logging crews. Just as he had done by the purchase of his own sawmill facilities, he would be bringing an important phase of the lumbering process under his direct control, and by eliminating an intermediary's profit he would of course add to the potential profits of the concern. While he recognized that for his first season of logging there was no practical alternative to relying on contractors, he sought to prepare for the future by engaging an experienced Maine man, Charles Harthan, to come out to Michigan as his logging superintendent. Hired at a salary of $50 a month and expenses, Harthan thus became the first employee of the firm.[15]

The winter of 1856–57 must have been a trying one indeed for Crapo. With the exception of brief visits to New Bedford in November and January, he remained in Michigan from the end of September through mid-April. Harthan joined him in December, and much of their time was no doubt spent in the woods urging along the logging contractors. Almost certainly he wrote frequently to his son during these months, but the letters have not survived among the Crapo manuscripts and we can only guess at the many difficulties which he must have encountered during this first season. One thing we do know: not one of the contractors completed the full amount of his job. By the end of the season, instead of the 5 million feet of logs on which Crapo had counted, less than 3 million had been gotten in. This was a discouraging beginning, particularly when contrasted with his original anticipation (from the comfortable distance of New Bedford) of 10 million feet a year. While the failure of the jobbers to complete their contracts permitted Crapo to dictate compromise settlements with them on terms more advantageous than those called for in the agreements, this was little comfort from the standpoint of getting operations under way on the scale he had planned.[16]

Logging, however, was only one of the many problems demanding his attention. The Walkley mill required repairs and alterations which he estimated would cost some $3,000, and this work had to be completed by the first of April to permit starting up the mill as soon as the logs were run down into the booms. Also, steps had to be taken to recruit a work force for the mill, and provisions made for housing and feeding the men (the customary method of compensation in addition to the payment of a monthly salary). To meet the latter problem, Crapo succeeded in getting a New Bedford couple, W. L. Gee and his wife, to come out to Flint to run his boarding house. To fill the post of mill superintendent, he had his choice of some half-dozen appli-

cants from the surrounding towns. After careful consideration, on March 9, 1857, he hired George W. Burrell to
start the following week at a salary of $50 a month and
board. Burrell, he noted in his memorandum book, was
"to have charge of running my mill, cutting the lumber,
looking after men, going into the woods logging in the
winter, etc., etc., in short either to saw in the mill or do
whatever I wish." [17]

With Burrell's assistance, Crapo set about hiring a crew
to run the mill. Two lists in his memorandum book indicate
that from nine to twelve men were required: an engineer
in addition to the foreman, a head and a tail sawyer for
each of the two saws (a mulay and a circular), a fireman, a
man to run the edging table ("to be as good a man as in the
mill"), a man to haul logs, one or two men to pile lumber,
and perhaps two men to run the lath machine. Wages for
the men ranged from $15 to $18 a month and board for the
least skilled to $38 a month and board for the head sawyers,
and Crapo estimated his wage bill for seven months of operation would run close to $3,340, allowing for the cost of
operating the boarding house. By running the mill for one
shift of twelve hours, he figured he could saw about 15,000
feet of lumber a day or a total of perhaps 2½ million feet
for the season.

By early in April the mill was in operation, and eager
though he was to watch over its progress personally, he
found it impossible to delay returning to New Bedford any
longer. Leaving Harthan, Burrell, and Gee in charge, he
departed for the East, arriving home on April 17.

Despite the press of business which confronted him on
his return, he could not hide his anxiety over the way things
were going at Flint. "I wish you to keep me posted on everything about the mill," he wrote to Gee:

> State how the men work—what time in the morning
> the mill starts—when she shuts down at night—how
> much she cuts per day—when the edging table started,
> also the lathe machine, etc. . . . In short, everything.

Gee's replies were more than satisfactory. If anything, Crapo
suspected overstatement in the report that the mill was turning out 25,000 feet of lumber a day and feared that a short
spurt of such brisk activity might be followed by a slack-
ening of pace. "The mill must be run constantly and steadily. . . . She must be run through the season into cold
weather; and if one gang gets to lagging another must take
their place." His lack of experience as a lumberman continued to worry him. Defensively, he wrote Gee:

> I suppose the other mills have the advantage of us in
> doing up the business right, as why should they not;
> they certainly with years of experience in all depart-
> ments of the business should by this time have every-
> thing reduced to the most perfect order and system,
> and make the most out of the mill, labor and every-
> thing else, whilst we can only feel our way, and no
> doubt, in numberless instances, fail where they suc-
> ceed. But all that energy can do shall be done; and
> with prudence and care, I shall hope ultimately to
> keep somewhere in the wake of my brother manufac-
> turers.

He drew confidence, however, from the men whom he had
left in charge at Flint. He assured Gee:

> I am pleased with the zeal with which you enter into
> my interests there; and from your manner of writing
> I am led to suppose that I am faithfully served by Mr.
> Burrell. Harthan I know to be faithful and devoted to

my interests. With such men to aid me I hope yet to
save ourselves from being an object of ridicule by our
more practical and experienced neighbors.[18]

After a month in New Bedford, his affairs there were in
sufficiently good order to permit him to return to Michigan.
In Flint he found things running well, and emboldened by
his success in the operation of the Walkley mill, he yielded
to the temptation of acquiring yet another mill. The owners, McQuigg, Turner and Company, had been anxious to
sell out for some time. Six months earlier, he had declined
their offer, feeling that it would be "extremely injudicious
—not to say rash" to undertake running two mills before he
had even proved to himself that he could operate one to advantage. "The thing would be entirely beyond my control
and management," he had written them, "and derangement,
if not positive loss, would in all probability be the consequence." At the time, however, he had expressed his interest
in considering the purchase later if "after one season of
trial with my own mill I shall find myself equal to the task
of managing a more extensive concern." [19]

By June, though hardly half through his first season as
a sawmill proprietor, Crapo had apparently gained that confidence. Finding the owners of the McQuigg mill even more
eager to sell than before, he feared he might never have a
better chance to make the purchase and decided to seize the
opportunity. Returning to New Bedford, he secured the
agreement of his partners, and the purchase was made for
$20,000, with one-third down and the balance to be paid off
over the next five years.

"I suppose you will think this is a wild scheme," Crapo
wrote to Harthan who had returned to Maine to spend
the summer with his family. Nevertheless, it was a logical

step for expanding his operations, since the property lay just below the Walkley mill on the river, being separated from the latter by a three-acre strip of land which was acquired for an additional $2,000. Operating the two mills together, Crapo would have facilities for sawing some 7 million feet of lumber a year. The purchase concluded, he took immediate steps to get the new mill into operation by mid-July, to run for the balance of the season alongside the Walkley (or "upper") mill. Even before returning to Flint, he instructed Burrell to seek out some good men to make up a crew, cautioning his Michigan lieutenants only that "we must endeavor to hire the men for reasonably *low* wages . . . to economize in every possible way." [20]

three

DEPRESSION IN THE LAND

I

Crapo might well have been concerned with economy, more so than he could know. The year was 1857, and the country was on the verge of a serious depression from which it would not fully recover until well after the outbreak of the Civil War. Almost two years had passed since the purchase from Driggs, and he had barely begun to get his new enterprise into operation. When he had arrived in Michigan during the winter of 1855–56, confidence in the future of the lumber industry had been at a high pitch. On every side he had been assured that it would be impossible to overstock the market.[1] He had encountered unforeseen obstacles and delays, but despite them he had succeeded in making a start. Just as lumber was beginning to come from his mills in a steady stream, he found himself faced with a rapidly deteriorating economic situation.

Ostensibly the troubles began with the failure on August 24 of the mis-named Ohio Life Insurance and Trust Company, a banking institution active in both eastern and western money markets. Shadows on the economic horizon had appeared earlier, however, and Crapo himself was among those to note them. In May he had written Gee from New Bedford:

> Times are getting very hard here; money is very hard
> to be obtained on any terms, and everyone predicts

a financial crisis at hand. Failures are frequent and heavy. It is attributed here to a failure of western merchants to pay their eastern bills, and to western speculation; but I think that eastern extravagance has something to do with it. At all events business was never duller here, nor money scarcer. The west has entirely drained the east of money, and I fear that we shall have to pass through a season of "hard times."[2]

Despite these danger signals, Crapo had gone ahead with his plans for expansion. Throughout the summer and early fall, his mills continued to turn out lumber, adding steadily to the piles in his yard. Less than a month after he had taken possession of the McQuigg property, Crapo noted with pleasure in his memorandum book that the two mills together had cut 44,033 feet of lumber in a single twelve-hour day. By the end of the sawing season, he had some $40,000 worth of lumber on hand.[3]

With his manufacturing thus well under way, Crapo had begun to face in earnest the problems of marketing. The sawmills at Flint had been built up almost solely on the basis of the local demand for lumber in the town itself and in the surrounding country. In acquiring first one and then another of the four main mills at Flint, Crapo had naturally fallen heir to a major share of this local market. Largely with an eye to improving sales there, late in 1857 he added a planing machine to the equipment of his upper mill. The new machine, which cost him $680 delivered from Massachusetts, permitted him to offer dressed lumber as well as rough boards just as they came from the saws. His customers, he wrote, could now "select just what lumber they want and have it shoved into the mill and planed with very little detention." It was apparently the first such installation at Flint, and improved his competitive position considerably.[4]

Nevertheless, there were limitations on the market for lumber at Flint. For one thing, the demand there was principally for "common" lumber, which brought less than half the price of "clear." * Even more important, no merely local market could be expected to sustain operations on the scale called for by the size of the investment Crapo and his partners had made in their pine lands.

From the inception of the enterprise, his goal had been the more distant and more profitable markets in Detroit, in Chicago and other rising Midwest centers, and of course back in the East where native lumber resources were rapidly being exhausted. New Bedford in particular appealed to him as an outlet for his lumber, for obvious reasons. While there during August, 1857, he spent many hours visiting the city's lumber yards to observe the quality of lumber being sold in the various grades and to compare it with what he was turning out in Flint. He was pleased with the result, and in a long letter to Burrell, his mill foreman, he instructed him to saw and sort the firm's "clear" lumber and "seconds" so as to meet the requirements of this market.†
Detailing the way inspection rules were applied in New Bedford, he wrote:

> Much poorer boards go into these two qualities than I
> had supposed. The constantly increasing scarcity of

* The names assigned to the various grades of lumber varied somewhat from one lumber center to another. Broadly speaking, however, they can be listed as (1) clear, (2) seconds, or second-rate clear, (3) common, and (4) culls. The term "uppers" was used to denote the grades above common.

† On his way back to Flint, Crapo had the opportunity of making a similar study of the mills and lumber yards at Lowell, Massachusetts. Once again he found the comparison with his own operations more favorable than he had dared hope, "whether we consider the quantity of lumber cut—the way in which it is manufactured—the manner in which it is taken care of when sawed—the quality of the lumber, etc."—HHC, Flint to WWC, NB, Sept. 13, 1857.

the two upper qualities of lumber here for the last few years has had the effect, in the survey, to crowd in a great many boards which a few years since would have been rejected. . . . I think as poor lumber will sell here for clear and 2nd rate as in Flint, but it must be well sawed and of even and uniform thickness.[5]

Some practical method of shipping lumber was required, however, if these markets were to be reached. Crapo had chosen Flint as his manufacturing point in the expectation that the Port Huron railroad would soon be completed to that place. But when the Panic of 1857 put a stop to virtually all railway construction, including the Port Huron road, he found it necessary to cast about for some alternative means of reaching a broader market.

The nearest existing rail line was the Detroit and Milwaukee, which passed through the village of Holly, sixteen miles to the south of Flint and linked with the latter by a plank road. On giving the matter some thought, Crapo realized with surprise that not only he but all other local lumbermen as well had completely overlooked the possibility of using this route to send out their lumber from Flint. His plan, as he explained it in a letter to his son, was

to purchase 2 or 3 acres of land directly on the R.R. at Holly for a lumber yard, and then make a contract with the Detroit & Milwaukee R.R. directors—which I can do on very favorable terms—to put a side track through the yard, and to haul my lumber . . . for such prices as we shall agree upon. . . . I shall then send my clear and 2d rate lumber over the planks 16 miles to my yard in Holly where it will be stuck up ready to be loaded onto the cars at any time.

. . . I am not going to set down and peddle out

lumber here in Flint solely, when there is a market at far higher prices for any amount that I can make, which can be reached by only 16 miles of good plank road, with a short route afterwards by Rail Road. With my lumber in Holly piled immediately on a side track I can send it over the Road E. or W. to supply every lumber yard from St. Johns, in Clinton Co., to Detroit —or, if preferable, to ship it East from Detroit to any point I choose, or sell to Lumber Merchants in Detroit.

The plan seemed perfect. "I must secure a monopoly if possible," he wrote William, adding that he expected no trouble in securing from the railroad "such terms and accommodations . . . as will for all practical purposes secure to me such monopoly." [6]

In submitting his proposal to the railroad, he pointed out that the quantity to be shipped the first year would be limited, "as I have manufactured the present season principally common lumber for sale at Flint." His timber, however, he continued,

> is of a quality and is so situated that I can increase or diminish the proportion of the upper qualities at pleasure. . . .
> Should I succeed in making such arrangements with you as will justify my doing so, I shall cut such quantity and quality of timber for the coming winter as will enable me to send over your road hereafter several million ft. per annum.[7]

We have no record of the terms of the agreement finally arrived at, but a bargain was made, and Crapo proceeded to establish lumber yards not only at Holly but also at Fentonville, another stop on the railroad five miles away.

Very likely his decision to use both points was calculated to maintain his monopoly of the plank road route for lumber shipments out of Flint.

With these arrangements made, he was now able to proceed with plans for the season's logging. He made contracts with jobbers to cut 3½ million feet of logs. In addition, this year he also put a crew of his own at work in the woods under Harthan. Between both groups of men, he hoped to get in between 6 and 7 million feet, enough to keep both his mills going without letup throughout the coming year. To Harthan's crew, he entrusted the cutting of his best timber, explaining to William that while it "will cost me quite as much and perhaps more than if I had let [it] out by the thousand, . . . in the end it will be more economical—even at a trifling more cost," because it would be cut well and without waste. "It does not however require so much skill, judgment and care to cut common, sapling timber," he continued, "and this description it is that I put out by the job." [8]

It was a busy winter for Crapo, for everything seemed to require his personal attention: the mills and lumber yard at Flint, the two new yards at Holly and Fentonville, the logging camps in the woods. A typical report on his activities reads:

> I must leave here for Marathon [where Harthan's camp was located] as soon as I can wallow through the snow, and after inspecting everything there and at the jobbers' camps, push out south after hay, &c. and teams to haul logs in the woods, as well as lumber to Holly and Fentonville.

"These constant and almost daily rides in an open waggon over hard roads this cold weather are rather tough," he wrote William, "but there is no dodging it." "It is certainly very different from the old Coml. Ins. office," he added wryly.[9]

II

As we have seen, the Panic of 1857 had in an indirect fashion forced Crapo to find a new way to get his lumber to market. Its direct effects on the enterprise were even more important. For nearly two years, the Michigan venture had been steadily absorbing the capital of the New Bedford partners without bringing in any return. First there was the purchase of the Driggs tract itself. Acquisition of the Walkley mill in 1856, and of the McQuigg mill the following year, had required an unforeseen additional investment. Repairs and improvements to the mills had added to the expense. The first season of logging, during the winter of 1856–57, had cost Crapo almost $6,500, while running the mills during 1857 had required nearly as much. A small amount of lumber had been sold during the summer, but as things stood in the fall of 1857 the firm was still largely dependent for its working capital on money siphoned off from the partners' other resources. Between October, 1856 and July, 1857 a total of $18,000 was paid in, coming equally from each of the three men. Yet even this did not provide any margin of safety, as was graphically indicated when Crapo wrote his son in September, 1857: "I shall be obliged to draw upon you tomorrow for funds for future expenses, as we cleaned out everything in the shape of money last night." [10]

As the depression deepened, however, it became clear that it would be increasingly difficult to turn to New Bedford in time of need. Arriving there for a brief visit in

November, Crapo found business very bad—"much worse than I expected," he wrote to Gee in Flint.

> Property is worth nothing, and from what I can see the present financial difficulty and derangement are very far from having passed away. In fact I see everywhere around me such evidences of "hard times," "bankruptcy," etc. as to feel very little of that small share of courage left which I was permitted to take with me from Flint.

It would be impossible, he feared, to get "another dollar" from New Bedford for operating expenses in Michigan; the winter's activities would have to be limited to what could be paid for with the proceeds of lumber sales.* Since plans for the winter included not only logging, but also hauling lumber to the Holly and Fentonville yards, the situation was doubly awkward. "I shall turn my steps towards Flint as soon as possible," he assured Gee, "and there labor to dig through—looking forward and hoping for the 'good time coming.' " [11]

In Flint the depression was taking its toll just as it was in New Bedford. Business was at "a perfect standstill," Crapo wrote his son in December after his return; "no one buys and no one sells." Farmers, finding markets for their surplus only at ruinous prices—or finding no markets at all—were quite naturally inclined to put off purchases until some more

---

* Harthan had twenty-four men at work in the woods, and three times within the space of six days Crapo wrote him expressing surprise and concern that so large a crew should be employed so early in the season. He was worried, too, that his wages were too high, particularly the premium rates he was paying for men who had been hired from Maine. "There must be thousands of men in Michigan," he wrote Harthan, "who would be glad to get work at $10 a month."—HHC, NB to Charles Harthan, Marathon, Nov. 25, 28, Dec. 1, 5, 1857, in LPB 6.

propitious time. Weather compounded the influence of "hard times." An open winter, with frequent thaws and little sledding, made it difficult to haul lumber into the surrounding countryside and provided another deterrent to sales. The one factor that eased Crapo's situation somewhat was his ability to accept provisions in exchange for lumber. Hogs, beef, corn, oats and butter were among the commodities taken in at one time or another during the winter, and either sent up to the logging camps in the woods or held for use the following summer in boarding the sawmill gangs. "In consequence of my being able to take produce," he reported to William in January, "my sales of lumber are larger than all the rest of the dealers here." [12]

The quantity of lumber sold even in this fashion, however, was very disappointing, and the amount sold for cash still less. Throughout the winter he had a constant struggle to keep his head above water financially. While barter sales helped make it possible to keep logging operations going, the need for some cash was inescapable. This was even more true of hauling lumber to the inconvenient railroad than of logging. "All of the teamers must have *some* money," he wrote, "and some of them must have *all* money for drawing." Yet it was vitally important, he felt, "to get all my clear and 2d rate lumber over the planks to the R.R. this winter, so as to be able to reach a market with it—in quantity—when spring comes." [13]

It was a perplexing situation indeed for Crapo. He was plagued constantly by a fear that he would be forced to suspend operations entirely for want of money. Weighing his situation in a letter to William, he wrote that "I can't fully satisfy my own mind whether it is best to struggle on and try to get in logs, or to stop that expense so far as I can." Yet on sober reflection, he could not escape the fact that any economy would be self-defeating if it meant failure to get in a stock of logs for sawing during the coming season. Only "two or three concerns in this entire region" were doing any logging. McFarlin, one of his principal competitors at Flint, was not putting in a single log, intending to stock his mill only with "what small lots [of logs] he can pick up of the farmers up river." In these circumstances, Crapo could not help but feel that perseverance would bring its own reward if he could only keep on building up his stock of lumber for the time when market conditions would return to normal.[14]

The only answer was to sink still more capital in the business, capital which—so far as he was concerned—could come only by applying to the lumber enterprise virtually every penny he could raise from sales of his western lands. He had been determined "to get along if possible without help," and had largely succeeded in doing so during the fall and early winter of 1857. Between September and December of that year he put more than $3,700 of his own funds into the business, while calling on Arnold and Prescott for a total of only $600 apiece. As payments for logging began to fall due early in 1858, however, and as his labor bill for running the mills mounted during the summer, he was forced to ask greater assistance from his partners. Between January and July their contributions totaled $3,550 each; in the same space of time Crapo himself put in just over $6,000.[15]

III

Crapo's original concept of a venture in lumbering had been of an enterprise operated as a sideline to his other interests and requiring no more than perhaps three months of his time out of the year. When the Driggs purchase was made, and particularly after his first trip to the Michigan pine lands, he began to see that it would require a far greater expenditure of both time and effort than he had contemplated. He clung nevertheless to the belief that he could run the business by "commuting," as it were, between New Bedford and Flint. Early in 1856, writing to tell his brother of the purchase, he explained that "I shall have to spend about half my time there . . . but have no idea of moving my family." [16]

As his business plans expanded to include the running of two sawmills, and as he learned the necessity of close supervision of logging operations, he was forced more and more to realize that the enterprise could not be run by remote control. During all of 1857 he had found it possible to spend scarcely more than a hundred days in New Bedford, and even when he was at home much of his time was taken up with matters related to the lumber venture. The hard times which prevailed by the end of that year proved to be the last straw. His struggle to get through the winter convinced him that the only possible hope of ultimate success lay in moving permanently to Flint. "Unless all my powers of body and mind and all my time are devoted to my business here," he wrote William, "I must inevitably lose what little I may have acquired during many years of care and anxiety and some little toil."

Accordingly, he proposed that his wife and children should join him in Michigan. They were not at all eager to leave their comfortable New Bedford home, but a prolonged separation appeared to be the only alternative. The thought of this was more than he could bear.

> Alone here and separated from all those influences of home and affection which have sustained me through many years of toil . . . [he wrote William], few can tell or will ever know or realize how much of fortitude and resolution has been required to carry me through the two last years of my life.

"Nothing," he continued, "could afford me so much support and encouragement in the years of toil now before me, as the presence and the society of [my family]." After several exchanges of letters, it was finally agreed that he would return to New Bedford briefly at the end of February to wind up his affairs there, and that his wife and daughters would return with him to establish their home in Flint.[17]

If he had earlier suspected that the purchase of the Driggs tract had been a mistake, he was now firmly convinced of it. "But then if it be a mistake," he wrote, "there is only one way ever to retrieve it, and that is by making the best of what remains." He was now, he thought, "somewhat wiser . . . than I was in the outset in regard to the nature of this business as well as to its details," and he saw his constant personal attention to these details as an absolute necessity.

> I find now, as the lumber is overhauled and sorted, etc., what has been lost by trusting to foremen; and although it will compare more than favorably with the lumber manufactured here by others, yet I shall for the future superintend personally everything in relation to the hiring of the men, the running of the mills, the manufacture of the lumber, etc. These things cannot be submitted to hired help—foremen though they be—without great loss; for men cannot be

found who will for mere wages do that which an employer's interest requires.

To his dismay he had discovered that he had on hand at the mills "more planks and common boards and a certain class of scantling than I shall sell for years," while his stock of fencing, flooring, and other types of lumber was only a fraction of what he would be able to sell. During the previous summer he had repeatedly called Burrell's attention to the kinds of lumber which should be sawed. The instructions had been ignored, however, simply because "it required less care on his part for the saws to run on day after day cutting out the simplest kind of lumber than it would to have fencing and flooring, etc., etc., sawed from all such logs as were best adapted for these purposes." [18]

Because of this and other incidents in the operation of the mill, he determined if possible to do without a foreman, and to hire instead a clerk who would free him from some of his duties in the counting room. With so many other things pressing upon him, he had found it impossible to keep up his accounts and he was worried that the problem would become unmanageable if left too long without attention. He therefore sought William's aid in securing the services of some ambitious young man from New Bedford, someone who "can work, and is not afraid of the weather, or the mud, on an occasion." He warned that whoever was hired should come "with the expectation of seeing a new country—bad roads—things laying about in an unfinished state, and altogether a different looking place from New Bedford." Crapo did not expect that keeping the accounts would require more than half the clerk's time once the books were written up to date, and he was careful to specify that any candidate should understand that his services might be used "on any work in connection with my business which would be proper and reasonable." He would be required to build the fire in the office, and to be up in the morning for breakfast at 5:30, the regular hour in the boarding house both winter and summer. By way of compensation, Crapo offered $300 a year and board—"certainly great wages at these times." Burrell, who had served as Crapo's mill foreman for less than a year, was discharged in January, and arrangements made for a young man from the East, Zachariah Chase, to join Crapo in March as his assistant in the office.[19]

With these plans completed, Crapo was set to make the best of a bad situation. "The future is uncertain," he recognized, "and no one can tell when trade will revive and business generally be restored to a healthy active state." But he was able to see some bright spots even in the dark picture presented by the prevailing hard times. For one thing, he expected to be able to hire mill hands for considerably less than in the past. Even more important, he saw some basic changes being wrought in the lumber business in Michigan:

> Such has been—and to a certain extent is now—the wonderful facilities for getting pine timber into the numerous streams leading from almost every part of the northern portion of the lower peninsula of this state into the navigable waters of the surrounding lakes, that every man for the last few years who has had a 40 acre lot of pine land and could raise three shillings of cash and the "balance" on "Bond and Mortgage" has built a saw mill somewhere and commenced sawing lumber—and has then sold it for just what it would bring, without any reference to cost of manufacture or the worth of timber on the stump. They have started in debt and have then manufactured at every disadvantage, and have finally sold

their lumber for less than cost to meet payments that trod constantly upon their heels from the very outset.

But this class of men, who have not only fouled their own nests but have prostrated and crippled the business by their unreasonable competition, with which the solvent and judicious and prudent manufacturer has had to contend, are now effectually "done up," and are buried and sunk so low that no line can ever be found long enough to reach them and to bring them to the surface again.

"They are disposed of," he rejoiced, and "for a time, at least, the business will be left to the control of skill and capital judiciously applied." The "regular" manufacturers —in whose number he of course counted himself—he hoped would be able to conduct their enterprises "at less expense and more in accordance with the laws of trade and economy than it has been possible to do for the last few years." *

* "Three-fourths of the men now in the business are mere 'one horse concerns,'" he wrote in another letter; the cleansing effect of the hard times would soon bring about a situation in which "the whole business must and will be carried on by not over one-third of the men now in it, and at a good profit."—HHC, Flint to WWC, NB, Jan. 25, 29, 1858.

four

THE PROBLEMS OF A LUMBERMAN: II
(1858 - 1859)

I

Late in March, 1858, Crapo arrived in Flint with his
family to take up permanent residence there. This move,
perhaps even more than his initial venture into the lumber
business, would in retrospect prove to be the turning point
in his life. No longer was he a New Englander at work in
the West. As his fate and fortunes became increasingly in-
tertwined with those of his adopted state, he truly became
a Michigan man.

The years 1858 and 1859 form a distinct period in his
Michigan career. The dominant theme of these two years
was his struggle to make the lumber enterprise profitable
in the face of continued economic stagnation. In this task
he was, as we shall see, only partially successful. But through
his efforts in this critical period he laid the foundations for
ultimate success on a grand scale.

Immediately on his return to Flint, he energetically took
hold of the problems of preparing for the coming season's
operations. Harthan was already engaged in running the
winter's cut of logs down the river, and securing them in
the booms required long and arduous labor. The two contractors had cut more than 2,150,000 feet of logs, and with
the amount put in by Harthan's own crew and the logs left
over from the year before, Crapo had a stock of more than
6 million feet of logs. Getting the mills ready to run also

required a great deal of care. Repairs had to be made, piles of lumber shifted in the yards to make room for the new cut as it came from the saws, a crew of men hired, and so on. Thanks to the depression, from the moment of his return Crapo found himself "bothered constantly with applicants for work, in my counting room, in the streets, and everywhere." He had dispensed with his foreman, and the entire task of recruiting men for the mills fell on his shoulders along with the many other details requiring his personal attention.[1]

In less than three weeks, however, he was ready to start up the saws. The first day, he was on his feet constantly from four in the morning until seven at night. "You may be assured," he wrote William that evening, "that it is no small matter to start two such mills at the same time with a gang of nearly 50 men—outside and in—many of them ignorant of what you really want of them, and all of them at more or less loss as to their work." Crapo's description of the first day's activity reveals clearly the pace which he had set both for himself and for his men:

> The principal difficulty is in getting the logs into the mill and the lumber out of it. . . . The sawyers are of course men of experience and know what they have to do, and are in fact fixtures; but as to the logs that come to their saws, or the edging of the lumber, or the sorting and piling of it, they know nothing and care nothing; and what is more they are to be watched and drilled constantly to be made to cut certain qualities of logs into certain descriptions of lumber; and these descriptions are very numerous, much more so than you can possibly imagine without positive knowledge on the subject.

But when you come to sorting and piling, then it is infinitely worse to manage. With 10 raw, green, thickheaded Irishmen to take lumber that is passing back from the saws in a steady stream, in every possible shape and form and quality, and have it conveyed to more than 50 different piles by them, is I can assure you no trifling matter. You must jump and spring and shove and lift yourself and be all over the mills and throughout every part of the yards until all the piles get fairly started, and every man learns his place and can tell to which pile out of more than 50 any given board or class of lumber should go; and at the same time see to the edging table that the lumber is properly dressed and the sawyers that it is of the proper thickness, etc., etc.

But you may inquire why all this at once? I answer for the simple reason that very much depends in starting right. Men have to be taught in the very outset what is required of them and what they must do and how it must be done, if it is ever expected that they will do it. . . . The natural tendency of men who are employed is to drop, little by little, below the standard taken at the start, but never to rise above it.[2]

Understandably, Crapo had been somewhat skeptical of his ability to operate without a foreman. Only a year before, he had been utterly ignorant of the problems of operating a sawmill. Nothing in all his varied experience before embarking on the lumber venture had even vaguely resembled the active management of a crew of workmen. Yet after a few weeks' trial he felt more than satisfied with the result:

I have succeeded beyond my expectations in reducing things to system. The men are all cheerful—everyone is on hand promptly to the minute—and all seem anxious and willing to enter into my views and to yield up to my arrangements.

His own work day was invariably fourteen hours or longer, and he drove his mill gangs "as they were never drove before." He demanded from his men the same effort that he himself exerted:

> As soon as I find a man disposed to waste time he is paid off and discharged at once, and a new man put in his place. This of course applies to the common hands. My head sawyers, engineers, edgers, etc. and prime men whom I know and who know me, still they are liable to lose their place, and that risk, if nothing more, ensures faithfulness.

By constant supervision of every detail, he expected to be able to cut his lumber at no more than two-thirds what it had cost him the year before. "By keeping a little short of hands and shifting them where work crowds the hardest," he wrote William, "I am able to save the labor of 2 or 3 men." He was already meeting a large part of his wage bill with provisions taken in exchange for lumber. To conserve his cash even further, he secured a stock of such items as coffee, tea, sugar, rough clothing, etc., to pay out to his men in lieu of money wages, figuring that he might in this way make a 25 per cent profit which would otherwise go to the storekeepers of Flint.[3]

Throughout the spring and summer of 1858 he continued to be harrassed by a shortage of operating funds as acute as that which had plagued him during the preceding winter. The market at Flint was dull, and sales there were next to nothing, a situation which was aggravated by price-cutting on the part of the other dealers. To his surprise, he was selling more than four times as much at his Fentonville yard, although it had been established primarily to serve in connection with his plans for shipping his upper grades of lumber out by rail to paying markets. The sales at that point to the farmers of the surrounding region, however, were principally of common lumber in exchange for provisions. While this barter trade helped him pay his mill men, some cash was needed for this purpose as well, and all cash was required to meet the bills for logging. The stock of "uppers" which had been hauled over the planks to the Fentonville and Holly yards offered no prospect of rapid return. It could only be worked off to advantage by patiently seeking out buyers who would pay satisfactory prices.

Yet desperate as was his need for money, Crapo felt that it was "no time to sell." "Many persons having lumber on hand," he explained to William, "are obliged to sell at ⅔ cost, and that we are not going to do. Their lumber, however, is disappearing, and by another year the market must be nearly bare." Only a very small stock of logs had been cut in the region during the preceding winter, and few concerns were doing any sawing at all. Only one of seventeen large mills at Saginaw was running. "Now," Crapo felt, "is the time to manufacture; labor and provisions are low, and good men can be found, which cannot be done when all the mills are running." [4]

The only way he could keep going, however, was by sinking still more money into the business. "Tell Arnold and Prescott," he appealed to William in April, "that I must have means to keep the saws constantly in motion, whether we sell or not." Their aid, together with what he could spare himself, tided him over each crisis, but the crises kept recurring. In July he reported that he had had to resort to paying his men in store orders, and that the storekeepers were now dunning him for their money. He had received two payments of $50 and $75 from land sales, he wrote, "which barely carried me over last night (Saturday) with my men, and without which I hardly know what I should have done." [5]

In his determination to keep the mills running full blast, with or without sales, Crapo was acting in the firm belief that the long-awaited rail connection to Flint would soon become a reality. His plan to use the Detroit and Milwaukee Railroad by hauling lumber over the plank roads to Fentonville and Holly—under the circumstances an excellent step—was nevertheless in the nature of a stop-gap arrangement. Although it met the immediate need for some kind of outlet to a broader market, inherent difficulties in the operation made it clear to Crapo that a direct rail outlet was still important. For one thing, the expense of the plank road route was all out of proportion to the distance involved. The teamsters had to be paid $1.75 per thousand feet for hauling the lumber some sixteen miles to the Fentonville and Holly yards, while the cost of unloading and piling the lumber, and then later loading it onto freight cars, added another $1.00 per thousand. In contrast, the rail charges for the fifty-two miles from Fentonville to Detroit were only $1.71 per thousand feet, and would doubtless have been little more could the lumber have been sent directly by rail all the way from Flint. While the upper grades might command prices high enough to warrant this expensive transportation, the plank road route could do very little to open wider markets for Crapo's common lumber. Equally important, it lacked the flexibility which a direct rail connection would have afforded. Again, lumber could be hauled to the yards at the railroad only at such times—

generally during the winter months—when the farmers were free enough from their own tasks to be able to hire out as teamsters.[6]

For these reasons, Crapo continued to watch eagerly for any signs of renewed life in the railroad project that was to link Flint with Port Huron. Under the impact of the panic, construction work had been abandoned the previous autumn. In the spring of 1858, however, new arrangements were announced which made it seem certain that the line would be completed to Flint by the end of the following summer. This news encouraged Crapo greatly as he struggled to keep going in the difficult months after his move to Flint.[7] Yet now just as before, he was due for disappointment. Indeed, one is inclined to wonder whether he could have found courage to keep on at all had he known how long the realization of a direct rail outlet would be delayed. Not until 1862 would Flint have any rail connection whatsoever—and the line which was opened in this year was the Flint and Pere Marquette, which ran between Flint and Saginaw and was of only minor importance in Crapo's operations. The anticipated railroad from Flint to Port Huron —the route whose planned construction had persuaded him to locate his operations at Flint—would in fact not be built within his lifetime.

Still, whatever its weaknesses, the plank road route did offer an outlet of sorts for his lumber, and even as he watched for signs of progress on the Port Huron railroad, he sought to make what use he could of the means at hand.

He kept his mills running steadily throughout 1858, much to the surprise of others in the region who thought him "a strange man" indeed and marveled that any lumberman could be found having "either the means or the courage" to continue sawing without prospects of sales. By the end of the season he had cut out all but one million of the 6 million feet of logs with which he had begun the year. In preparation for the next season's sawing, he had Harthan and his men put in nearly 3 million feet of good logs during the winter of 1858–59, and the sole contractor whom he engaged cut a quarter of a million feet of sapling logs to add to this amount.[8]

From the standpoint of mill operations, 1859 was uneventful. He had been obliged to make extensive repairs on his piers and booms in the river, and before starting the saws the engines, boilers and other machinery in the mills had to be carefully overhauled. "Mills are like old ships," he observed to his son, "and like old ships will require at every fresh start many times the outlay that was anticipated." He had, however, "constantly added to and improved" their condition until they were in better shape than when bought, better even than at any time under their previous owners. Personal supervision of the mill demanded more time than he could properly spare from his other responsibilities, yet he felt that it was time well spent:

> No one but myself can manage the men employed and have them cut the lumber right, and work up to time. No hired person can do it, for no hired person can maintain any influence over them for any length of time, no matter how well they may be disposed. What I see coming under my own observation I can talk about and charge upon the guilty, and correct; but whatever comes to me through a hired foreman in any sense is sure to make a fuss. They will receive reproof from me with submission for anything that I personally see or know, but if reported to me they regard it in the light of "spying" and "watching," and very foolishly resent it. I have good men—nearly 50—

but they are of all nations, and tempers, and prejudices; and they will work well so long as *I* can manage
and look after them, and hold them square up to
their duty.

The result of his unremitting efforts gave him great satisfaction, however. It was with no small pride that he reported
that his lumber was generally considered to be of excellent
quality, "notwithstanding the fact that it has been manufactured by myself, who never until within the last two or
three years knew one board from another—and in a region
proverbial for the bad manufacture of lumber." [9]

II

Despite Crapo's desire to avoid competition with those
who were forced to sell at sacrifice prices, the problem of
finding paying markets for his own lumber could not long
be postponed. As matters stood in the spring of 1858, more
than three-fourths of the lumber sawed during his first
season of mill operations remained on hand. In the thirteen
months between February 26, 1857 (when he had opened
his accounts), and April 1, 1858, barely one million feet of
lumber had been sold, bringing in a total of just $9,535.
Operating expenses had already come to many times that
sum. Even without taking into consideration his own $3,000
a year salary, the receipts from sales had fallen far short of
maintaining the business, let alone justifying the extensive
investment which had been made.[10]

These sales, of course, had all been made to his local
retail market, either at Flint or at Fentonville. Now, however, he was running into serious trouble there, as the other
dealers sought desperately to unload their lumber by cutting
their prices. The problem had first cropped up in the

months immediately following the Panic of 1857, when Alexander McFarlin and some of the other local lumbermen retreated from the long-standing Flint price of $8 a thousand feet for common lumber. At first Crapo attempted to stand aloof, relying on the quality of his lumber to carry him through. "At present," he wrote William in January, 1858,

> I am selling nothing, as all the other dealers here have within the last week assumed the attitude towards each other of the "Kilkenny Cats," and seem more decidedly bent on eating up each other than conducting their business like rational business men. They have some 4 or 5 "sharks" each on the streets and it is almost impossible for a teamer to get into my yard even if he wished to. They will for the sake of underselling each other take almost any price. I of course have nothing to do with this. My lumber is good, is well sawed and well stuck up, and when they, like the "Kilkenny Cats," have destroyed themselves—all but the tail—I hope and believe that my lumber will bring an advance on present prices.[11]

The pressure of cut-rate competition continued, however, and after long deliberation he concluded to come down $1.00 on cash sales, while holding to the old prices on barter sales. When he did this, though, he found that he got all the trade because his lumber was of better quality, and that in consequence his competitors lowered their price still further. He concluded that it was fruitless to try to compete in price, and finally resolved to maintain the former prices, "sell or not sell." The situation drifted along in this state throughout the summer, but in the fall McFarlin renewed the competition with a vengeance, prompting Crapo to call on him "with a view to have some understanding in regard to prices." Receiving no satisfaction, and having determined that "I must and will control this market," Crapo went in for all-out competition to drive McFarlin to the wall. After a week during which McFarlin secured all the trade of the farmers coming to Flint with their teams for lumber, Crapo decided to adopt a new tactic:

> I commenced sorting my lumber [he wrote] so as to keep back all the best of it for dressing, etc., and selling the balance at his prices, and even less where we could not secure a purchase without, and for the last week we have again cut off nearly all his sales. I am fairly in for a regular trial of strength and have no fear of the result. My lumber is so much better than his that I can sell the poorest part of my common at $6 and with my planing machine work up the better part so as to reach a figure much above him.[12]

The battle continued throughout the winter. McFarlin kept six or eight "sharks" on the streets of the village who would meet prospective buyers and "tell every teamer to go to all the yards and get the lowest prices they can and then come to him and he will sell .25¢ per M. less." When he persisted in this course, Crapo at once changed his own policy "so as to sell nothing and at the same time compel him to sell at the lowest possible prices." By February, 1859, he found that he was making some headway in the competition, with McFarlin's assortment of good lumber depleted while his own remained intact. While conceding that the old price line could no longer be held, Crapo had settled down to a policy which was to serve him for some years to come in dealing with his local market:

My common lumber I am selling for $5 and $6 per M
—very low—but no lower than the others, nor in fact
not so low, for we have no regular prices. When a
man wants nothing but common or culls *we sell* at
some price—if we can; but when he wants common
with fencing and flooring and the upper grades then
we make those qualities sell the common at our own
prices.[13]

This struggle for the local retail market was important.
Crapo's real problem, however, was to push his lumber
into the broader currents of the lumber trade nationally.
Only here could he expect to sell in quantities large enough
and at prices high enough to make the enterprise a paying
proposition. Inefficient as they were, his arrangements to
reach the railroad at Fentonville by the plank road from
Flint had provided him with the physical means for reaching out to more distant markets. His efforts during 1858
and 1859 to develop the possibilities of this outlet are
a story of steady exploration and experimentation. He had
succeeded in a relatively short time in mastering the many
problems of manufacturing lumber; he now had to find his
way in the competitive race to market it.

During the winter of 1857–58, he had begun sending
his clear and "second-rate [clear]" lumber over the planks
to Fentonville. Piled up there in his yard on the railroad,
it was ready to be shipped out whenever a purchaser might
be found. His first encounters with the lumber buyers who
traveled through the sawmill regions, however, were most
disappointing. These dealers, who bought to ship to Albany,
Chicago, and other lumber centers, were eager to take his
lumber, but despite his urgent need for cash he could not
agree to sell at the prices offered. In disgust, he wrote his
son that "they want all the profits and the cream of the

lumber." He decided instead, as his first move, to make the trial of sending a small lot of his "uppers" directly to William in New Bedford. He recognized that such a course would require more effort than dealing with a traveling buyer, but he could not accept the idea "of selling what little clear and 2d rate clear lumber I have on hand to others to send over the same course, and thereby make a profit of $5 to $8 per M."[14]

By mid-May, 1858, he had his first shipment ready to go east from the Fentonville yard. The eight carloads—65,000 feet—were to go by rail to Detroit, by lake vessel to Oswego, by canal boat to Albany on the Erie Canal, and then again by ship to New Bedford. At prevailing Flint prices the lumber would have been worth from $16 to $18 per thousand feet, had there been any buyers. In New Bedford, Crapo hoped, "it should bring $42 certainly." Since the total cost of shipping from Flint to New Bedford was just a little over $12 a thousand feet, it seemed at last that there would be some prospect of profit.[15]

When the shipment arrived in New Bedford, however, it proved difficult to sell even at $40. The urgent need of western lumbermen for cash, together with unusually low freight rates to the East, had combined to glut the market at Albany and other eastern points, and by the end of July Crapo was regretting that he had not been willing to take $38 for the cargo when it had arrived. Despite his need for money, though, he felt that the lumber should not be sacrificed. He instructed William to sell in quantity for $38 if possible, but not to be alarmed if this could not be done. "We can get our price in time," he assured his son, "but may have to keep [the lumber] a year" to do so.[16]

With prospects dim for any immediate returns from the New Bedford shipment, Henry continued to search for other markets which could be reached from his yard at Fenton-ville. It remained a slow process, however, since "so many who have lumber are unable to hold it that those seeking to buy with cash can make their own price." One sale of 100,000 feet of clear siding to go to Albany brightened the picture somewhat in July. The price of $12.50 a thousand feet delivered in Detroit seemed low to Crapo, particularly since the lumber would have to be drawn from Flint to Fentonville in mid-summer, but the money was needed to keep the mills going. Crapo also felt some justification for the deal in that it would serve to introduce his lumber to the Albany market. One unforeseen result of his arrangements with the Detroit and Milwaukee Railroad was that the railroad itself turned to him for several sizable lots of lumber. The quality of the lumber which he furnished was so satisfactory that soon he was supplying all the lumber used along the entire line from Detroit to Grand Haven, despite the fact that Detroit dealers had offered to furnish it for $1.00 a thousand feet less.[17]

By the fall of 1858, the number of traveling buyers from Chicago, Cincinnati, Cleveland, Syracuse and other cities had increased measurably, and the market had begun to pick up somewhat. In October, Crapo had several offers to buy up all his clear and "seconds" at prices considerably above those which had prevailed in mid-summer, but he still felt it was to his advantage to hold out for a rise in prices. Short as he was of funds, his enterprise was none the less far better financed than most in Michigan at that time, and he aimed to take full advantage of this fact. With most of the lumber which had been drawn to the railroad still on hand, he continued throughout the winter and spring to add to the piles at his Fentonville yard in the hope that 1859 might bring better opportunities for selling at a profit.[18]

He was playing a waiting game. In February he wrote William:

> I have now more than two bona fide cash customers for my clear and 2nd rate clear lumber, but I will not give prices until spring opens. Mine is in fact the best lot of seasoned lumber—in manufacturer's hands—that can be found anywhere in this region, and all the lumber buyers on this side of the peninsula know it.

By mid-May, 1859, he had some 600,000 feet of "uppers" at Fentonville, and had still reached no decision on selling it. In his chaffering with prospective purchasers, however, he had learned much about the pitfalls awaiting the unsuspecting lumberman. To his son he wrote:

> The buyers of lumber here are all sharks. They are a class of men that have ever stood between the manufacturer and the regular dealer, and they intend to buy of the poor manufacturer at their own prices, and sell to the dealer at about $6 per M higher rates. There is not nominally that profit made by the shark, but in reality it is. For instance, he obtains an inspection that uses up inevitably the manufacturer who deals with him, buying No. 2's at quoted prices, but taking nothing that is not perfect, and No. 3's the same—and then selling both grades to the dealer for No. 2's—and so of lower grades, through the entire inspection. The manufacturer can't live unless he can get the same inspection by which the dealer sells lumber.
>
> The regular lumber buyer of the manufacturer— he who buys to ship and sell to certain dealers by cargo—is certainly the hardest man . . . that I ever had any conception of. I won't sell them my lumber,

unless they pay me for it, and that they won't do.
They have worked hard to buy my lumber for the last
3 months, and thought in the start that I must do just
as they said, and sell at their prices—but I'll send the
whole to New Bedford—anywhere—first, before they
shall have it.[19]

At first he had expected that the lumber jobbers who visited him at Flint would be forced with the passage of time to
give him satisfactory prices for his stock of "uppers." He now
began to see that these hopes were futile. The "sharks" were
well aware that the average sawmill operator was in no position to leave his mills for the purpose of selling his lumber
in some outside market. Crapo was no exception; indeed, if
anything he was more restricted in his movements than most
manufacturers, because of his insistence on rigid personal
supervision of all details of his mill operations.[20] Yet if he
refused to sell to the "sharks" on their own terms, there
seemed to be but two alternatives. He might ship the lumber to some eastern point to be sold for him on commission
by a resident wholesale dealer, or he might himself accompany the lumber to Albany or some other center, and there
personally take charge of its sale.

For some time Crapo had been considering the former
possibility. In January, 1859, one Ezra D. Fogg, a lumber
dealer of Providence, Rhode Island, had written him proposing to take his entire stock of good lumber on consignment and to sell it for a commission of 5 per cent. Crapo's
first reaction was favorable, as he had been thinking of the
desirability of selecting some point "to which all my lumber
going East might be sent, so as to get a reputation for it
that would secure future sales." He wondered, though, if it
might not be more valuable to make several shipments to
different cities, so that they would serve as samples of his

lumber in various markets. What caused him to hesitate more than anything else, however, was his fear that extras would make the 5 per cent commission more like 10 per cent, and that Fogg would not take any particular care to see that good prices and a fair inspection were secured. He had also been considering a second shipment to William in New Bedford, but his experience the year before made him cautious about committing much of his stock in that direction either.[21]

By the end of May he felt it was time to have the lumber moving somewhere. Still unsatisfied with Fogg's proposals and with prospects for sale in New Bedford, he concluded that his best move would be to ship his entire lot from Fentonville to Albany, meeting it there himself and either selling it or re-shipping it from there to whatever point seemed desirable in the light of conditions at that lumber capital. He did not like the prospect of leaving the mills, but he felt that in no other way could he secure an adequate return for his lumber. On second thought, however, he decided first to make an exploratory trip to the three principal lumber centers—Chicago, Cincinnati, and Albany—to make a first-hand check on conditions at each city and to see whether one of the western points might not prove a better market than Albany. While he found Chicago men willing to buy his lumber, one day there convinced him that he could probably do better elsewhere. In Cincinnati, he found the picture considerably more cheerful. The day he arrived he received a better offer for his clear lumber than any he had had before, and he regretted very much not having visited that city earlier in the season, before the dealers had purchased their stock for the year. He found that he could ship his lumber there from Detroit cheaper and with less trouble than to Albany, the charges totaling $4.00 per thousand feet as against $5.12½ per thousand to the latter point. After making conditional arrangements to ship a large quantity of his "uppers" to Cincinnati if no better opportunity developed, he pushed on to Albany.[22]

Arriving in the lumber capital of the nation, he was subjected to a rude shock. It was virtually impossible, he found, to sell any lumber there except through the services of one of the many wholesale dealers or brokers. In a long letter to William, he described the way the trade was carried on:

> Here everything is regulated by a Board of Trade, either in fact or by the mutual understanding and uniform practice of every man in the business, and against which no one manufacturer . . . can successfully compete. Almost without an exception the dealers here buy no lumber. . . . They are large and no doubt wealthy concerns, receiving lumber from the manufacturers on consignment, and selling on commission. . . . The regular commission is 10% on the gross amount of sales with every possible "extra" that a "sharp" man can stick on to a dull or inexperienced one in the final settlement.

How could the manufacturer escape these heavy charges? Perhaps by selling his lumber outright to the Albany dealers; but this could be done—if at all—only by taking prices which would in effect afford the dealers at least 15 or 20 per cent commission instead of 10. The only possible alternative would be to reach the retail lumber yard dealers and consumers who looked to Albany for their supply. In this, however, there were "very serious obstacles":

> A manufacturer stands no chance whatever in selling to them whether in the city of N.Y. or elsewhere be-

cause they will not bother themselves with purchasing of a man whom they do not know and of the character of whose lumber they cannot readily inform themselves, and of the present ruling prices for which they are perhaps ignorant, so long as they can come or send directly here and at once see just what they can do— the best that can be done, get just what they want, and at the lowest possible prices.

Although this "system" by which the Albany market operated was well established, Crapo rebelled against it. "I cannot . . . conform to the course adopted by 19 out of every 20— not to say 99 out of every 100—of the lumber manufacturers. . . . Men that will continue to manufacture lumber and quietly submit to such a system deserve to be poor, and should be poor all their days, as they most certainly will be."

Although all the burden and toil falls upon the poor manufacturer, and although he is compelled to furnish all, or nearly all, the real capital required to be permanently invested—and which is really "locked up"—in the lumbering business, still he is . . . the slave of a class of men, who with very little real capital are enabled to live at their ease and like gentlemen, and who stand between him and the yard, retail dealers, and consumers, receiving from them and at their hands just what they in their tender mercies are disposed to give him.

"A manufacturer," he told William, "must either submit at once to the 'system' however it may operate against him, or as the only alternative seek some point where he can get the confidence and the trade of the retail yard dealer." To do this would require time, perseverance, and "no small amount of energy and business tact." Yet, he felt, "*we* must succeed in this effort or abandon the business at the first possible moment."

> My aim is to save the commission—the profits—of the dealer here, the lumber brokers everywhere, to myself as a part of the value of my lumber, and to reach the dealers or consumers beyond or outside of this class. . . . If it can't be avoided in any other way we must have a yard of our own at some suitable point.

At the time of his visit, prevailing prices to the trade at Albany were $19, $23, and $33 for "the three higher grades of Canada and N.Y. lumber." Crapo felt sure that his lumber, if sent there, would bring $20, $25, and $35, since it was a choice lot and seasoned. But after taking off the inevitable 10 per cent, these prices were distinctly too low for his views:

> I must and think I shall do better; in fact I can do better by falling back on Cincinnati, where I made certain conditional arrangements the other day. . . . I was favorably impressed with the appearance of the dealers there; they want just such lumber as I shall have to sell, and I can reach them there, as soon as they find out who and what I am, without paying some white-gloved gentleman dealer or broker 10% for the privilege of selling my lumber to them.[23]

III

On June 29, Crapo returned to Flint, after ten days' absence during which he had traveled 2,172 miles. However discouraging his experience in Albany, it nevertheless was extremely valuable. He now knew what he was up against in seeking markets for his lumber, and the conclusions which he drew were in large measure to shape his course for the rest of his career in the lumber business.

He was physically exhausted by the trip and on his arrival was confronted once again by the strenuous routine required by the ordinary operations of his enterprise. He now felt, however, that he was at last on the road to success in disposing of his lumber on satisfactory terms. During the ensuing weeks he devoted all the time he could spare to building up a market "peculiarly my own,"

> that is, a market by which I could hope to sell hereafter to men desirous of buying my lumber without the intervention or aid of jobbers; and to a certain extent without having my prices influenced by the weekly quotations in Chicago or other places, indeed by accidents and uncertainties of heavy shipments at certain times made by men compelled to sell at just what they could get for the time.

Although he still hoped to find means of reaching directly to eastern markets, Ohio seemed to offer the most in immediate possibilities. Within a few months after his return to Flint, he had sold not only a large shipment of 200,000 feet of clear lumber to Cincinnati, but also a great many smaller lots, including some of his better grade common, to go to Toledo and other points to the south. "By unremitted efforts," he wrote William, "I am pushing out and securing markets, every day almost, where no one here ever thought of sending lumber." [24]

Achieving these results required a vast amount of care and labor. On one occasion he spent four full days at his Fentonville yard supervising the loading of 60,000 feet of lumber for shipment to Toledo and Cincinnati, personally measuring and inspecting each board to guarantee that it would meet the expectations of the buyers and encourage further orders. Much time was taken up in arranging the details of transportation, and in bargaining with the various railroad companies to secure the lowest possible rates. The effort was worth it, however; small orders continued to come in from many different places despite a generally dull market. "Wherever I have been able to sell a carload," he wrote, "orders for more have quickly followed." One small lot went to Decatur, Illinois; another to Milwaukee, Wisconsin.[25] Selling and shipping in small quantities demanded extra effort, but it paid off—he was realizing from $2.00 to $3.00 a thousand feet, and sometimes more, over his neighbors who sold at wholesale.*

Equally important, in view of the dullness of the retail market at Flint, was the fact that he was finding an outlet for a considerable amount of his common lumber as well. At the beginning of the year he had undertaken to have the top third or so of his common sorted out from the piles and hauled to Fentonville along with his clear. It would be, he wrote William, "not quite equal to Albany select box [lumber]," but he hoped that it might sell in such manufacturing centers as Lowell, where much lumber was required for packing boxes. Since he was paying teamsters largely with the poor common, he felt he could make good progress to-

---

* His lumber going to Cincinnati brought him $33 and $24 for the two upper grades (No. 2 clear and No. 3 or "second-rate" clear), while at Toledo he was getting $28 and $22. With the cost of transportation from Flint $8.00 and $4.50 respectively to the two points, the lumber was netting him at Flint $25 and $16 for his Cincinnati shipments and $23.50 and $17.50 for those to Toledo. Since No. 2's and No. 3's usually had to be sold together, this made the market about equal at the two places. Inasmuch as the long-standing retail prices at Flint for these two grades were $16 and $12, breaking into these Ohio markets was a significant advance.—HHC, Flint to WWC, NB, Oct. 5, 1859.

wards working off his entire stock if he could make this "box" pay to ship outside. Having failed to find satisfactory prices in the East for his "uppers," however, it was obvious that this class of lumber would be even more of a problem to dispose of there, since the cost of transportation would remain the same. In Ohio, however, he was finding buyers for it who were willing to pay prices more than ample to justify the shipping charges.[26]

In another move to dispose of common lumber, he had decided in March, 1859, to make the attempt of rafting some 500,000 feet down the Flint River to Saginaw. Most of his neighbors fully expected that the rafts would be broken up on the rapids in the river, and the lumber lost. Crapo could see that it would not be sold at Flint for a long time to come, however, and he needed to clear his yard if he was to continue to run the lower mill. Weighing the loss of another year's interest on the money tied up in the lumber, the cost of moving the piles, and the danger of fire, on the one hand, against the risk involved in rafting the lumber, on the other, he decided to take the chance. To the surprise of the skeptics, the job was completed virtually without incident. When the lumber arrived in Saginaw, however, there was little demand, and Crapo decided to hold it there in the hope that conditions would improve. Since he was able to devote relatively little attention to disposing of it, in the midst of all his other activity, by August only 185,000 feet had been sold. This lot had gone to Connecticut, though at a very low figure. Lacking any better outlet for the balance of the lumber at Saginaw, he finally decided to send it to Fogg in Providence, Rhode Island, as a test of what that dealer could do. In reviewing the results of this experiment, Crapo recognized that he would probably wind up taking a loss on the lumber, as against Flint prices, but he still believed he would be ahead by having made the attempt. In demonstrating the feasibility of rafting lumber to Saginaw, he felt he now had a solid argument against any possible attempt by the Detroit and Milwaukee Railroad to raise its charges on carrying his lumber from Fentonville to Detroit.[27]

In still another instance he succeeded in working off a quantity of common outside of Flint, with a sale in May of more than 200,000 feet to a man in Detroit. The price received was $10 a thousand feet for dressed lumber and $8.00 for undressed, delivered at the railroad at Fentonville. Since getting lumber hauled over the planks during the summer cost Crapo $2.00 a thousand feet, the price was low enough, but it still netted him the same as the reduced retail prices prevailing at Flint.[28]

Despite the fiasco of his Albany trip, Crapo continued to hope that he could sell some of his clear lumber in the East. He felt it was important to work his lumber into every market he could reach, so as to establish a reputation for it and put him in a position to take advantage of the inevitable variations which made one market better at a particular time and another at some later date. Throughout the summer of 1859 he negotiated directly and through William with the principal dealers in New Bedford. His former neighbors there were interested in his lumber, but like other eastern men he had contacted, they had been unwilling to offer prices he considered satisfactory. Once he had succeeded in getting several important sales in Ohio, however, he felt ready to put New Bedford to another test, though he still lacked any definite commitment from the dealers there. Late in August he shipped William 146,000 feet of his clear and second-rate and 24,000 feet of clapboards, hoping that once it arrived it would be taken by either Wilcox or Greene and Wood, two of the principal dealers at New Bedford. In the fall he also made a small sale of 60,000 feet to a house in Boston, and sent another shipment on consignment to Fogg, this time consisting of 150,000 feet of his "uppers." [29]

In the middle of September, 1859, there was a sudden turn downwards in the lumber market generally, forcing him to give up hope of working off the rest of his stock at Fentonville until the next year. The shipments already made, however, were sufficient to give him a fair trial of the various markets. His efforts in Ohio had proved an unqualified success. In October he had word from a house in Toledo that they would want their entire next year's supply from him, some 800,000 feet. Despite unfavorable conditions, he was receiving orders every week from Cincinnati, Dayton, and other Ohio cities. Triumphantly he wrote his son, "I have now reached a point—by much toil and hard labor certainly —where my lumber is and will be sought after." [30]

The results of the several shipments East, on the other hand, were uniformly discouraging. The New Bedford dealers were bent on taking every possible advantage, both in price and in inspection, and William finally decided the best interests of all would be served by holding the lumber until spring, a view with which his father was forced to agree. Meanwhile, of course, the heavy transportation charges had to be paid, once again putting Crapo in a tight spot for funds. The shipments to Fogg had been no better. Fogg had

> held out great prospects to me of what he could do with my lumber in Providence if I would ship it to him, and when I done so he sold it—as I learn by others, not by him—in Albany as it arrived; and of course sold it at Albany prices which will not net me hardly one half which I am getting for what I sell here and at Fentonville and South.

Even on the sale to Boston, which had been made at relatively high prices ($40 for the clear), Crapo found he had been cheated in the inspection to the tune of some six or eight hundred dollars. It is little wonder that he concluded:

> I do not feel like sending any more lumber East, for it is too long a road, and is lined with too many who live by plundering the manufacturer of everything. I have learned too late that [he] is a prey to everybody.[31]

five

YEAR OF DECISION: I
(1860)

I

While Crapo was at work in Michigan, his two partners in New Bedford watched with concern the slow progress of the enterprise which at the outset had seemed to offer such great possibilities for profit. They already had been called upon to furnish considerable sums of money beyond their original investment, and Arnold in particular was anxious for an accounting. All during the summer and fall of 1859, while Crapo was desperately seeking to develop markets for his lumber, Arnold nagged him constantly to balance up the books so that they might see where they stood. The request was easier made than complied with. Although Crapo had actively carried on the logging and manufacture and marketing of lumber for more than two years, he had had time for only the barest minimum of work in the counting room. Original entries of transactions had of course been made from the start, but the task of setting up the various books of account and getting them properly started had necessarily gone by the board in the face of other, far more pressing duties. Since the spring of 1858, much of the day-to-day detail work had been taken over by Chase, the young man whom Crapo had hired from the East to be his clerk. But until Crapo himself could find time to work on the books and bring them up to date, there was little that Chase or anyone else could do.[1]

Arnold, far removed as he was from the actual scene of operations, found the delay hard to understand, but to Crapo the situation was crystal clear. "It would have been perfect folly," he wrote his son, "for me to neglect vitally important matters for the purpose of figuring up balances and counting up losses and profits." With the burden of appeasing Arnold's clamor for accounts thrown largely on William, Crapo took care to explain his position fully to his son:

> My time has been devoted not only to . . . logging—which is of itself a most difficult and laborious as well as a distinct branch of business, and would require all the time of any one man to look after it—but in employing and overseeing almost an army of men—in superintending the manufacture of my lumber and the running of two large mills, with all the machinery, and with the procuring of all the necessary supplies of every description . . . and also in employing competent men and discharging incompetent ones, which of itself is a work of great magnitude. . . . You know not the care that is required to keep these men straight and to obtain from them the greatest amount of labor; and also to have the lumber sawed right and taken care of when sawed. But all this is hardly a beginning of my cares. The lumber is to be sold when made, and for the last two years I have labored to create a market where there was none, and to reach markets where there was no means of transportation.

For one man to attempt to carry on all these various aspects of the business, he wrote, "is more than has ever been undertaken here, or elsewhere." He reminded his New Bedford colleagues that there were concerns in Michigan which, "with three active partners," were engaged in the manufacture of lumber alone, and on a far smaller scale than his own operation at Flint. That the enterprise had survived thus far was due only to the way in which he had devoted his every moment to it, a fact which had caused him at one point to comment bitterly to William that "I am just about as much cut off from all social communion and intercourse with the world—and even my own family—aside from my business, as though I were incarcerated in a jail." He had done the things which had seemed most important, and if other things (such as the accounts) had been neglected, at least there was now some chance that when a balance should be struck, it would show that something had been accomplished.[2]

By the fall of 1859, however, Crapo did not need a set of accounts to tell him that the concern could not well continue on its original basis. Piles of unsold lumber made it painfully clear that the enterprise had been conceived on a scale entirely too large for realization under the business conditions which had prevailed since its inception. Qualitatively speaking, Crapo had achieved success in every aspect of the undertaking; but, quantitatively, his achievement was far from sufficient to warrant or justify the tremendous investment which had been made in the Driggs pine tract. The original plan had been to convert 10 million feet of logs into lumber each year. In the four years which had elapsed since the purchase of the lands, however, he had accomplished little more than the anticipated results of a single year's work—and he had been unable to sell more than half of the lumber.

With the investment in the pine lands so far out of proportion to the rate at which they could feasibly be worked, the concern would necessarily be operating under a most serious handicap. To Crapo personally, though, the pinch was even more acute. His own $50,000 share in the original investment for the lands had been advanced by Arnold. In promoting the venture, he had counted on a prompt realization of profits to enable him to pay off this debt. Instead, after four years he was less able to meet this obligation than he had been at the outset, having found it necessary to put every cent he could raise from sales of land into the lumber enterprise as working capital. Even his other investments—in whaling and in New Bedford real estate—had deteriorated in value. In the face of this situation, he recognized that drastic measures were required.

Even as he was working on taking inventory and writing up the accounts, therefore, he decided to broach the question with his New Bedford associates of altering their partnership arrangements in some way that would relieve him of the burden of his indebtedness for the pine lands.[3] He knew that Arnold, an elderly man, was already apprehensive as to the future of the concern, perhaps even anxious to see the venture terminated before further losses should be sustained. While the enterprise was nominally an equal three-way partnership, Arnold had actually provided the entire initial investment, having advanced the shares not only of Crapo but of Prescott as well in the purchase price of the Driggs lands. Prescott, it was true, had repaid a major part of his $50,000 share, and both he and Crapo had put in lesser amounts along with Arnold on various occasions when the need for additional capital had arisen. Nevertheless, it was Arnold's money in the main that was at stake. It is hardly surprising that he was worried about the safety of this investment, in a business which was foreign to his experience and in a country equally foreign to his New England mind. The plan which Crapo suggested was one which was calculated to relieve these fears of Arnold's, as well as to permit him to escape his own difficulties.

In brief, he proposed that a division of interests be made, with Arnold (either alone or together with Prescott) taking over the Driggs lands, while Crapo would operate the mills on his own, paying rent to the other partners for their two-thirds interest in that property. He would cut no more logs from the Driggs tract, but instead would stock the mills either from his own pine lands in the area or by buying logs from others. Such a course, he argued, would actually best serve the interests of the other partners, and Arnold in particular, by preserving the value of the investment in the Driggs tract. During the current "mania for the indiscriminate destruction of pine timber," he explained, when every owner of pine land was frantically cutting logs

> with a view to realize something . . . at once to meet . . . pressing debts, it is more than folly to cut off such a tract of pine as that upon the Driggs tract and bring it into direct competition with the immense quantities of pine now being cut off and sold at prices barely sufficient to meet the expenses of cutting, hauling, and running the logs to market.

He had no doubt, he wrote Arnold and Prescott, that "in a very few years . . . the 'stumpage' of the pine on the Driggs tract will bring better prices than the lumber now commands when manufactured."

> No living man is, I am sensible, aware of the rapidity with which our pine forests in Northern Michigan, Northern Wisconsin, and Minnesota—the only Western states and locations in which pine abounds—are

disappearing; and the almost unlimited demand that very soon must exist for pine lumber throughout southern Michigan, southern Wisconsin, Ohio, Indiana, Illinois, Iowa, Kansas, and in fact the entire west, all of which must be supplied from that—after all—comparatively limited pine region.[4]

The causes which would inevitably increase the value of the pine lands many fold, however, could have little if any effect on the mills, and Crapo was careful to point out that the latter were by far the least desirable part of the property of the concern. At best, an improvement in business conditions might bring their value up to original cost, though even that was doubtful since they were already old and were rapidly wearing out. In proposing to take them over in a dissolution of the firm, Crapo was acting—he assured his associates—not from desire but from the necessities of the case:

> I am here and can see no possible way of getting in a position prudently and judiciously to return to New Bedford, [and] I must be content to forego all those first hopes of profit and gain on the pine lands, to get rid of the debt created by their purchase.

He reminded them that from "any point of view . . . I must be the greatest loser" by first having engaged in and then terminating the partnership in the way proposed. He had been well situated in New Bedford, and his salaries there had "afforded me a decent support for myself and numerous family." These things were now lost beyond recall, to say nothing of the disruption to his personal life and to his other financial interests occasioned by his removal to Flint. In this pleading, Crapo perhaps overlooked his own initiative in promoting the venture. Yet there was no denying that he had done all that was humanly possible to make the enterprise a success, in the face of the most adverse conditions imaginable. Were he able to find any way of paying for his share in the lands, he explained, he would certainly do so, "for the stipulated salary and commission allowed me for services would enable me to do infinitely better than by giving it up and adopting the course suggested." [5]

II

While the question of revising or breaking up the concern was being discussed, Crapo worked steadily to get the accounts written up. This, he soon discovered, was a task of major proportions, and the work dragged on far longer than he had ever expected. Again and again in his letters to his son, the phrase recurs: "I have written Arnold to keep him quiet."

In the various aspects of the business there had been a great variety of transactions, involving for the most part small sums paid to or received from a multitude of different individuals. Crapo's aim in writing up the books was not merely to show the current financial position of the firm, but also to provide an analysis of costs sufficiently reliable to serve as a guide for future planning. Because of this, accurate distribution to the various accounts was essential. The original entries, however, had often been made in a manner which obscured the proper assignment of charges. As an example, payments for work performed on repairs to mill property had frequently been mixed in with the manufacture of lumber accounts. To remedy this situation, Crapo found himself forced to go over the entire body of records, item by item, from the very beginning, transferring entries when necessary so that everything would be charged in its proper place. The records of sales were confused by "the endless variety of dicker, barter, and retail" in which the business had become involved, as well as by sales on commission and on credit, and all this made more work. In addition, there was the problem of physical inventory, complicated by the profusion of grades and classifications of lumber.[6]

By the end of December, 1859, Crapo was able to send off his statement of lumber on hand, and during the next two months he prepared and sent East nearly thirty separate accounts * illustrating various phases of the business.[7]

The story told by these accounts was hardly one to cheer Crapo's partners. During the three winters of 1856–57, 1857–58, and 1858–59, just under 10 million feet of logs had been cut from the Driggs tract, and close to 3 million feet of logs had been purchased from other sources. By the close of the 1859 sawmill season, all these logs had been sawed, yielding (after wastage) about 12¼ million feet of lumber. Slightly more than 5½ million feet had been sold and payment received. Most of an additional 700,000 feet which had been shipped on consignment probably had also been sold, though Crapo had as yet received no accounting for it. Though it was an item of minor importance, 1½ million shingles had been marketed in addition to the lumber sold by the board foot. But a total of nearly 6 million feet of lumber remained unsold in Crapo's yards at Flint, Fentonville, and Holly. This included nearly the entire amount sawed during 1859, and some even from the very first year of operation.[8]

Although the total value of the lumber which had been sold was $56,273, actual cash receipts had been but $41,330. (Just under $5,000 of the difference between these two fig-

---

* The record of sales, showing a breakdown by grades of lumber, is given in condensed form in Appendix B.

ures represented money due for lumber sold, but as yet uncollected. The balance of nearly $10,000 was accounted for by the fact that considerable quantities of lumber had been exchanged for produce, grain, cattle, horses, wagons, harnesses, and other articles either used in the business or paid out to the men in lieu of cash wages.) The lumber on hand in Crapo's yards was worth $66,289 at prevailing prices. The rub was, of course, that this represented far more than a normal inventory, and under existing conditions it could be converted into cash only at a severe loss, if at all.

On the expense side, the cost of labor and supplies for manufacturing the lumber (including logging, driving, sawing, and selling) had come to more than $46,000, not counting the $15,376 due Crapo for his $3,000 annual salary and 6 per cent commission on sales. Besides these actual expenses, Crapo quite correctly had provided in his accounting for a stumpage credit to the Driggs tract of $1.00 per thousand feet of logs, and for a credit to his mill property account of $1.00 per thousand feet of lumber sawed. These two items were bookkeeping transactions rather than cash outlays, but the amounts they represented ($9,831 and $12,638 respectively) were quite properly charged to the cost of manufacture, constituting (in the first instance) a depletion reserve, and (in the second) a depreciation allowance.

Thus, after three full years the income from sales had not even equalled the day-to-day cost of operations, nor provided anything for Crapo's salary and commissions, for depletion or depreciation, or for profits on the investment.

The biggest part of the investment, of course, was the $150,000 purchase price of the Driggs tract. In addition, however, the partners had invested $44,991 in their mill properties. The two mills themselves had cost $10,038 and $20,000 respectively. Another $2,488 had been spent for the land which lay between them and for several other lots on which a barn, a lumber shed, a storehouse, and an office had been built. The cost of erecting these buildings and of making repairs and improvements to the mills, the various piers and booms, and other parts of the mill properties had totaled $11,627. The purchase of a planing machine and a shingle machine for the mills had added $680 and $155, respectively.

The acquisition of the mill facilities and the continued operation of the concern had been made possible only by the willingness of the partners to sink still more money into the venture, hoping that in this way they could still make the original investment in the lands pay off. Between 1856 and 1859 the three men had put in more than $47,000, in approximately equal shares, while Crapo had also abstained from drawing either salary or commissions due him. Even so, some $13,800 remained due on the purchase price of the second mill.

Meanwhile, the investment in the pine lands continued as a heavy drag on the firm. The notes given Driggs in part payment of the $150,000 purchase price had borne interest at 7 per cent, payable semi-annually. In advancing the shares of the other two men in the land, Arnold insisted that the same interest be credited on the entire cost of the tract, whether or not the notes to Driggs had been paid. Thus, by January 1, 1857, a year after the purchase, the lands were charged with $155,792. By January 1, 1858, after still another year, the amount was $168,197, and by January 1, 1859, it was $181,703. By January 1, 1860, the investment in the lands represented $195,153.[9] Neither this sum nor the original purchase price of $150,000 figured in Crapo's books or balances at Flint; the only way the lands had entered into his accounts was in being credited with $9,853 for stumpage and debited for $3,426 in taxes. But even with this net credit of $6,427, nearly $39,000 had been lost on the lands in interest alone.

As the interest piled up, Crapo's indebtedness to Arnold for his one-third share of the lands grew also, from $50,000 at the start to $60,568 on January 1, 1859. By July 1, 1859, it had risen to $62,770, and by the end of the year it was $65,051. No wonder Crapo feared the very passage of time, and sought to escape this mounting obligation as rapidly as possible!

III

If Arnold had been uneasy before the accounts were completed, he became even more disturbed as he saw revealed the full picture of what was involved in the business. Crapo would have preferred to continue the existing arrangements during the 1860 season so far as manufacturing operations were concerned, if he could meanwhile be freed of the burden of the Driggs land. This would give him a chance to sell out more of the lumber on hand, and perhaps to realize enough profit so that he would be in a better position to buy out his partners' interest in the mills later on. Arnold, however, insisted that if any change be made, it be one which would relieve him immediately of all responsibility for the manufacture or sale of lumber.[10]

The negotiations in New Bedford between Crapo's son and his partner Prescott, on the one hand, and Arnold on the other, were finally brought to a conclusion by the end of March, 1860. Arnold submitted a proposition which was, in effect, an ultimatum. He agreed to assume Crapo's share in the Driggs purchase, as well as that part of Prescott's share for which he had not been reimbursed as yet. This would leave him with a nine-elevenths interest in the tract, while

Prescott would hold a two-elevenths interest. Both Crapo and Prescott would then be released from all further obligation for the advances which had been made on their behalf. In return, however, Arnold demanded that the other two men buy out his interest in the mills and manufacturing operations.

Arnold had figured the total credit due him as $29,992, and in making the division of interests he was willing to settle this sum for the compromise figure of $24,000. To Crapo, however, this was a hard bargain. In his original proposal he had not contemplated adding to his own holdings, which he was financially as ill-equipped to do as he was to pay for the Driggs land. Should he be forced to take a larger interest in the manufacturing business than he held already, he felt it would be only just under the existing circumstances if he could make the purchase at a sizable discount from original cost. Instead of this, however, Arnold demanded not only the return of his investment in the manufacturing end of the business, but also the payment of interest on it as well. He would make no allowance for some $3,850 which Crapo had finally been able to pay him towards the pine lands during 1859, and he was to be reimbursed for his share of the stumpage due the Driggs tract for logs taken off.

Whether the settlement was what Crapo wanted or not, however, made little difference. Explaining its terms, William wrote him:

> I have tried and Prescott has tried to make it more favorable, but it is impossible, and we fear delay. If Mr. A. should die leaving matters in present shape, you would have no mercy, and he is so old we fear the delay of a day.

Accordingly, William had accepted the settlement for his father, a step with which the elder Crapo heartily agreed in view of the circumstances.[11]

Before the arrangement could be formalized, however, several matters included in Arnold's proposal remained to be settled. As a condition of making the change in the partnership, Arnold had stipulated that he should be satisfied as to the "quantity, quality, and title" of the Driggs tract, and also that Crapo should furnish a complete accounting for certain western lands which had been purchased jointly by the two men as a speculation (with Arnold, as usual, having provided the money, and Crapo undertaking their management and sale). Explaining the reason behind these provisos, William wrote that "Arnold wants to know how all his western matters stand—he wants to close all up, he is now arranging as he thinks his will for the last time." [12]

Crapo was in the midst of starting up the mills, and plagued as he was for want of time, he found it extremely difficult to make up these accounts. As in the case of the accounts of the lumber venture, he was forced to go over his records for years back, picking out the various items relating to these lands. Finally, by the end of May, he had completed the task and submitted the accounting to Arnold. The matter was still not disposed of, however. After receiving Crapo's statement of sales and receipts from the lands, Arnold decided that he wanted to be freed entirely from this interest, and he therefore added to his earlier proposal for settlement the demand that Crapo purchase the balance of the lands which remained unsold for the sum of $12,000. This Crapo was not at all eager to do, particularly in view of the fact that he was already undertaking a larger obligation than he desired for Arnold's interest in the lumber business, but as he saw room for possible profit in the proposal, his protests were relatively mild.[13]

A more serious obstacle was posed when Arnold began to voice fears as to the value of the Driggs tract. From some inquiries he had made he had gathered the idea that the amount of pine on the land was actually far less than he had thought, and for a time the whole settlement seemed endangered. His informants, it turned out, had been connected with rival Michigan pine land interests, and the specific statements made were easily refuted by Crapo. Moreover, another element had been introduced to delay final settlement. In July, Prescott made a quick trip to Michigan to discuss with Crapo both the negotiations with Arnold and their own relationship in the future operation of the firm. Bargaining back and forth continued right up to the end, with Crapo seeking to gain further concessions and Arnold stubbornly holding to his original position. Failing to secure any reduction in the amount, Crapo attempted to get six years' time in which to pay off the debt, and stood firm on a demand that no more than 6 per cent interest be charged. (Arnold had charged 7 per cent on the earlier advance for the lands.) The final agreement, however, called for payment within four years. Despite the earnest efforts of Crapo and his son, only one significant modification in Arnold's terms was won. In the latter's original proposition, he had agreed that should he at any time sell his nine-elevenths interest in the lands, any excess over $128,000 should go to Crapo and Prescott. The final settlement, concluded on August 22, 1860, reduced this amount to $61,585. While this concession was of no immediate importance, it did at least hold out the hope to Crapo that he might yet reap some advantage from the lands, should they increase in value as he anticipated.[14]

As the prolonged negotiations were brought to a close, William indulged in a bit of moralizing at his father's expense. Expressing his relief that the burden of the Driggs land purchase had been lifted, he wrote:

> I hope [now] to see the great mountain of my life—your large indebtedness—removed some day. This will surely happen if you will stick with me to the doctrine of *selling* and not *buying*. This we must do. Let us get out of debt. We can do it. And then perhaps there will be some enjoyment to life. The accomplishment of this settlement brings a little daylight.[15]

six

A FRESH START
(1860 - 1861)

I

The settlement with Arnold in 1860 marked the start of a new phase in Crapo's business. Despite the continuing partnership with Prescott, Crapo was now in effect his own master, for Prescott was content to remain wholly in the background, accepting without reservation whatever course Crapo should feel most desirable for the firm to pursue. Crapo's path was still far from clear, however. Although the intolerable burden of the Driggs land debt had been lifted, he still owed Arnold $12,000 for the latter's share of the manufacturing business, and $12,000 more for the wild lands formerly held jointly by the two men. His job was now to make the Flint enterprise profitable enough to enable him to meet these debts.

This was not his only worry. Quite apart from his interest in the Flint concern, his other financial involvements were both complicated and embarrassing. Before undertaking the lumber venture, he had made many speculative purchases of land in Michigan and other western states, holding some of it alone or with his son, and the rest in company with different New England associates. The taxes on these holdings were an annual drain on his already strained finances. He also had investments in whaling and Massachusetts real estate. Both these interests and the western lands required personal attention which he was unable to give so long as the Flint concern demanded every minute of his time. Furthermore, he had many debts back in New Bedford, presumably incurred in connection with these earlier ventures, and these obligations had been a constant source of concern to him as he struggled to make the best of a bad situation at Flint.

Although by separating the manufacturing business from the Driggs pine tract he had put the former on a more workable basis, he still could see no great prospects of profit ahead. Accordingly, even as he was arranging the settlement with Arnold he had concluded that his goal would be to sell out at the first opportune moment. If a purchaser could be found who would take the mill property at cost, he could then concentrate on selling off the accumulated stock of lumber to realize whatever might be salvaged from the ill-starred venture. Once freed from his responsibilities at Flint, he would be able to devote the necessary time to disposing of his widely-scattered land holdings. With the money thus raised, he would at last be in a position to wipe out all his debts and have enough left over for a comfortable retirement.

This, of course, was a long-range orientation. Crapo knew that business conditions would have to be much improved before a buyer for the mills could ever be found. Even then, his only chance for success in selling out would be to show by his books that money could be made in lumbering at Flint. This thought was never far from his mind as he struggled with the thousand and one details that demanded his personal attention in operating the concern.[1]

Even before the settlement revising the partnership, the uncertainty of his prospects had not hindered his vigorous prosecution of the business. During the winter of 1859–60 he had concentrated on cutting good logs which would yield a high proportion of "uppers." By thus building up a stock of lumber which it would pay to ship out, he planned to be in the best possible position to realize quick cash returns, whatever the final arrangements with his partners might be. Nearly 4 million feet of logs were put in, which, together with several lots of logs purchased on the river in the spring, were enough to keep the mills running steadily all season.[2] This would have been no great achievement had it not been that Crapo's logging superintendent, Charles Harthan, had suddenly been called back East, right at the height of the season in January, by the death of one of his children. He had left with a promise to return in two weeks, and it was only after nearly two months had passed without word from him that Crapo learned he did not intend to return at all. Meanwhile, Crapo had been forced to shoulder the entire burden of supervising the crews in the woods and the log drive down the river to Flint. Even under ordinary circumstances this added responsibility would have put him in a difficult position. Coming as it did when he was buried in work trying to get the accounts completed and some kind of settlement arranged with Arnold, it created an almost impossible situation, from which he extricated himself only by the severest exertion. During the summer of 1860, therefore, in planning his course under the new arrangement, he resolved never again to undertake the operation of his own logging crews. In deciding after three years' experience to rely instead solely on the services of contractors to put in his stock of logs, he felt that he would be streamlining his operations and making them more manageable.[3]

Once the mills were started in the spring, Crapo immediately turned his attention to getting his stock of lumber under way to market. The previous year he had hesitated so long before shipping that he had been caught with higher freight rates and the competition of green lumber from the current year's cut. Now, he hoped to avoid a repetition of this difficulty by shipping his lumber early in the season. Late in April he sent off some 83,000 feet to William in New Bedford. A number of shipments, totaling 500,000 feet, went to Fogg, the Providence, Rhode Island, lumber dealer, who had apparently overcome Crapo's dissatisfaction over their earlier dealings by a visit to Flint during the winter. Although Crapo did not expect to receive as good prices East (after allowing for transportation cost) as he was getting for the smaller lots that went to Detroit and south into Ohio, the fact that the lumber could be sent off in large quantities meant a very considerable saving of time and labor that in some measure compensated for the lower return. Two large lots were purchased in May by buyers from Massachusetts—200,000 feet to go to Lowell, and 100,000 feet for Springfield. Although the prices were low, these sales nevertheless netted Crapo $4.00 a thousand over prevailing yard prices at Flint.[4]

By the beginning of summer all signs appeared favorable. His local trade at Flint was better than it had ever been before. William had written asking for another cargo of lumber, and for once there were sufficient funds on hand to meet operating expenses before the payments fell due. The mills were running steadily, and more than two-thirds of the lumber coming from the saws was of a quality which would pay to ship. By August, Crapo was getting more orders than he could fill from Detroit and Ohio, and he regretted ever having made the shipments to Fogg. On receiving accounts from the Providence man, he found that his net return on the lumber, after figuring transportation, commissions, and other charges, would be $3,000 less than the same lumber would have brought in Detroit, Toledo, and

Cincinnati. The second shipment to William—some 78,000 feet—did not turn out well either. Since it was less than a full cargo, he had had trouble engaging lake transportation for it, and it laid on the docks at Detroit for over a month. When it was finally gotten off, grain shipments were at their peak, and canal freights from Buffalo had risen to $5.37½ a thousand feet as against the $2.50 rate which had prevailed in May and June. "I am sick of sending lumber East [on consignment]," he wrote. The uncertainty as to the prices which it would bring was aggravated by unpredictable charges for transportation and handling, not to speak of delay and damage en route. In contrast, definite orders received at Flint for delivery "at a certain point within my own reach and management" (such as Detroit or Toledo) were "a certain thing." "I then know what I am doing, and what I sell the lumber for, I get." [5]

This was the trade which Crapo sought, and it was increasing rapidly in the summer and fall of 1860. In October, he wrote William that "things look well here—infinitely better than at any previous time for the last four years." Lumber prices had been rising in Chicago, and Crapo was encouraged beyond all measure. "If we could only have one or two more seasons like the present," he wrote his son, "there would be no fear of the West." [6]

This rosy outlook, however, was destined to be short-lived. On November 6, 1860, Abraham Lincoln was elected President of the United States. Years of sectional controversy and conflict were being brought to a head. In the economic sphere there was an almost immediate reaction, as a sharp financial panic struck in the weeks following the Republican victory at the polls. Basically, the causes of the panic were threefold. The intimate commercial relations between the North and the South were threatened with disruption, and there was widespread repudiation of debts owed by southerners to northern business houses. The possibility that active war would break out caused a general state of apprehension and indecision, which the *New York Tribune* called "the severest trial to which a business man can be subjected." Under such conditions, the paper continued, "he knows not whether to contract or to expand; to take credit or to give it; to buy or to sell; to continue manufacturing or to stop." Finally, there was a dangerous weakening, soon leading to virtual collapse, of the wildcat banknote currency which formed the major part of the circulating medium in the West.[7]

To Crapo these developments came as a rude shock, quickly putting a damper on his hopes for a rapid improvement in his position. At first he hoped the panic might prove a transitory phenomenon, which having come "like a sudden tempest" would as quickly pass away. Yet he was fearful that it might embarrass him in paying for the extensive logging operations already laid out for the winter. In his letters to his son his irritation is obvious. His first reaction was that the disturbance had no legitimate economic roots, but was due to efforts

> by Northern politicians and Southern slaveholders
> . . . to make good . . . their charge that such would
> be the result of Lincoln's election, but more seriously
> to drive the North into making more concessions to
> the South, and to obtain more compromises to our
> own disadvantage for the sake of peace.

However injurious to his business the turn of events might be, this was one point on which his mind was now fully made up:

I say [he wrote] *no concessions, no more compromises,*
nor toleration or forbearance towards secessionists and
traitors. We have been harrassed and annoyed by
"Northern doughfaces" and "Southern fireaters" quite
too long, and I am tired of it, as are the great mass of
the Northern people.[8]

II

Before considering the effects of the panic in more detail,
it may be well to turn for a moment and see what lay behind
Crapo's uncompromising attitude on this question. Although
he had spent many years of his life in New Bedford in public
office, he was not by nature a politically-minded man. His
intense preoccupation with his business affairs had left him
little time for concern with politics. Still, he had not been
able to hold himself wholly aloof, and he had followed
political developments with at least a corner of his mind.
Until the early fifties he had been a Whig, almost as a matter
of course, considering his environment and associations. As
early as 1855, however, he had become an ardent adherent
of the new Republican party. During the Fremont campaign of 1856 he expressed his stand vigorously in a letter to
an Ohio friend:

> Success to the Republican cause everywhere. . . .
> Here [in New Bedford] there is no fear; we are wide
> awake and in earnest. There is a North—the prin-
> ciples of Freedom must yet triumph—and Kansas will
> yet be free. The aggressions of the Slave power have at
> last aroused the People, and they are for once at least
> in earnest.[9]

Yet however earnest the Republicans may have been, it was
Buchanan and not Fremont who emerged victorious from

the canvass, and while the slavery controversy continued in the ensuing years from 1856 to 1860, it did not always hold the center of the stage. The Panic of 1857, the depression which followed it, and the gradual recovery of the economy: these were the aspects of national affairs which absorbed the attention of businessmen like Crapo. Not once during these years does a reference of any kind to political matters appear in Crapo's voluminous correspondence.

All the while the basic tensions were growing, however, and by early 1860 their reflection in partisan politics had become so strong that even he, deep as he was in critical business negotiations, could not ignore or escape it. "I have had the misfortune," he announced most unexpectedly in a letter from Flint to his son in April, 1860, "to be elected Mayor of this city." He had allowed the nomination to be pressed on him over his protest because "a sentiment very generally prevailed throughout the Republican party that they could elect no other man." His Democratic opponent, the local postmaster, was widely respected, and was one of the oldest residents of Flint, and Crapo's victory was a tribute both to the growing strength of the Republican party and to Crapo's own personal popularity in a city which he had made his home only two years before. Regardless of party loyalty, however, his willingness to be drafted had rested largely on the fact that the duties and responsibilities of the office were nominal. Indeed, the city government was so rudimentary, he explained to his son, that the mayor of the year before had "entirely abandoned the office, after receiving the honor of an election, and left the public business to the Recorder and the Board of Aldermen." This the newly elected mayor had no intention of doing, although he did feel that he could discharge his obligations quite adequately by sitting as chairman at council meetings, and seeing that others performed their assigned duties efficiently. "Do not fear," he assured William, "I shall spend no more time than my interest will warrant. . . . I shall not let it interfere with my business in the least degree." After three weeks in office, Crapo had come to the conclusion that his election might not be a bad thing after all. "It gives me a moral influence here," he wrote, "which I think will be no detriment to my business." [10]

As political events assumed a more rapid pace after the fall elections, pungent comments on national affairs began to appear more frequently in Crapo's letters. In the face of secession by the slave states, already undertaken by South Carolina and threatened elsewhere throughout the South, many northern leaders were vacillating, but Crapo's convictions were starkly simple: no retreat from principle.

> We have asserted our manhood at the north [he wrote William] in electing the man of our choice for President. I hope really we shall not disgrace ourselves by being frightened out of our own senses and manhood, and like whipped curs instead of independent and enlightened Freemen, yield up our own success.

A week later he continued on the same theme:

> The Republican party *must stand firm* . . . nothing now can possibly be gained by an offer at compromise and conciliation, to say nothing of the folly and impropriety of offering terms of concession to men in open rebellion and in an attitude of treason. We have in fact nothing to concede. The only issue in the late Presidential contest was that of slavery extension; and the verdict of the people has been recorded that slavery should be confined to its present limits, that it

> shall not be extended. This is already a matter of
> history, and if 5 or 500 leading and prominent men
> of the Republican party should rise up and say that
> the south although in rebellion should be pacified,
> even at the surrender of our victory, and the sacrifice
> of our principles, still for the next four years at least
> this verdict of the people would stand unchanged—
> and its moral power would remain the same.[11]

Despite all efforts of the compromisers, however, the
breach between North and South widened rapidly during
the interregnum between the November elections and Lincoln's scheduled inauguration on March 4. By February,
seven states of the lower South had actually seceded, and had
organized the Confederacy. To Crapo the southern course
seemed sheer madness: "They are bigger fools down south
than I supposed could be found anywhere in this age." He
found it hard to take the whole business seriously. "All we
want," he wrote, "is to say but little, keep cool, support the
government, . . . make no concession, and let treason de-
stroy itself." [12] But treason was not weakening but growing
bolder, and by April, civil war was a reality.

Once hostilities had actually broken out, the effect on
the North was electrifying. Only a few weeks before, Crapo
and other Republicans could hardly find words enough to
denounce their Democratic opponents, who, he wrote, "in
their determination to break up the Republican party and
again obtain political power will aid southern rebellion, to
the final overthrow of our government and the ruin of our
country." Now men of all parties rallied to support the
Union. In Michigan as in the East, he assured his son, "all
party lines are destroyed and the entire population is determined to break up Southern Rebellion at any cost and

sacrifice." What that cost and sacrifice might be was as yet but dimly seen. Crapo's own views were perhaps typical of many in the North:

> This war can't last always and even should it continue for two years things will very soon settle down and move on again in their usual channels, at least to some extent. Men must be active here in the North in pushing forward their various plans of improvement and enterprise . . . the people must eat and drink and wear and build; and as a circus with all its paraphernalia will draw not only all the boys from their work but even the men whilst it is passing by, so this war excitement for a period will engross the attention of everybody, yet just as sure as all the men and boys will return to their work again when the circus troup is out of sight, so sure will all hands turn their attention to business again as soon as war is fairly inaugurated and its novelty has passed away and it becomes an established thing. . . . War or no war the country can't subsist long with all mechanics and operatives idle, for very soon everything "on hand" will be used up, and there will be a scarcity of everything.[13]

III

Despite Crapo's hopes for a quick revival from the disruption of civil war, business conditions continued to be somewhat depressed until well into 1862. There was a slow recovery from the initial shock of the post-election panic, but once the reality of war replaced mere uncertainty as to the future, the economic scene remained clouded while the necessary readjustments to the new situation were taking place. For Crapo's business, the first year and a half of the war proved little better than the years which had preceded it.

Encouraged by the flourishing sales of the summer and fall in 1860, he had let contracts for a total of 10 million feet of logs, the timber to come from his own pine lands rather than from the Driggs tract as it had in the past. This was several million feet more than the annual capacity of his mills, but he planned to run the excess down to Saginaw and either sell the logs outright or have them sawed for him there. With this large stock of logs on hand, he hoped that he might be in a position the following year for a concentrated selling effort which would produce enough cash over and above the needs of the business to enable him to pay off at least some of his most troublesome debts.* Financing such a program was no small matter, since getting in this quantity of logs would require $25,000, all of which would have to be paid in cash by the end of the following spring. When the logging season opened, however, Crapo had already been able to lay by for this purpose some $4,000 in cash and a like amount in short-term paper. With this and the expected proceeds from the winter's sales, he felt that he would be in good shape to meet the demands of his loggers as they came due at the rate of approximately $1,000 a week.[14]

These plans for making 1861 a year of profit-taking were rudely upset by the financial panic which broke in the wake of Lincoln's election and by the unsettled business conditions which followed. One of the immediate results of the panic was to check purchases of every kind. It was only with difficulty, and thanks to his long efforts in nurturing his

---

* He was also hedging to be certain that he would get at least a full season's supply of logs for his own mills. "These logging contractors are 'hard fellows,'" he wrote, "and cannot be depended on for the fulfillment of their contracts, so that we have to calculate for failures if the winter is unfavorable, and if otherwise then a full stock, just the reverse of what we could desire."—HHC, Flint to WWC, NB, Nov. 25, 1860.

home market with the farmers, that Crapo was able to keep abreast of the heavy obligations arising from this ambitious program of logging. During the winter, all his 1860 cut of the upper grades had been hauled to his Fentonville yard, and was ready to ship. But although he had made good progress in the two preceding years in developing an out-side market for his lumber, with the coming of spring he found opportunities for satisfactory sales few and far be-tween. When buyers could be found, in most cases they de-manded three or four months' credit. Since one of Crapo's troubles in meeting his logging bills had been his inability to collect at maturity on a number of notes he had taken for lumber sold the previous year, he found it necessary to be doubly cautious in trusting anyone for payment.[15]

The economy of the entire West was disturbed by the de-preciation of the banknote currency which formed the major part of the circulating medium. Michigan itself had practi-cally no banks, due to stringent restrictions enacted after the Panic of 1837 brought an end to a wildcat banking spree in the state. But the liberal laws of Illinois, Indiana and Wisconsin had encouraged the formation of great numbers of banking institutions during the fifties, many of which had as their sole purpose the issuance of banknotes to meet (and profit from) the need for currency in an expanding economy, and in particular in states like Michigan which had no banks. These issues were required by law to be backed by the de-posit of state bonds, but a major part of the security depos-ited was in bonds of certain southern states which, even before the secession crisis, were selling well below their nominal value.

With the outbreak of war, these southern bonds soon became almost worthless, bringing rapid depreciation of the banknotes for which they were supposed to provide security.

Taken in conjunction with the other elements of instability in these banks, the result was failure on a mass scale. In April, 1861, the first month of the war, thirty-seven banks closed their doors in Illinois alone, and before the crisis had run its course eighty-nine in that state had failed. Thirty-nine Wisconsin banks went under, as did twenty-seven in Indiana. The chaotic state of the currency which resulted was an impediment to commercial transactions of all kinds, and this state of affairs lasted for several years until finally the new national banking system drove the state banks out of the business of issuing banknote currency.[16]

Aside from the general effect on the economy of the crash of the wildcat banks, it had a specific effect on the lumber industry which greatly increased Crapo's difficulties for a time. The lumber trade at Saginaw had for years been carried on with the aid of advances from Chicago lumber merchants. With the virtual general closing of the Illinois banks, these advances stopped abruptly, forcing the Saginaw dealers to sacrifice their lumber at ruinous prices. The tremendous quantity thus thrown on the market quite effectively cut Crapo off from sales in Detroit, Toledo, and Cincinnati, where he had previously been working off his "uppers." [17]

Despite the difficulties which he faced on account of the plight of the Saginaw lumbermen, the hard situation of the latter underscored for him his faith in Flint as the best location in Michigan for lumbering. In fact, his mills at Flint were nearly the only ones in the region that were running. Of some fifty mills on the Saginaw River, only three at East Saginaw and three at Bay City had started up for the season, and by May he noted that they either had or were about to shut down for lack of funds to pay wages. "My market," he told his son, "though 'down'—'bad'—is nevertheless the best there is in this state at the present time, for I maintain my prices and sell some, all the time, every day, whilst others sell nothing." Indeed, he was, he thought, "selling more lumber than all the rest of the manufacturers almost in Michigan, for the farmers are all right and buy, and they are the only ones that can buy." [18]

Although his own situation was awkward, he was gratified by the difference between it and the plight of the Saginaw men, and felt that some good would come of the contrast "in establishing the fact among lumbermen that I have the best lumbering point in all Michigan."

> Ever since I have been here the Saginaw lumbermen have made it a point to speak disparagingly of my mill property and to depreciate its value, to every man they could get hold of, simply because I did not locate myself there, and give them the benefit of my business. I have however always argued that all things considered this was the best spot for manufacturing and selling lumber that could be found. Now the fact is demonstrated and all admit it. Lumber is worthless in Saginaw and they are obliged to stop with all their logs in the river that must be disposed of before the ice of next winter takes them out, whilst here I am selling my coarse lumber—right along—at my old prices, only by crowding on to the price here and there a little, and crowding down the inspection at the same time, I am selling common lumber here now at double the price they can get for it in Saginaw.[19]

The major factor sustaining Crapo's business was his success in capturing the patronage of the farmers of the region. By 1861, he boasted that "to a very great extent at least" he had won "the control of the market in Flint." Many of the farmers he considered *"my customers,* for when they leave

home they start for *my yard* and come here without any regard to 'street runners' or 'sharking.' " It was a matter of
some pride when he declared that

> I never depart a cent from my regular prices for the
> sake of taking trade from McFarlin or anyone else.
> They can buy of me at my regular prices or go else-
> where; and in the end—even for what may be re-
> garded as transient custom—I think this system gives
> me quite as many customers as it takes away; and with
> my regular customers it is everything, as they are not
> fearful of having to pay more to make up for some
> person who has "screwed down" and bought for less.[20]

Crapo's yards at Fentonville and Holly afforded him a
distinct advantage over his local competitors for the farmers'
trade, both because there he had the market to himself, and
because these yards gave him "the 'first cut' " at teams bound
for Flint from the south. During the winter months, when
snow and frozen ground allowed the farmers to haul their
lumber home by sled, many would travel as much as one
hundred miles to Flint with their teams. This trade, of
course, came to a standstill in the spring, as roads turned
into rivers of mud, and even an open winter, with warm
temperatures and little snow, meant a serious curtailment
in sales.[21]

Over the years Crapo had developed a system of handling
his retail yard trade which permitted him the maximum
volume and profit possible under the circumstances. "I have
worked as hard as ever one man did to get prices back to the
old notch," he wrote his son early in 1861. William had been
disturbed to hear that his father was selling common lumber at $6.00 a thousand feet, but in a long letter Crapo

explained that this was only his nominal price, and that in actuality he was receiving as much or more for his lumber as at the old established prices:

The lumber which I now call common and sell for common, would not pay freight to New Bedford; it is in fact no better than what they sell for "shipping culls" in Saginaw for $3. I sort and pick, and crowd the inspection down, little by little (until I dare not go much lower) and they will stand it, but the moment I touch the price there is trouble. And after all, I am selling at prices ranging from .50¢ to $2 per M above McFarlin and others. I have however advanced my price for fencing $1 per M—now selling it at $8— because there is no fencing North except green; I also sell my parallel or stock lumber—which is common, and no better—for 3 prices; the poorest at $7, the next best which answers to surface but is a little better than the $7 or lowest kind, and has knots on the edges, @ $8 rough, and if surfaced, at $10—and that which has no knots on the edges but otherwise no better than the preceding I sell for $9 in the rough or $12 if dressed and matched. And then also of my common lumber of all widths and wider at one end than the other, I sort that into 3 parcels, selling the very poorest of it as common at $6, and the next as "selects" at $8, and the best of it at $10, calling it "Box." In regard to the upper qualities I pursue this course. The old prices of $16 for clear, and $12 for 2d rate I maintain, whilst McFarlin sells for $15 and $11 and even for less, as he sells for just what he can get; but even with this I secure an advance from old prices of from $3 to $5 and even much more. For instance I sell no really clear here, that Detroit, Albany, Toledo or any other regular inspection would make clear. All this I draw out and send off to Fentonville, and that which by regular inspection is sold for 2d clear elsewhere I sell for clear here, and that which is sold for "select box" elsewhere I sell for 2d clear here, and by this means really advance my prices without seeming to do so.

This has not been done all at once as a matter of course; I have in fact been years about it; and I am enabled to do it now in spite of opposition by having my yard in the best possible condition, with an assortment of everything all nicely put up, and in a shape so that we can take purchasers to anything ready assorted, and the pile looking as though nothing had ever been taken out of it. We have to deal with all sorts of men—some very ignorant, and some very suspicious, and some who do not care much what they buy if it is only cheap. They want to think that they have bought cheap, and they want their money to go a great ways, and it won't do to put the price up and keep the inspection up, and then argue them into the belief that they will fare equally well or better by paying a higher price and having a better inspection. As there is no standard of inspection here, and as the extent of my business is such that I can make my own inspection, I endeavor to fit everybody in some way. For instance I have piles of my regular Flint 2d rate clear at $12 (being in fact nothing but Albany selects) but a very close man, or a man with a very slight purse comes and wants 2d clear; but when we say $12, he starts back; we then take him to a pile selected out of our common, which we call No. 2 second rate and show it to him as $10 lumber, and he is then all right and we have just suited him. The only drawback to this is the extra labor in sorting and handling, but after all, if I had pursued the old beaten track of having only 3 grades—clear, 2d rate, and common—I should have been no where long before this.[22]

Another feature of Crapo's business during 1861 was his establishment of a general store at Flint. It was a logical extension of his practice of receiving produce in payment for lumber, and by stocking some manufactured goods "in addition to what I am now obliged to deal in, by way of barter," he was certain that such an enterprise would "pay well and be . . . of no risk."

> I pay out to my men a large amount of cash which goes directly to support other stores, whereas nearly every dollar of it could be paid in trade, besides helping me very much in the shingle trade, and in the general barter trade of the place. There is now only one small store on that side of the River where my mills are (Ward 1) which has a population of over 1000, which if in New Bedford would have 10 to 15 stores certainly.

From the start the store was a success, and on many items he boasted that he was able to make 100 per cent profit over cost.[23]

IV

As the year 1861 drew to a close, Crapo reviewed his situation in a long letter to his partner, Prescott. The latter had asked whether any funds would be forthcoming from the Michigan enterprise to help meet the January interest payment on Arnold's mortgage. Crapo was forced to reply in the negative. His stock of clear lumber was larger than ever, and it was all paid for, but he had been able to do no more than meet his expenses for the year, which between logging and running the mills had come to from $50,000 to $60,000. Local sales of common lumber had enabled him to meet operating expenses while his stock of "uppers" continued to grow, and so long as this went on he was increasing the potential profits of the enterprise. But until he could find sales in quantity and at satisfactory prices for his better quality lumber, he could not free himself from the treadmill of merely turning over an old dollar for a new one.[24]

seven

THE PROMISE OF PROSPERITY
(1862 - 1863)

I

The first real signs of improvement in Crapo's business came in the second half of 1862, coincident with the general upswing of business activity then taking place.[1] In June he had told his son, "My sales are good for the season, and are ample to meet my running expenses, but do not leave much beyond that." By November, however, he was writing that "my trouble is, not as to what I can do with my lumber, but as to how I can get as much as I can sell." [2] The lumber trade at Chicago, a significant barometer of conditions throughout the Middle West, had been in a steady decline since the Panic of 1857, and in 1861 it had hit its lowest point since 1854. In the latter year receipts of lumber at the Great Lakes metropolis had totaled nearly 230 million feet; by 1857, this had grown to almost 460 million feet. In 1861, however, receipts were at a seven-year low of less than 250 million feet. As the country gradually became adjusted to wartime conditions, the trend was reversed, and in 1862 receipts had jumped to over 305 million feet. From this point onward, the annual totals mounted steadily under the influence of war-inspired prosperity and renewed expansion, until by 1868 the figure was more than 1,028 million feet.[3]

A local factor of great importance in spurring Crapo's sales during 1862 was the outbreak of a salt boom at Saginaw. The presence of strong brine in the region had long been known, but it was not until 1860 that the manufacture of salt was successfully undertaken at Saginaw. The spectacular success of this first enterprise led to rapid expansion of the industry, bringing in its train a flow of eastern capital and a burgeoning prosperity. The boom brought a heavy demand for lumber for house building, as eager settlers began to pour into the Saginaw Valley.[4]

Even more important to Crapo was the urgent need for seasoned lumber in the construction of salt vats and salt works generally. After long years of struggling, here he found a virtual bonanza, as few of the other lumbermen in the region had anything but green lumber to offer. He suddenly discovered that he was in the most unusual position of being able to set his own price. In November, 1862, he sold some 50,000 feet of seasoned lumber to a Saginaw man at $20 a thousand, $4.00 a thousand more than he had ever received for such lumber before. The price was considered steep, but the buyer had no alternative except to pay what was asked if he was to get the kind of lumber he needed. Only a few days had gone by when Crapo raised his price $2.00 more on another sale, and set his men to work sorting out every piece of lumber suitable for salt works. Since it was not necessary that boards for this purpose be clear, but only that they have sound knots and be free from sap, the gain in price over the $16 figure which had long been the top for clear lumber in the Flint market was even more striking.[5]

Other markets, too, were improving rapidly. Within a week after his first large sales to salt manufacturers he raised his yard prices $1.00 on all grades, with "hardly a single word" said about it by the buyers. Another week passed, and he went up $1.00 more on his tariff; two months later, in January, 1863, he repeated the step once again.[6] Despite an unusually open winter with little sledding, his local sales and those at the Fentonville yard held up remarkably well. In February he sold his entire 1861 cut of "uppers" at Fentonville to a Troy, New York, firm for more than $20,000. Lumber continued to rise in price at Detroit and Chicago, and by the coming of spring he began to think he had jumped too fast at his first opportunities for large sales, high as the price had seemed at the time. In March he calculated that he had already lost some $4,000 by the advance since the Troy sale the month before, and by April he placed the loss at between $6,000 and $8,000. The Flint and Pere Marquette Railroad, after years of delay, had finally been completed between Flint and Saginaw in December, 1862, and Crapo quickly took advantage of it by shipping an average of 25,000 feet of lumber daily to the rival lumber center, where it found a ready sale at good prices from a yard which he established there.[7]

The result of this new turn in Crapo's business was that for the first time since becoming a lumberman he was able to build up a substantial and uncommitted cash balance. In January, 1863, he had nearly $7,000 on deposit at a Boston bank, with another $6,000 in good paper due during the first five months of the year. Two months later, his cash had mounted to $15,000 in Boston and about $5,000 in Flint and Detroit. By May his eastern deposits totaled $37,-945, passing the $30,000 mark at which he had earlier thought he would declare a dividend for himself and Prescott. As sales continued heavy, however, he raised this goal first to forty and then to fifty thousand, and finally, by the end of the summer, he was able to make a dividend of the latter sum. His own share of $25,000 he directed William to use in New Bedford "in the payment of such of my debts there as you think most advisable and proper."[8]

The favorable conditions prevailing during 1863 did not mean, of course, that Crapo had no problems. The preceding winter he had contracted for 6 million feet of logs, which, together with one million feet held over from the previous year, would have been ample to keep his mills busy all year. The lack of snow during the logging season, however, had greatly hindered his operations, and as the winter wore on he was fearful that he might not be able to get any sizable amount of logs down the river. When spring came he found himself with only half the stock he had hoped for. The low water created difficulties in running logs to Saginaw and this enabled him to buy up several lots of logs at sacrifice prices, but to get a stock large enough to keep the mills going he was forced to turn to a purchase of timber rights some four miles upriver from Flint, contracting to have the logs cut and hauled to the river on wheels during the summer.[9]

His mill hands, too, were causing him much trouble, the result of the manpower shortage occasioned by the war and of the steadily rising cost of living. "They are continually clamoring for more wages," he complained to William in June, "and the more I raise on their wages the less they do." How much he had actually increased his rates is open to question, however, in view of his statement in the same letter that "last spring I took a stand that I would not raise another cent on the wages of anyone, and they could go or stay." In any case, those who stayed, it seemed, grew "more independent and slack every day." The problem became worse as the months went on; in September, he wrote:

> There are a great plenty of men, but they are perfectly shiftless and lawless; that is, these transient ones that I am obliged to hire to keep my business along. And I do not only suffer on account of their slackness, but

they drag down all my regular help, as one man will work no faster or better than another.[10]

Despite these annoyances, Crapo was well satisfied with the way matters stood at the end of the 1863 season. In November he wrote William telling how, with lumber both scarce and high, he had climaxed the year by a carefully planned coup to consolidate his control of the local market:

> About 10 days ago I slipped off up North [presumably to the small mills along the river between Flint and Saginaw] and purchased all the lumber there was on hand—in one day—and got my contracts all signed before anyone was aware of it. I purchased some 700,000 feet of one concern. There is now no lumber in this region not in my hands except what McFarlin has, and as a matter of course I have matters somewhat my own way.
>
> Upon closing the above purchases, I waited one week and then put up my prices—all around—$2 per M. There was . . . some little grunting, but we sell just as much as though I had not raised.

Despite his heavy sales, he continued, "I have a nice little stock of lumber on hand," and he looked forward to selling it at prices which were now far more attractive than those which had prevailed between 1857 and 1862:

Prices of '57 to '62		*Present Price*
$ 4.00	Roof boards	$ 9.00
2. to 3.00	Culls	8.00
6.00	Common boards & planks	13.00
7.00	Fencing and common parallel boards	14.00

10. to 12.00	Second-rate clear lumber	20.00
15. to 16.00	Clear lumber	24.00
10. to 11.00	Dressed & matched flooring, Box	20.00
3.00	Lath—now taken as fast as made	10.00

And all other descriptions and qualities in proportion.[11]

While Crapo's operating expenses began to increase as well during 1863, the lumber he was selling at these new prices had been manufactured when costs were low. The figures which would be needed to compare the increases in lumber prices with changes in the cost of production are not available, but it is extremely doubtful that the latter came at all close to keeping pace with the price rise. Even more important, since he was now selling lumber rapidly and in quantity, the expenses of maintaining his inventory and of selling lumber were cut sharply.

Ever since the settlement with Arnold and reorganization of the firm in 1860, Crapo had looked forward to the time when he would be able to sell out and close up the business. Discussing this question in June, 1861, he complained to his son:

> I am old and am now working far beyond my strength, and have no rest day nor night, and am constantly pressed down with cares and anxieties and responsibilities enough to crush out and subdue the energies of a much younger person.[12]

He recognized, too, that it would be utterly impossible for him to do anything toward settling up his land operations and other business affairs so long as he was immersed in the day-to-day responsibilities of the lumber enterprise. In July,

1863, he reflected: "Had I shut down last fall and done nothing about another stock of logs and hired no men, only to sell lumber, I should now have had $80,000 at least of cash on deposit." Perhaps, he thought, it was just as well to run his mills through the current season, but he was determined that it would be his last despite the fact that the business, in his words, "never looked as promising as it now does." By the end of September, however, he had succumbed to the lure of further profit, writing William:

> If I could run everything right up to the handle for the next two years, I ought to make as much clear money as I could now sell the mills for; in which case —if I could not then sell the mill property—it would have cost me only two years more toil and care.[13]

II

Two other projects claimed much of Crapo's time in the midst of his new-found success in the lumber business. The first was an ill-starred attempt at sinking a salt well, for he was not immune to the salt fever sweeping the Saginaw Valley. Many people at Flint believed that the salt deposits which had been tapped at Saginaw also extended under their own city, and although this was only speculation, Crapo was sufficiently convinced to make the trial. Drilling operations were begun in November, 1862, as soon as the sawmills had shut down for the winter. With an enthusiasm reminiscent of his hopes for the lumber venture back in 1855, he visualized a rich flow of profit. Assuming that brine of sufficient strength should be found, he calculated on a production of one hundred barrels a day which at a cost of $20 a day would yield over $200 net profits daily. His original estimate of the cost of drilling was $2,500, and he figured that even a short period of production would repay this initial outlay. Further investment would of course be required for evaporating kettles, vats for solar evaporation, storage buildings, and so on, if the well proved successful. He was confident, nevertheless, that he could do as much with $12,000 as any outsider just setting up could with $40,000, since much of his sawmill equipment and property could be employed in the operation without additional expense, even to the extent of scrap lumber from the mills providing fuel.[14]

The drilling continued steadily throughout the winter and spring without any decisive results, but with sufficient indications of progress to sustain not only Crapo's hopes but those of the townspeople, whose interest in the success of the venture was such that the result of each day's boring was considered "almost as important as the expected news from the Army of the Potomac." By mid-May the well had nearly reached 1,200 feet, the limit of the original contract for the job. The seepage into the shaft was brine of high strength and purity, but as yet the drilling had reached no porous sandstone layer in which the brine could accumulate in sufficient quantity for practical commercial exploitation. More than $4,000 had already been spent, and Crapo felt that he could not afford to go further. Discouraged though he was, the thought that success might lie but a few feet deeper was too much for him. In an appeal "to the public spirited citizens of Flint and those interested in its growth and permanent prosperity," he proposed that a subscription be raised to continue the drilling, the money to be repaid in the event of success, and lost along with his own outlay in case of failure. Within a week some $900 was contributed, and the boring went on without interruption. All was to no avail, however. At 1,360 feet the drill became stuck fast, and all efforts to dislodge it proved fruitless. The project was abandoned.[15]

Crapo's disappointment was tempered, however, by the rapid progress of another project, the success of which was ultimately to be as spectacular as the failure of the salt enterprise had been dismal. His original plans for the lumber enterprise, it will be recalled, had been made in the expectation that Flint would soon be connected with Port Huron by a railroad, permitting easy access to water shipment for his lumber. On several occasions attempts were made to revive this project, but the line, as mentioned earlier, was not to be completed during Crapo's lifetime. He had, in the meantime, made arrangements for hauling his lumber over the plank road to Fentonville, loading it there on cars of the Detroit and Milwaukee Railroad. Meanwhile, another enterprise was undertaken in the region, the Flint and Pere Marquette line which was to run from Saginaw to Flint. This road was completed in December, 1862, just in time to be of immediate advantage in the sudden boom brought about by the development of salt works at Saginaw. The importance of an extension from Flint which would link the new line with the Detroit and Milwaukee at Fentonville or Holly now became obvious to all concerned.[16]

To Crapo, the construction of such a line would mean a solution of one of his most critical problems. The plank road route to Fentonville had never been more than a makeshift arrangement for him. It was slow, costly, and uncertain. With steadily increasing opportunities for sales of lumber, he was finding it more and more difficult to keep his Fentonville yard supplied. The manpower shortage resulting from the war had aggravated the situation, and now many of his former teamsters were finding more profitable employment with the salt works at Saginaw.[17]

In these circumstances, it was only natural that he should turn his attention to the possibility of taking an active part in promoting the construction of a railroad between Flint and the line of the Detroit and Milwaukee. Such a road, he felt, was certain to be undertaken soon, and it would pay big dividends to those who controlled it.

> The Saginaw Valley [he wrote his son] is destined to contain a large population, much wealth, and a great deal of business, and Flint stands at the very door of the whole valley. There is no other outlet to it, and no way by which the trade, travel, etc. to and from Saginaw can be diverted from it.[18]

Crapo had another reason for taking the initiative in the construction of the road, quite apart from the profits which might be expected. Such a link would be of considerable value to his lumber business, no matter by whom it was built, but it would mean much more to have it in friendly hands. The Saginaw management of the Flint and Pere Marquette Railroad hardly met that requirement, and he was fearful of difficulties if they should undertake the new line as an extension to their own road. If they should control the rail outlet from Flint in both directions, he would have to pay them "just what they see fit to charge" for carrying lumber. On the other hand, he wrote,

> if I can control to some extent the road from Flint to Fentonville I can say to the Saginaw Road—"let my lumber go over your road in summer to be shipped in Saginaw for Chicago, or to any of the Lake ports, for Cincinnati or the 'East,' at fair rates, and we will take your salt and lumber in the winter over our road to Fentonville, and thence to Detroit, etc. at fair rates." I can also say "let me carry my lumber 32 miles

over your road to the docks in Saginaw at fair rates,
or the D. & M. R.R. will let me over their road to
Detroit on terms that will take my lumber out in that
direction for shipping east and you will consequently
lose it over your road."

By controlling this link from Flint to Fentonville,
with the Saginaw road one way, and the D. & M.
Road the other way, both taking my lumber to navi-
gable water, and each of those roads being thus
brought into competition with each other, for our
benefit, my lumber prospects will be more flattering
than can be well imagined, so long as we wish or are
compelled to carry it on, and our Mill Property, etc.
greatly enhanced in value, and its sale made certain.[19]

From the very start, when Crapo first began to consider
the possibility of promoting the railroad, he was firmly set
on one point. If he was to have anything at all to do with
the project, the line would have to be built with cash capital paid in by subscribers to the stock, so that when completed it would be free of debt and could pay dividends.
This was quite different from the way in which many (if
not most) of the western railroads had been financed. It was
common practice in railroad promotions for the stockholders
to make only small payments towards the nominal capital of
the company, raising the actual cash for construction by the
sale of bonds. The usual result of this procedure was a
chronic shortage of cash for working capital, heavy financing
expenses and interest charges, and frequent disruption and
delay in construction. Many of the lines which had sprung
up over the preceding decade had suffered from this practice,
and to see its deleterious effect Crapo had only to look to the
Flint and Pere Marquette, which was mortgaged to the
hilt.[20]

In considering the project, Crapo's mind turned naturally to New Bedford as a source of capital. During the fall and winter of 1862–63 he negotiated through William to get backing from his former townsmen. If the proposed road should be "built with cash and judiciously managed," he assured them, "there will be found no railroad in the country to exceed it in net earnings on the dollar." He had been careful to keep his plans secret from others interested in the route, but by January, 1863, he was ready to come out into the open. Articles of association under the Michigan general railroad law had been drawn up and signed by twenty-five prominent citizens of New Bedford and Flint, and with the filing of these papers and the deposit of $800, the route was secured.[21]

The next step was to secure stock subscriptions. Crapo drew up a printed prospectus outlining in careful detail the estimated cost and prospective revenues of the line, and assured interested investors that

> when built, [it] will be the natural and direct line of communication for all the travel and traffic from Detroit, and all places on the line of the D. & M. R.R., to and from Flint, as well as to and from the entire Saginaw Valley, and all the region of country tributary to said valley, which must necessarily have its outlet through Flint; and this travel and traffic, which is already very large, must increase almost in a geometrical ratio, as the vast resources of that valley shall become developed.

The cost of construction he placed at $194,575, which, with $46,000 for rolling stock, depots, and engineering, would make a total of $240,575. On the basis of the most conservative figures possible and with generous allowances for error, he estimated the annual passenger income at $44,090 and the revenue from freight—lumber, salt, produce, and manufactured goods—at $17,000. Against this $61,090 anticipated revenue, he set $12,000 as the estimated cost of operating the road. Then, to conclude the prospectus with an estimate of earning sufficiently modest to escape any danger of over-optimism, he rounded off the income figure to $60,000 and increased the expense figure by half, to give an estimated annual profit of $42,000.[22]

The main burden of raising the capital fell on William in New Bedford, since it was recognized that the major part of the financing would have to come from the East, indeed that it would be fruitless even to consider the project without strong support from that quarter. Soliciting the aid of his son-in-law, W. C. Durant, in selling some of the stock in Boston, Crapo wrote: "They are all ready to take here if they had money; but in a new country, where there are no banks or money lenders, people have to use all their means in their business." Despite all efforts, subscriptions were very slow in coming in, and on several occasions during the early months of 1863 Crapo began to wonder if the enterprise had not been a mistake. The situation was particularly embarrassing for him because "everybody in Michigan expects that I am going to build . . . as a matter of course, merely because I pay as I go along, and have succeeded in my business beyond expectation." The general belief that "if Crapo undertakes, the road will be built" was flattering, yet he knew that this local enthusiasm would not pay the bills. For fear of failure, which would react badly on his other interests, he hesitated to agitate the question in Flint until he had some word of progress from New Bedford. A telegram from William in April announcing that $170,000 worth of stock had been taken cheered him considerably, however, and he replied to his son that "I shall take hold of it here now with an assurance that the road will be built." Two weeks later he was able to report an equal measure of success: "the stock is all taken, and more is wanted." Although the capital proposed in the original articles of association was only $200,-000, when the lists were closed a total of $250,500 had been subscribed. New Bedford investors had taken $188,800, and Boston men, $22,200. Flint had subscribed $32,000, and Fentonville, $7,500.[23]

Assured of adequate capital, Crapo was now able to proceed with the formal organization of the corporation, effected in a meeting held at Flint on June 4, 1863. He was chosen president. Four of the New Bedford stockholders—Thomas Knowles, Pardon Tillinghast, J. G. Delano and Humphrey W. Seabury—together with J. B. Walker of Flint made up the balance of the board of directors. Crapo had already undertaken much of the preliminary work—procuring surveys of possible routes, drafting specifications for construction, discussing arrangements for connections with the Detroit and Milwaukee and the Flint and Pere Marquette, and gathering information on the thousand and one details involved in the construction and operation of a railroad.[24] As word of the project spread, no less than five eager applicants for the construction job appeared.* Seemingly, everything was in readiness for contracts to be let and for work to commence.

One vexing question remained unsettled, however—the southern terminus of the road. The two villages of Fentonville and Holly, five miles apart on the line of the Detroit

* "Ready *cash payments,*" Crapo wrote his son, "is the material with which to build railroads, and I have no doubt that it will . . . create ample competition to insure us the work at reasonable rates. When R.R. companies rely solely on the sale of bonds and are always 'hard up' and their bills unpaid, their expenses are increased necessarily to a very great percentage." —HHC, Flint to WWC, NB, May 13, 1863.

and Milwaukee south of Flint, were both eagerly seeking
the advantages to be secured as junction point for the new
railroad from the north. Crapo's original inclination had
been towards Fentonville. For some years he had maintained
lumber yards at both points, supplying them over the plank
roads from Flint, and his business at Fentonville had proven
far more important than at Holly; the new railroad would
obviously be of greatest value to him if it ran directly to
the more profitable market. With some reason, he felt that
the same causes which had made Fentonville a better point
for his own business would serve to make it the logical
terminus for the railroad from the standpoint of profitability.
Certain residents of Holly, however, seeking to gain the
connection for their own town, had brought their claims to
the attention of the New Bedford stockholders, and the entire project became bogged down for months as the controversy continued.[25]

Other frictions also developed between Crapo and the
New England men who were furnishing the major share of
the capital. After a visit from several of the eastern directors,
Crapo commented wryly that he wished they had "less of
the idea that knowledge and prudence and sagacity is confined to certain localities." "Your New Bedford friends," he
wrote William on another occasion, "have got an idea that
we must have more stock, and they have certain notions that
extra heavy iron, and *extra everything,* must be used." Even
when decisions had been reached, he complained, "new
views and ideas are constantly recurring." The insistence of
the New Bedford directors on discussing every small detail
at length irritated him greatly, and he protested that "I think
the interest of the road . . . will be quite as well in my
hands as in theirs." If the road was to be built, "it must

necessarily be by and through my constant and unremitted efforts and attention," and under these circumstances he felt that he should be "left somewhat at liberty to manage it in my own way."

> To make all the bargains and arrangements for the building of this road, with all the calculations, purchases, arrangements for depots, stations, side tracks, land damages, surveys, plans, bridges, the purchase of materials, locomotives, cars, etc. etc. would require the undivided attention of an energetic, competent man; but if a long correspondence with the New Bedford people is necessary in every particular case before a decision can be reached, the work could not be done to any advantage.[26]

For a time, the very advisability of continuing with the project was brought into question by some of the more cautious eastern investors, and only his urgent need for a rail outlet and his faith in the profitability of the line kept Crapo from throwing up his hands in disgust. At last, in August, the decision to proceed was finally made. By dictate of the New Bedford directors, the Holly route was chosen, but after the indecision of the summer Crapo no doubt felt this was a small price to pay. Proxies from the eastern members of the board granted full powers to Crapo and J. B. Walker, the other Flint director, to proceed with construction of the line, and on September 9, 1863, Crapo was able to announce to his son that "the Engineers commence work in the morning." [27] In a later chapter we will trace the actual work of construction, and see the success which attended the railroad's operations almost from the day it opened for business, November 1, 1864.

III

Salt and railroads were not the only matters diverting Crapo's attention from the lumber business during 1862 and 1863. The country was deep in civil war and while the majority of his letters to his son made no reference to political conditions, when he did turn to that subject there was nothing half-hearted about his comments. More than a year after open hostilities had commenced, the Union cause remained in doubt. Military defeats were demoralizing the North, while from Washington there came vacillation instead of leadership. "I fear for the result," he wrote William in July, 1862, "unless a more energetic and decided course is pursued. . . . Already we have almost entailed certain ultimate defeat by our 'half-way' prosecution of the war." Two months later he wrote:

> My dear son, we are *defeated* now, to all intents and purposes. Politicians and speculators, and brainless incompetent officers, and a President with a policy neither Peace nor War, with thousands of *Loyal Traitors* in high places, have ruined the country and destroyed the government. I would not be discouraged or find fault, and I do not publicly, but I cannot help feeling for the terrible condition of our country, and mourning as I see her drifting onto the rocks.[28]

Reverses in the field and confusion in Washington lent encouragement to anti-administration and anti-war elements in the North, and the Republicans needed all the strength they could muster. The vigor of Crapo's views on the war question was well-known, and it is perhaps little wonder that he should be considered by the local party organization as an outstanding possibility for public office. A move to enter his name as a candidate for Congress proved abortive, but it was quickly followed by his selection in October,1862, as Republican candidate for the state senate. As in the case of his earlier term as mayor of Flint, the nomination was made without his knowledge or prior consent. Once again the argument used to persuade him to accept was that he was the only man in the district whom the party could hope to elect, "and that in duty I was bound to make the sacrifice."

> You can regard it [he assured his son] as a distinction freely and voluntarily conferred upon me unasked and unsolicited, which goes to show, so far at least, that my conduct and business transactions since I have been in this state have been such as to secure the confidence and approbation of the more influential men with whom I have come in contact.

The diversion of energy from his business in the event he should be elected bothered him somewhat, and he feared that it would disturb his son and his partner Prescott even more. The session would last only forty days, however, and he rationalized that

> as I have some legislation of my own to effect, and as I can make it tell in various ways to the interest of my business, and as I shall be brought in direct contact with the leading men from every part of this large state, I am inclined to think after all that it "will pay."

His impression as to the reason he was chosen by the party makes an interesting comment on the political life of his day. "Among the people here," he wrote, "old political hacks are getting out of date, and hard working business men begin to be sought after to fill their places."

> I happen to be regarded in this part of the state as a thorough business man, and in every sense reliable, and not a politician; and am also popular among the farmers who regard me as a "working man" and one who is with them in tasks and habits, and who is doing much for the development of some of the great business interests, as well as for agriculture, in this part of the state.[29]

The campaign was bitterly fought. The opposition was a so-called "Union Party," started, Crapo wrote, by a "few proslavery, rebel-sympathizing Democrats . . . solely for the purpose of drawing all the Loyal Douglas Democrats and unsuspecting Republican votes they possibly could." At the outset the new party caught on "like wild-fire," denouncing the "Black Republican war," high taxes, and so on, and it was generally thought that they would win the state. The Republicans got a late start, holding their district nominating convention little more than three weeks before the election. To make up for lost time, eight of their lawyers volunteered to stump the district, and willy-nilly Crapo found himself included in the group. His assignment called for a heavy schedule of speeches nearly every night in a different town or village. It was a new role for him, and one which taxed his energy heavily. The results of the campaign, however, showed that he had done his job well. The Republicans carried the state, 67,816 to 62,102, while in the senatorial district Crapo ran ahead of his opponent in nearly every township.

Highly gratified with the results, Crapo wrote his son

that "we have saved the state, to stand by the side of Massachusetts."

> I am indeed proud to think that both my native and
> adopted states are true to the cause of free institutions,
> and our Government, in this time of peril to both;
> and am not now sorry that I lent my feeble aid to the
> support of our principles and the government.

He was pleased in spite of himself by his own victory, commenting that "this does well for a man who has drawn the
lines as tight as I have in my business operations for the last
five years, and who never yielded a point with my men."

> The "Boys"—to a *man*—all voted for me, and nearly
> every one of them (Irish) were strong Democrats.
> They say I work them hard, and two hours every day
> longer than anyone else, but that I board well and
> pay well and treat them all like gentlemen; and not-
> withstanding all the *hard work* they like me. This is
> gratifying to my feelings, and you can hardly realize
> how proud I feel of the kindness and partiality of my
> men, acquired under such circumstances.[30]

Two weeks later, with his mind full of the salt and railroad projects, to say nothing of his lumber operations, Crapo
began to regret that he had ever allowed himself to be persuaded to run for the office. He admitted to his son that his
business was "a perfect system," and that the four young
men whom he had trained as his lieutenants would be able
to keep everything moving along as usual during his absence
at Lansing. Nevertheless, he wrote with a worried tone, "I
alone can straighten out the 'kinks.' " For years he had been
so close to every detail of the business that he now found it

next to impossible to imagine it running without him. But the die was cast; he had accepted a new responsibility, and as always he felt obligated to carry it through to the best of his ability.[31]

When the legislature convened at Lansing in January, 1863, Crapo found himself unable "to avoid being placed in a position of hard work." He was named to three committees, and chosen as chairman of one of these, the committee on incorporations, which was, he wrote, "one of the most laborious" in the Senate. "Not being conversant with Legislation," he wrote his son, "and being anxious not to prove the weakest man in the Senate, I have to *study hard,* as well as *work hard.*" He approached his new duties with a due consciousness of his position as a freshman member:

> Although the machinery is somewhat complicated to a new beginner, I intend that by the time some of those who "start off" with great noise and bluster begin to be laid on the shelf and lose their influence, that I shall then be ready to take their places. . . . Some of our new members are very anxious to make great men of themselves the first week, and I suppose this is so in all Legislative bodies, but there is good common sense enough in the body to give those very vain and self-sufficient members a "wrap over the knuckles" when they get too troublesome.[32]

eight

THE CALL OF POLITICS

I

In allowing himself to be drafted for the senatorial nomination, Crapo had taken a step which was to lead him far deeper into politics than he either desired or imagined to be possible. A few days after his arrival at Lansing in January, 1863, he observed reflectively in a letter to his son: "I think that I should like this legislation if I had nothing else to do." This comment is a key to his attitude. He had no thought that his term in the state legislature would be anything but an interlude in a busy life which had been and would continue to be devoted wholeheartedly to business affairs. The party leadership had placed him in a position of prominence as chairman of the committee on incorporations, however, and he felt bound to justify their confidence in him. As he recalled it at a later date:

> Being a new member, and nothing but a poor lumber man among bustling lawyers and active political managers, I endeavored to confine myself strictly to the business at hand and treat everything in a fair, candid and straightforward business manner. This course I could see, very plainly, began to tell as the session advanced, until I became, by a sort of common consent, a leading member, and my opinions and views began to be sought on all important matters.[1]

When the session came to a close in March, Crapo was

confident that he had seen the last of politics. He was anxious to return home. "I have had a respite from my business," he wrote his son, "and can now take hold again with more resolution." [2] Back in Flint there was much to be done. The lumber business was booming. Work on his salt well was proceeding steadily, and as yet his confidence in its prospects had not been shaken. Most important, plans for the railroad project were beginning to take shape, and from the summer of 1863 onward, it occupied nearly every minute of time that he could spare. It was, therefore, no doubt, with considerable annoyance that he received the governor's call to a special session of the legislature in January, 1864. The growing need for men for the Union armies had led, early in 1863, to the establishment of a system of national conscription which would go into effect whenever quotas could not be met by voluntary enlistment. To encourage recruiting and avoid the stigma of being forced to draft, many Michigan cities and towns had turned to offering bounties to volunteers. Such municipal bounties were of doubtful legality, however, and the lack of uniformity in the bonuses offered frequently led to competition between various towns to secure men to meet their quotas. With this situation in mind, Governor Austin Blair had called the extra session for the primary purpose of enacting legislation which would both legalize and regularize the system of bounties.[3]

When the legislature convened in January, Senator Crapo found himself not only torn away from his business affairs, but—over his vehement protests—named as chairman of a special joint committee of both houses which had been created to consider the main question before the session. It was an exacting task, made all the more critical by the fact that the bounty question could not be divorced from the continuing active opposition to the war itself. More than one hundred petitions and memorials were laid before the committee; "every sort of legislation was asked for, and all sorts of opinions entertained by different members." The situation called for all the tact that Crapo could muster, but he emerged with his stature as a leader still further enhanced. His draft of the committee's final report was adopted with the change of but one word; he was charged with re-writing the accompanying bill when the committee rejected the draft prepared by one of the other members; and he was given leadership of the administration forces in carrying the bill through the legislature. After protracted debate, all amendments were defeated, and the law was passed substantially in the same form in which it had come from his hands.

While he was thus engaged, he also had to face single-handed a heavy responsibility growing out of his chairmanship of the standing committee on incorporations. A large number of railroad companies had applied to the legislature for what Crapo considered "very mischievous legislation." They had combined, he wrote,

> to secure the passage of a law authorizing towns and counties, by a mere majority vote, to become stockholders to these roads, or to issue their bonds to be loaned to these roads, or sold in the market, and the money loaned the several roads, and that too upon the simple "promise" of these companies "to pay"—and what was still worse, before these R.R. companies should have raised a single dollar on their subscribed stock.

At first he was almost alone in opposition to this plan, against "the whole force of the log-rolling of nine railroad schemes, from as many different localities and companies." If he could not defeat outright the railroads' plan "to get credit by taxation without security," he sought at least to secure some protection for the taxpayers of the state. While his success was not so complete as he might have wished, he was finally able to rally enough support in committee of the whole to secure (by a one-vote margin) the insertion of certain important limitations, in particular the provisos that bonds might not be sold for less than their par value, and that no bonds (or money derived from the sale of bonds) be delivered to the railroad company until the roadbed had been completed and the ties paid for and delivered.[4]

As a result of his course on these two matters, and his success in carrying others along with him, Crapo had made a strong impression on many of the Republican politicians in the state. It was nevertheless an occasion of great surprise to him when, towards the close of the special session, he was approached "by some of the leading men in the senate and house, as well as outside of them" with the suggestion that they put forward his name at the forthcoming party convention as their candidate to succeed Governor Blair. Since the state was safely Republican, the nomination would be tantamount to election, but Crapo regarded the very idea as both "strange and improbable," and hastened to assure William that there was no cause for alarm that he was "turning politician":

> I am no political man, and among the great number of eminent men who are even now, by their friends, seeking the nomination, I shall undoubtedly be lost sight of long before the convention is held. I do not therefore make myself unhappy through fear that I shall be troubled with the offer of a nomination for this high office.[5]

At first Crapo had regarded the proposal as a mere compliment from friends, but it soon became clear that it was meant in earnest. Professor J. E. Tenney, the state librarian, wrote him that "I have been actively corresponding with my well tried personal political friends in your behalf . . . and thus far have received very gratifying answers, much more favorable than I anticipated." [6] The Republicans of Genesee County had long planned to make Crapo their nominee for Congress. In 1862 the fear that he would flatly refuse the nomination had led to his being chosen instead for the state senate, but his partisans had been looking forward to sending him to Washington in 1864. Now, however, this plan was superseded by that of entering his name in the gubernatorial contest. Crapo took a dim view of either idea. He was at last making progress towards lifting the burden of debt which had plagued him ever since coming to Michigan, and to reach this goal he knew that he would have to give constant attention to his lumber and railroad projects. Yet if he had to choose between the two jobs, he wrote his son, he would far prefer that of governor, "since its duties could be discharged without so much inconvenience to my business." [7]

What were the reasons for Crapo's appeal to his fellow Republicans as a gubernatorial candidate? The question is particularly relevant in view of his utter lack of desire for political preferment. His own answer was that

> it is because I am supposed to be a man of *business* and *work,* untrammelled and unfettered with old political hacks—a man who says what he thinks—and believes what he says—firm and decided, and who will guard well the interests of the state, and make such appointments as her interests demand, and not such as political partisans clamor for.

Modesty compelled him to add that this view was "undoubtedly erroneous," and even if true, he could scarcely believe that it would go far "to give a man such an office to the disappointment of so many political cliques, and political aspirants." [8] Yet there can be no doubt that he was held in high personal esteem by those who had worked with him and had witnessed his impressive ability to grasp rapidly the details of complex and unfamiliar matters. Furthermore, in an age when the successful businessman was coming to be looked on as the natural leader of society, Crapo's credentials were of the highest order.

In the existing condition of Michigan politics, however, these qualifications in themselves would have hardly been enough to bring Crapo's name to the fore had it not been for another consideration, one which in the end probably proved decisive. Both of Michigan's United States senators, Zachariah Chandler and Jacob M. Howard, were from Detroit. Howard would be coming up for re-election by the legislature in January, 1865, and the retiring governor, Austin Blair, intended to challenge him for the post. In these circumstances the residence of the next governor would be of critical importance, since if a Detroit man should be chosen it would greatly strengthen Blair's chances and weaken Howard's. For this reason, support for Crapo's candidacy came not only from those who admired his personal qualities and his business background, but also from strong elements in the Republican party which opposed Blair and wished to continue Howard in the senatorship at Washington. Of the more than half dozen men mentioned as possible candidates, it had soon come to be generally accepted that the contest would lie between Crapo and H. P. Baldwin, a Detroit banker and businessman, and here the locality question came directly into play. The *Saginaw Re-*

publican, for example, stated editorially that while Baldwin would normally be its first choice, it could not favor his nomination because of his residence and instead was backing Crapo. "Detroit does not ask the nomination of Mr. Baldwin," the paper continued. "This is done by parties in other parts of the state who wish to take one of the Senators from Detroit, a proceeding which we . . . oppose." [9]

Still another factor working in Crapo's favor was the decision of John Owen, the incumbent state treasurer, to run for re-election. He was considered so popular that his nomination was taken for granted, and the fact that he, too, was a Detroit resident gave even more weight to the locality question. "It is understood," Professor Tenney wrote Crapo, that

> the secret reason why he consents to be a candidate again is that a rivalry has sprung up between the Second National Bank [of which Baldwin was president] and the Insurance Bank—the latter bank has the State deposits and I *guess* would not like to see them transferred to Mr. Baldwin's Bank. You understand! [10]

One of the main grounds advanced in opposition to Crapo's nomination was his relative newness to the state. The *Wolverine Citizen* of Flint, one of Crapo's most vigorous supporters among the Republican press, answered this charge by pointing out that although Crapo's actual residence in Michigan was of but eight years' duration, he had had large real estate holdings in the state for fifteen years, and had had the opportunity of studying her resources and interests on his annual trips prior to the time he had embarked on his Flint lumber venture. "His own interests," the paper continued, "have thus been so identified with the growth and prosperity of the State, as to prompt the search into what would most effectually promote the latter." The editorial added that Crapo "has already been the cause—either directly or indirectly—of bringing into the State as many settlers, as many active business men, and as much capital, as almost any other person in Michigan," and concluded its argument with the statement that Crapo not only was the largest taxpayer in Genesee County, but paid taxes as well in some thirty other counties in the state.[11]

As the jockeying for position continued in the months preceding the convention, Crapo kept his son informed on the progress of his own candidacy although he insisted that he had "no thought and little desire" for the nomination. In May he wrote that "I have no time to do a thing to secure my nomination, and it will undoubtedly go by default."

> I have abundance of strength in the state, and all over it; but it is from a class of substantial, high-minded men who will do little to head the necessary movements in the different counties to secure "Crapo delegates," leaving the field open to mere political men to secure delegates to suit themselves.

Up to the very eve of the convention Crapo remained skeptical, despite the assurances of his backers that his chances for the nomination were as good as or better than those of any of the other aspirants. His friends, by and large, were not "political workers" but rather "the old, staid, business men about the several county seats, and among the farmers, and nearly all the Republican senators of the last legislature," and he was sure that their support would not prove of much influence in the convention. With "a very little personal effort" he felt that he might have assured his election, but he had no regrets that he had not done so, since even at that date he had not fully settled in his mind whether he did or did not want the nomination.[12]

Two weeks later, however, when the convention opened in Detroit on July 7, Crapo had apparently overcome much of this professed indifference. He wrote his son that he had prepared a notebook listing each county alphabetically "with the names of the delegates, as well as prominent Republicans, and with their preferences."

> This book I made a repository of all the information sent me from all parts of the state, and from which I was able to direct . . . just who I wanted to look after certain persons. As a matter of business I took the whole thing into my own hands so that my working friends had only to take their directions from me as to any cases outside their own locality.

"When we came to the convention," he announced proudly, "the Army of the Potomac was not better organized than my forces." On the first ballot, Crapo led the field with 86 votes out of 207 cast, followed by Baldwin with 65. His strength grew as the supporters of other candidates switched their votes to one or the other of the two leading contenders, and on the third ballot he was nominated, defeating Baldwin 106 to 103.[13]

"Victory has perched upon the banner of my friends," he wrote William, "for it was their cause rather than mine." It is impossible to judge his sincerity in such protestations. Undoubtedly he had been torn between his sense of duty to his business and the appeal to his vanity inherent in the kind of support he had received. He had taken the leadership of his forces at the convention, he claimed, "merely to aid the efforts of my friends, and without a hope or even a wish to succeed." "I regret the result," he wrote his son, "but it is too late; I am now in for it." Indeed, he found it rather difficult to believe what had happened.

> It is only a little over six years since I could claim the right to vote in Massachusetts, and now I stand at the head of the Republican party in this state, which expects at the coming election to roll up a majority of 20,000 for the Union cause. My position is a very honorable one, speaking after the manner of political men, and one that a great many of the most prominent and intelligent men in the state would make great sacrifices to reach; and it is with no small degree of surprise, even to myself, that I recall my situation when a boy on my father's farm, toiling among the rocks and stones, without knowledge or even books, and without even the confidence and good manners induced by cultivated society; and my situation today.

"This certainly should teach all boys," he moralized, "that under our free Institutions industry and perseverance, with an irreproachable moral character, will place within their reach the highest political preferment." He admitted that his own case might be an exception, "but even if it be so, it shows what can be done by strong will, and unyielding efforts." [14]

In his acceptance speech Crapo outlined the political ground on which he stood. The Republican party, he declared, had been formed "for no partizan purpose . . . but as a great moral and political necessity" whose purpose was to prevent the extension of slavery. Slavery, however, had "demanded all," and the result had been the Rebellion, in which "slavery and not the Republican party has made the issue, and no other choice has been left us than that of abject submission to this gigantic evil, or a deadly conflict for its overthrow." With the outbreak of war, he continued, "another and nobler mission" had been given the party:

> We are not now merely to see that the polluting touch
> of Negro slavery does not extend itself to free terri-
> tory, but we are, in the deadly conflict now raging
> . . . to battle with this despotic monster slavery . . .
> until it shall be effectually overthrown and destroyed.

To this end, he urged a vigorous prosecution of the war and expressed his hope that along with victory there would come a Constitutional amendment by which "slavery shall be blotted from the Republic forever." [15]

II

As might be expected, Crapo's nomination was received with varying reactions. The *Detroit Advertiser and Tribune,* more or less the official Republican paper, praised the nominee but nevertheless commented with careful impartiality that the large vote for Baldwin had given him "much of the moral effect of success without its burdens and cares." [16] Not all those in the Republican ranks were happy with the selection which had been made. Baldwin and his backers were of course dismayed, as were those who had planned to support Governor Blair for the United States senatorship. Charles S. May, the incumbent lieutenant-governor, who fell in both categories, wrote to Blair from his home in Kalamazoo: "The ticket falls flat here—buried under Crapo's speech!" [17] But the real fury came from the Democratic *Detroit Free Press,* which coupled its political attack with a personal one. "Seriously," the editors wrote, "we cannot believe that a great party, numbering among its members so many leading men of the state, would have selected an entire stranger to the people, of no talent or distinction, unless they felt that the chances of his election were desperate." They were "sorely puzzled" as to the qualifications of the Republican nominee, whom they described for their readers in the following words:

> His personal appearance is anything but prepossessing. In height, he is a little over six feet, very spare, a thin hatchet face, stoops, wears green glasses, and like most New England men is particularly sharp in money affairs, and always ready if there is a chance to make a penny.[18]

No one familiar with the Republican party six months before, they wrote, would have thought possible the nomination of a man like Crapo.

> He is a recent emigrant to this State. He knows but few men in the state, and is well known by less. He may be a good merchant, a better lumberman, but what real knowledge has he of the State, its varied interests, the laws which have been enacted, and now in force? . . . Mr. Crapo was designated as the candidate, not from his peculiar fitness, not from his qualifications, but because of his locality, and the supposed bearing his nomination would have upon the selection of Senator next winter. He was nominated to serve the interests of the party, and not to look after the interests of the people.

They claimed that "the regency of the republican party, whose headquarters is here in Detroit," had decided that Senator Howard should be re-elected, and had dictated "every movement upon the political chessboard of that party . . . to produce that result."

These men had control of the State Convention, and defeated Mr. Baldwin, not because they believed he was not far better qualified to discharge the duties of governor than the stranger they nominated, but because they feared that it would be impossible for them to secure for Detroit the Governor, the State Treasurer, two United States Senators, two Regents of the University, the Sub-Treasurer, Receiver of Public Moneys, the Provost Marshal for this Congressional District, besides numerous other offices of large pay. They sacrificed Mr. Baldwin to save their own party and personal interests.[19]

It is impossible to determine the truth of this charge. If a Republican "regency" existed, it would have been dominated by Zachariah Chandler; it has been stated that by 1862, in the course of his rise to power, the senator "owned the Republican organization from the State Central Committee down to the most obscure caucus." [20] Crapo was no stranger to Chandler. The two men had had business dealings, and on at least one occasion the senator had been Crapo's overnight guest while on a speech-making tour in company with Ohio's Senator Wade. Crapo's grandson even suggests in his biography that Crapo may have been a political protege of Chandler. On the other hand, there is no reflection in Crapo's correspondence of any close relationship with the senator, and in his own account of the preconvention maneuvering he clearly gives the impression that his nomination was being promoted from outside the ranks of the active party workers. Indeed, the fact that the convention's vote was so sharply split seems strong evidence against dictation from the top.[21]

Whatever the true background to his selection as candidate, it did not take him long to win backing from many who had at first been lukewarm. Two weeks after the convention the *Advertiser and Tribune* commented that "there is not a Republican paper in the State that does not cordially endorse [the nomination]." Recognizing that the candidate was not so well known as were some of the unsuccessful contenders, the editors devoted considerable space to setting forth his virtues. As a counter to the unflattering picture presented by the *Free Press,* they wrote that

> Mr. Crapo is about five feet ten inches in height, of rather spare habit, with shoulders slightly stooping, from continued application in the counting-room. . . . He has a high forehead, well balanced brain, and a piercing black eye, indicating a quick, active intelligence, and largely developed perceptive faculties.

He was, they averred, "emphatically a man of the people," who "commenced life poor, with nothing but his hands and brains for a capital," but had "by persistent, persevering industry and unswerving integrity . . . achieved a proud position among our business men and acquired a magnificent fortune." As a measure of his success, they estimated his annual taxes at $10,000, and characterized his business as "one of the largest in the state, conducted by an individual." Pointing out that he had not sought political preferment, but that the offices he had held had "come to him for his eminent fitness to fill them," they wrote that in his term as state senator he had "left the impress of his solid capacity and large business experience upon some of our most important State legislation."

> He is now in the prime of life, is a man of solid abilities, much business experience, good acquirements, of sound political principles, an active sup-

porter of the war to crush the rebellion, and a man of the highest character. He will be elected, of course, and we predict for him an honorable and useful administration.[22]

Despite the general assumption that Michigan was safely Republican, however, a month after the convention Crapo wrote his son that victory was "by no means certain . . . without a desperate struggle."

The political horizon looks bad just now. This call for 500,000 men, with recent reverses in the Army when the public mind had assured itself of speedy and decisive victories, together with the retirement from the cabinet of Mr. Chase, the waning popularity of Mr. Lincoln, and the persevering efforts of the copperheads, will all combine to depress the spirits of weak-kneed, timid, and vacillating Republicans. The quota of the state in this present call will be 15,000 men, which will nearly all come from the republican ranks, as every effort will be made to avoid a draft; and this cannot fail to weaken the party seriously.

The responsibility of his position as head of the Republican state ticket weighed heavily on Crapo, and he determined to do everything he could to bring about a victory for the Union party. "If we cannot carry *this state*," he wrote, "we cannot elect Lincoln, we cannot save our Government, and then *all will be lost*." He resolved as his first step to canvass as much of the state as possible on his own before the start of the regular campaign in mid-September. The plan he laid out was

to go quietly into a village and take a good room at a hotel, and let some of my Republican friends know

that I am there. They then appraise the leading and
most reliable Republicans of the fact, who freely call
upon me. I thus have an opportunity of talking over
freely and familiarly our prospects, our embarrass-
ments and our difficulties; and also arrange for the
campaign, and the most efficient mode of carrying it
on, etc. . . . Wherever I have been thus far I have
held quite a levee for some hours, all hands turning
out to see and talk with me for the first time, and
especially editors, lawyers, politicians, etc.

These informal meetings proved to be well worth the effort,
and Crapo soon found that he was winning support from
many "leading men of the party, who otherwise would have
been cold and indifferent, and perhaps done very little for
the success of the ticket." [23]

III

With the opening of the regular campaign, Crapo's emphasis shifted to a direct approach to the party rank-and-file
and to the mass of voters generally throughout the state.
None of the other candidates on the state ticket was an
experienced speaker, and only one of them was willing to
take the platform at all. As a result, while candidates for
congressional office took an active part in the campaigning,
the main burden of "stumping the state" fell on Crapo's
shoulders. The sole issue in the campaign was the question
of national policy in the Civil War; state issues appear not
to have been mentioned at all, and personalities entered into
the debate only to a very limited extent. The Republican
platform called for support of the Administration and a
vigorous prosecution of the war. The Democrats, denouncing "four years of failure to restore the Union by the experiment of war," demanded a negotiated peace "at the earliest

practicable moment." In Michigan their banner was carried by William M. Fenton, a fellow townsman of Crapo and former lieutenant-governor of the state. The debate was bitter.* "The Copperheads," Crapo wrote, were working with "reckless desperation and . . . utter disregard to all truth."

> I have supposed that there were limits to degradation, and that Northern traitors and rebel sympathizers had found that line long since. But all they have done heretofore that was base and ignoble and treasonable was as nothing compared to their present wicked and dastardly course.[24]

Crapo approached his task with misgivings, for he had never considered himself much of a public speaker and was acutely conscious of his lack of formal education. He was successful from the outset, however, and during the month and a half preceding the election he was constantly on the go, speaking at some forty meetings in all parts of the state, and addressing a total of more than 40,000 people. The significance of the aggregate size of his audiences becomes evident when we realize that it equalled approximately one-fourth of the total number of votes cast. The *Free Press,* which at first had asked, "Who is Crapo?" now thought the question should be "Where is Crapo?" To meet some of his appointments, he had "to ride by waggon over the worst kind of new-country, woods roads 80 miles—out and in—for a single speech." [25] At the very time he was following this

---

* The Republicans denounced Fenton for a treasonable speech which he allegedly made in 1862 while an army colonel. On the occasion of General Hunter's order freeing the slaves in certain southern states in that year, Fenton was supposed to have said that he would rather go over to the enemy than to serve in an army committed to such an order.—*Detroit Advertiser & Tribune,* Sept. 25, 1864.

arduous schedule, it must be remembered, he was also struggling to get his railroad built, and had on his mind the general problems if not the specific details of his lumber business.*

On some occasions he shared the platform with local candidates, but frequently he spoke alone, often for two hours or more. In preparation for the canvass, he wrote,

> I laid out my work by taking certain propositions, and
> fixing upon certain points, and then at my leisure
> and nights when I should have been in bed wrote out
> the arguments in reference to each of them.

Having thus drafted "sufficient matter for three speeches at least," he then drew up a brief, "and with these I went into the field." This intensive study enabled him, after his first few appearances, to speak entirely extemporaneously, adding greatly both to his self-confidence and to the impression which he made on his audiences. Working from the same basic material, he found it possible to vary his address so as to give each speech the appearance of being entirely original.

His main emphasis was placed on a refutation of the Democratic charge that the Republicans had started the war, an examination of the antagonism between the two great principles of democracy and aristocracy, and a call to all

* An indication of the pace of his tour is given by this partial compilation of his speaking dates from the *Detroit Advertiser & Tribune,* Sept. 24, Oct. 1, 5, 12, Nov. 2, 4, 1864: Sept. 22, Vassar; 23, Pontiac; 26, Flint; 27, Grand Rapids; 28, Ionia; 29, St. Johns; 30, Lansing; Oct. 1, Corunna; 3, East Saginaw; 4, Bay City; 6, Fentonville; 8, Lapeer; 11, Charlotte; 12, Hastings; 14, Newaygo; 18, Monroe; 19, Adrian; 20, Hillsdale; 20, Jonesville; 21, Coldwater; 22, Niles; 24, Dowagiac; 25, Paw Paw; 26, Kalamazoo; 27, Marshall; Nov. 2, Port Huron; 3, Ortonville; 4, Saginaw.

loyal Union men to put aside party labels and support the Administration until victory was won.[26]

The crowds which came to hear Crapo when he spoke were often so great that people had to be turned away. The personal attacks which had been aimed at him after his nomination made people curious, wrote the *Wolverine Citizen,* and after coming to listen they stayed to applaud.

> Talking and arguing to the People as a Man of the People, his influence and popularity continue to grow as he becomes more extensively known. The masses recognize intuitively that there is no *bogus* about Senator Crapo, and they value him accordingly.[27]

The *Lansing State Republican,* which had originally supported Baldwin for the nomination, was equally pleased. Reporting its impressions of Crapo's speech at the state capital, it described him as

> of good size and height, of dignified appearance, and of a nervous-bilious temperament—a combination usually connected with much mental application, strong feelings, earnestness of purpose, and great hang-on-ativeness in business. We noticed his characteristics more closely, because we had observed the attempt . . . after his nomination to run him down as a mere *"hatchet-faced money-making Yankee"* with merely that amount and kind of ability which would be adapted to drive good trades in buying logs for his saw mills, or be very sharp in measuring out a load of lumber to some poor teamster. But all impressions of this kind vanish at once upon hearing him speak for a few minutes. He speaks rather slowly, loud, distinct, emphatic, earnestly, candidly, without any slang ex-

pressions, with no attempt at witticisms, and with an appearance of elevated sentiments. . . . Instead of arguing from single points, [he] puts his facts in groups and masses, and then hurls them upon his antagonist, with force and effect.[28]

On November 8 the people went to the polls, and Crapo rejoiced that the result showed "a united North in the great work of maintaining, against all enemies, the integrity of the Union, and the maintenance of free institutions, at all and every cost." The official returns read 91,356 for Crapo, 74,293 for Fenton. He felt satisfied with his own role in the campaign. "By a great effort (for me) I have achieved a reputation of which I am not ashamed; and today I am regarded as one of the *strong men* in this rapidly growing and prosperous state." He had not, however, conquered all his qualms:

> I am aware that I am *greatly* wanting in *ability* to meet and properly discharge the duties of this high office; and I constantly fear that I shall not meet the expectations of my friends. If I had leisure to study out and prepare myself it would be different; but I have hardly a moment to prepare myself for what is before me, the demands of my business being imperative and constant.[29]

nine

GOVERNOR OF MICHIGAN:
FIRST TERM

I

On January 4, 1865, Crapo took office as Michigan's first businessman governor. All of his predecessors had been lawyers by profession, excepting only the young "boy governor," Stevens T. Mason, who had been carried over from the territorial government when Michigan was admitted to the Union in 1837. There was a definite place in the governor's chair for a man with practical administrative experience. "The governors for six years past have been *Orators*," Crapo wrote his son shortly after the inauguration, "but I would not exchange what little business knowledge I have for their eloquence in managing the affairs of a large and new state like this." [1] During the four years of Crapo's two terms as Michigan's chief executive, his business background helped him greatly in coping with the multitudinous details which demanded his attention.

The governorship was not yet the full-time job which it has become in modern times; it had vastly increased in complexity over the ante-bellum years but without a commensurate increase in administrative machinery. When Crapo took office the war was nearing a close, but even at that late date military matters made heavy demands on his time. With the end of hostilities, a new set of problems came into being, necessitating frequent trips to the national capital. In addition to the tasks arising from the war and its aftermath, there was still the ordinary state business which required careful supervision. The governor was chairman ex-officio of the various state boards, and Crapo soon discovered that nothing would be done unless he was in attendance. He was determined to be an honest and conscientious executive, and on his arrival in Lansing he had found "many things in a bad shape, which I am bound quietly to straighten out." Commenting on the new governor, the *Sturgis Journal* wrote that "if we are not mistaken, the sharks and pirates that are always hanging around the Capital, endeavoring to get their hands into the Treasury, will have very poor pickings during his administration." [2]

II

When the legislature assembled in joint session to hear the valedictory message of outgoing Governor Blair and the inaugural of Crapo, everyone was "eager and anxious to know how a lumberman would be able to meet the demands of the occasion." Crapo feared that his address would suffer by comparison with that of Blair, "one of the most eloquent and gifted men of our state," and wrote disparagingly to his son of his own production, although he did consider it a "plain, straightforward, practical document." [3]

The message contained few high-flown phrases and was concerned in the main with Crapo's views on the interests and needs of the state. After a brief review of the condition of the state treasury, and an admonition to continue the pay-as-you-go policy adopted in 1861, he turned his attention to the resources and prospects of the state. Michigan, he declared, was still in her infancy, and had a tremendous potential for future development. He was confident that her agriculture, lumbering, fisheries, copper, coal, and salt would in years to come make her "one of the most prosperous and populous . . . States in this Union." To achieve this goal, he urged the legislature to take steps to encourage the flow into the state of the two essentials for economic growth, labor and capital. He asked in particular that measures be undertaken to popularize Michigan as a place to settle among "the hardy emigrants from the over-populated countries of Europe." Declaring that "Michigan in the future is destined to become an important manufacturing district," he enumerated among its advantages a ready supply of raw materials, ample quantities of agricultural products to sustain an industrial population, and a vast market in the state itself and throughout the West. "The idea of depending upon New England and the East . . . for our manufactured goods, is simply against all the laws of trade and in direct violation of all the principles of political economy." As a further measure to encourage the economic development of the state, he proposed prompt action to complete for the entire state the geological survey so ably begun years before by Douglass Houghton, but abandoned after his death. He gave warning that he disapproved of the promiscuous pardoning of convicts which had been practiced by many of his predecessors, and announced his intention to make most sparing use of his powers of executive clemency. His stand on the "swamp lands state road" issue was equally a break with precedent. In 1850 the federal government had ceded to the state some 6 million acres of so-called "swamp land" (much of which was not actually swamp but merely inferior land) with the proviso that the state should apply the proceeds from its sale towards the task of drainage. In 1859 the legislature had passed a law authorizing grants from this fund for the purpose of constructing state roads. Crapo was sharply critical of the results thus far obtained and, indeed, expressed his opposition to the very concept that road building would provide drainage. He recognized, however, that the policy was perhaps too well entrenched to permit its abandonment but urged, at least, that great care be taken in its further application.

He concluded his address with a brief but vigorous call for the prompt and successful conclusion of the war, citing the 1864 elections as proof of the "determination of the American people that slavery shall cease to exist" and that the Union should stand over and above state sovereignty.[4]

The message met with a far warmer reception than Crapo had expected. It won him praise not only from his own party but even, albeit grudgingly, from the Democrats, whose chief journal, the *Detroit Free Press,* conceded that it "gives us a much better opinion of the man than we had before."

> He says what he has to say with a good deal of directness, and has evidently given much more attention to ascertaining the resources and business interests of the State than to politics, and from this we draw a favorable inference as to his future. His suggestions in the main are evidently dictated by his judgment of what will be for the welfare of the State.[5]

The first order of business for the legislature was the election of a United States senator, and while the Blair-Howard rivalry was, as we have seen, a factor in the preconvention maneuvering that led to Crapo's nomination, there is no evidence that Crapo himself played any part in securing Howard's election. Once this matter had been disposed of, the legislature settled down to the ordinary business of the session. There were, the *Free Press* had noted, "no existing questions involving great principles" to come before it, and the bulk of the legislation enacted was of a routine nature. The one occasion on which its even course was disturbed was when Crapo vetoed a bill authorizing the Houghton County board of supervisors to draw "swamp land" funds for the construction of a state road in the Upper Peninsula. The measure had made no provision for supervision or control of the expenditure by any state officer, and the new governor felt that this was a dangerous precedent which might "become an entering wedge for bolder schemes and the absorption of larger powers by boards of supervisors, already sufficiently extended." His action called forth the comment from the *Advertiser and Tribune* that vetoes "have been rare in the history of our legislature for some years past, but the present one shows that the Executive keeps a vigilant eye on all measures affecting the public interests, and subjects them to a wise and searching scrutiny." [6]

As the session progressed, Crapo gained confidence. He strove to inform himself on all the details of the state's business, explaining to William in one letter how he had "worked hard all day, shut up in my office in the State House":

> I have . . . written quite an important special message for the legislature, to be in tomorrow morning, signed some 300 blank military commissions, wrote four land contracts, and about 20 letters, besides tracing through the whole length of our statutes several important subjects.[7]

He took pride in his independence:

> One thing is giving me no little distinction. I rely upon myself, and although I do not reject the advice of others, yet I do not permit the mere politicians to interfere with my policy, or with my appointments.

. . . I keep my own council as to what I purpose to
do, and have no confidants. My appointments are only
known when made; and although some will be dissat-
isfied, yet in the end I give general satisfaction, and as
the fact becomes apparent that I am not the tool of
politicians, I find that my hold upon the Legislature
increases. My opinions are formed not so much by petitions, and advice voluntarily given, as by observation, and a quiet way of "picking up" isolated facts
bearing upon the measures and purposes to which I
am aiming. I talk very little but work unceasingly.[8]

By the end of the session in March he was more than ready
to return to Flint but declared, "I have succeeded to my own
satisfaction, and I believe to that of the Legislature." [9]

Noting his arrival home, the Flint correspondent of the
Detroit Advertiser and Tribune wrote that "hard work being the constant habit of his life, the cares incident to his
official duties have left no trace on him." To a son-in-law,
however, the situation appeared in a somewhat different
light:

He has an immense load on him now and I think it is
counting very fast on his constitution and mind and
what makes it worse it tends to more close confinement, and he neglects those old practices or pastimes
of his in the line of horticulture, etc., open air exercise.[10]

It was but a passing comment, but it foreshadowed difficulties to come.

Crapo's official responsibilities were not over with the
adjournment of the legislature. In May, in June, and again
in October he found it necessary to go to Washington on

state business, in particular the mustering out of Michigan regiments and the settlement of the state's claim for $700,000 spent in raising and equipping troops early in the war. Secretary of the Treasury McCulloch at first attempted to stall him off on the claim, but a newspaper leak that Massachusetts had succeeded in collecting from the federal government led Crapo to take a strong stand. When McCulloch told him that "Gov. Andrews [of Massachusetts] was a very disagreeable, arbitrary man," that he had made frequent trips to Washington "to quarrel with Secy. Stanton and others," and "that they paid him to get rid of him," Crapo countered with the threat that if his claim was not met he would feel justified in acting likewise, "to an extent which, under other circumstances, might be deemed ungentlemanly and discourteous."

> Michigan [he wrote his son] has put into the field over 91,000 of her best men, being one in every eight of her entire population; and our loss by the war will be 50% of our entire capital of productive labor. We are a new state and compared with Massachusetts are poor. We have not yet emerged from the hardships incident to the settlement of a new country, and have no surplus capital, and our taxes fall with terrible weight upon us; and I shall not quietly submit to remain passive and wait the slow tedious process of the Govt. paying our claim until it is perfectly convenient for them to do so when it permits itself to be *bullied* into the payment of the claims of Massachusetts, one of the richest states in the Union.[11]

Almost immediately upon his return from Washington in July, Crapo set off on a self-imposed task, visiting the Upper Peninsula

to post myself and become familiar by personal observation with the vast resources of our state in that
region, that I might be able—from the important position which I occupy—to so shape the policy and so
foster and protect those great and inexhaustible
sources of wealth there, as to protect and preserve the
interests of the state.[12]

On the trip he traveled long distances on foot and on horse-
back, inspecting mines, state roads, railroads, and harbors.
The tour was suddenly interrupted, however, when he was
stricken with an acute attack of a bladder ailment which had
troubled him since 1861, but which he had been able to
keep more or less under control since that time. He was
taken ill at Houghton, and it was not until several days
later, after reaching Marquette by steamer, that he received
proper medical attention. Before he could return home
safely, Dr. Willson, a son-in-law and his personal physician,
had to be summoned from Flint to accompany him on the
trip, and for more than a month his activities were severely
restricted as he sought to regain his strength.[13]

The following year, he took advantage of another opportunity to promote the interests of the state in the economic
sphere. On a trip to Washington in February, 1866, he met
with the entire Michigan delegation in Congress to enlist
their support for a duty on salt and copper, and to encourage their opposition both to the extension or renewal of
a reciprocity treaty permitting duty-free entry of Canadian
lumber and to a proposed revenue tax on lumber.[14]

III

The influence which state governors had wielded in national politics at the outset of the Civil War faded rapidly

as the federal government assumed a more and more positive role under the stress of the wartime emergency. If anything, this situation was more pronounced in Michigan than elsewhere, since the state's senior senator, Zachariah Chandler, was one of the main leaders of the radical party in Washington. Nevertheless, Crapo was able on a number of occasions to make valuable contributions in support of the radical Republican program.

In his inaugural address he had repeated the call in his acceptance speech for a Constitutional amendment which would abolish slavery, and had urged the legislature to adopt a resolution asking its adoption by Congress. Before any action could be taken, word was received from Washington on February 1, 1865, that the Thirteenth Amendment had been passed. At once Crapo sent a message to the legislature calling for its immediate ratification, holding forth the hope that Michigan might be the first state to approve the amendment. The delay of a day, however, gave that honor to Illinois, and Michigan had to content itself with second place on the roll.[15]

After the end of the war and the death of Lincoln, a new kind of problem dominated the national political scene. Crapo shared the deeply felt belief of many Republicans that President Johnson's policy towards the defeated rebel states constituted a betrayal of Civil War ideals. In Johnson's eyes, the task of reconstruction was completed by the end of 1865, when, under his initiative, state governments had been organized throughout the South committed in only the most limited way to acceptance of the results of the war. By acknowledging the authority of the United States government, by recognizing that legally slavery no longer existed, these governments were free to perpetuate in substance most of the characteristics of pre-war southern society. By their actions, in particular the passage of the so-called "black codes," they soon made clear their intention that the Negro was to continue a slave in fact if not in name. Still more important, as events were proceeding under the Johnsonian plan of reconstruction the South would be returning to the Union with even greater political power than it had held before the war. As slaves the Negroes had counted for three-fifths their number in the allotment of Congressional representation; now, as freedmen but still disfranchised, the Negroes of the South would give their erstwhile white owners twelve new Congressional places in addition to the eighteen seats they had held in 1860 by virtue of the three-fifths clause! It is little wonder that many Republicans felt that the victories of the battlefield were being bartered away by a President who was playing the southern game.

When Congress met in December, 1865, the Republican majority immediately took issue with the Presidential plan of reconstruction, and throughout the session the conflict grew in intensity. On February 19, 1866, Johnson vetoed a bill to extend the life of the Freedmen's Bureau, and on March 27 he took the same step with a civil rights bill. In Michigan, Crapo had been watching these developments with increasing concern, and on March 31 he acted by issuing a proclamation appointing April 19 as a day of fasting, humiliation and prayer. His purpose, he explained to his son, was "to say that the great work of reconstruction is not yet done, when Johnson says it is, . . . and to appeal to the highest attributes of our natures for a proper consideration of the whole matter." He acknowledged that in calling for the Fast Day, he sought "to affect and mould public opinion in this state, . . . to counteract the influence of the Johnson-Copperhead party here, and to keep the Republicans true to the great work of maintaining their principles to the end." [16]

In the proclamation he warned the people of Michigan:

> Let us not vainly imagine that all danger is past, and that we are now, as a nation, securely rooted in those principles of Liberty and Equality for which our Fathers contended. . . . The work is not yet finished! We have a mightier victory still to achieve in the reconstruction of a united country. . . . Now, when our political skies are clouded by antagonism . . . between the ruling powers at the Capitol of our Republic, . . . when great statesmen are apprehensive, and millions of freedmen are trembling and weeping for the safety and security of our Government, it is most proper and fitting that we should assemble in our respective places of worship, and there penitently confess our weaknesses and our sins, both as individuals and as a nation.
>
> . . . Our nation is yet in peril! The great triumph of breaking and subduing the power of the enemy—of tearing down—has been completed; but the greater triumph of rebuilding again our fair fabric of Human Government, recognizing the inherent right of all men to the enjoyment of "Life, Liberty and the Pursuit of Happiness," is only just commenced. Let us seek, then, the Divine aid, to subdue our pride—to surrender our wills—to abandon our prejudices, and to reconstruct the Republic upon the broad principles of Right, of Humanity, Justice and Eternal Truth; when all men, irrespective of caste or color, shall be equal in the eyes of the law.[17]

The proclamation was generally well received throughout the state, but in Detroit it created a tremendous stir among the Democrats, who had given their wholehearted support to Johnsonian reconstruction. The *Free Press* denounced it as a "flagrant outrage," a "public manifestation of disrespect and insult to the President of the United States." The Wayne County Democratic Association resolved that it was

> a direct attack upon the President for the exercise of his constitutional powers, an insult to the majority of the citizens of this State who are his supporters, and a blasphemous attempt to pervert the religious faith of the people for a wicked and partizan purpose

and called for an outpouring of the public at a protest meeting to be held on the Campus Martius.[18]

Although Crapo had not expected the violent reaction, he was by no means displeased with it, for he felt that the "Johnson Copperheads" had let the public know where they stood. The proclamation, he told his son, "was like firing a whole battery of grape into the bushes where a thousand rebels lay concealed." He congratulated himself that because of the fury of the Democratic attack his message would be published in Republican papers throughout the West and thus brought to the attention of thousands who would otherwise not have seen it.[19]

In charging that the governor was inviting the people to gather in their places of worship to "invoke the Lord to side with the Republican party," the Democrats had misjudged the public temper, and they soon found it expedient to change the ground on which their meeting was called to the simple support of the President's two veto messages, saying not a word about the alleged blasphemy of Crapo's proclamation. Meanwhile, however, the Republican papers were having a field day. The *Advertiser and Tribune* wrote that it "had not presumed that the prevalent piety of the Democratic masses was so sensitive." Carl Schurz's *Daily Post*, with a more historical turn of mind, wrote:

> There was a time when the Democrats pressed the Bible into service in their search for arguments in favor of slavery, [taking] advantage of the religious feelings of the masses for the purpose of prolonging the existence of the most revolting and most damnable of all known wrongs. It is no wonder indeed that . . . they should not be able to restrain their wrath when they see the formidable weapon turned against themselves, and find their wicked schemes dragged before the tribunal of conscience. They must have come to the conclusion that the people cannot be called upon to pray without injury to Andrew Johnson.[20]

When "certain irreverent persons appear[ed] disposed to jeer at the piety" of the Democratic leaders, the *Daily Post* sought "with becoming seriousness, and disclaiming any intentions of levity," to inquire as to the "particular tenets of these conscientious gentlemen, whose quick religious feelings have been . . . 'outraged' and 'insulted' ":

> These gentlemen . . . have been engaged in spiritual and spirited protesting for the last six years. . . .
> They protested against young men volunteering in the Union armies, lest the temptations of the camp should lure their feet into the paths of sin.
> They protested against disturbing the institution of slavery as a pernicious meddling with divine laws. . . .
> They protested against the churches, because of

their manifold heresies on the subject of the universal brotherhood of men.

They protested against the proclamations of Thanksgiving issued by the late President Abraham Lincoln, because they were wicked rejoicings over advantages gained in the unholy strife of war.

Their organ protested against the jolly old custom of Thanksgiving itself, as a Puritanical, New England notion, calculated to foster the wicked and fanatical heresies of Abolitionism.

They protested against any and everything that *other* Christian denominations considered of good repute and proper to be encouraged.

When the appointed day arrived for the Democratic protest meeting, wrote the *Daily Post,* "the masses assembled served only to show how large the Campus Martius is." The site of the meeting was moved indoors to the City Hall, where some four hundred people gathered in the Council chamber, that "narrow hall where once a week Aldermanic wisdom flaps its drowsy wings." There they heard an assortment of speakers applaud the President's defense of Constitutional principles and denounce the "politically pious" radicals. Outdoors, the *Daily Post* continued, "those that remained true to the original idea of filling the Campus Martius with a stalwart crowd, modestly confined themselves to the sidewalk, warming their enthusiasm in the melancholy glare of a lonesome woodfire." [21]

Three months later Crapo returned to the attack, delivering the main address at a huge celebration in Detroit combining the observance of the Fourth of July and the presentation of the battle flags of Michigan regiments to the state. Originally he had intended merely to make a five-minute speech receiving the flags. To prevent the Democratic city administration of Detroit from taking over the occasion to propagate their "Johnson-Vallandigham-Copperhead ideas and sentiments," however, he resolved to make his speech "of sufficient length so that there shall be no occasion for them to crowd in," and to show how the causes which led to both the War for Independence and the Civil War involved "the antagonism of the same principles and purposes." [22]

Tracing the early history of the nation in his address, he recalled how slavery, admittedly an exception to the free institutions established by the Revolution, had at the outset been "tolerated through misguided expediency, in the confident belief that it must speedily die out." Instead, he continued, this "natural enemy of Freedom and Free Institutions in every form . . . was permitted by degrees to establish and build up, over a vast area of our otherwise free and prosperous domain . . . one of the most despotic and arbitrary aristocracies which the world has ever known." He paid tribute to the men who stood before him for having put down the slaveholders' rebellion, but warned that even yet "the spirit which seeks to make slavery the cornerstone of empire . . . is neither dead nor sleeping. . . . Having failed so utterly in the resort to force, it will but recuperate its energies for a more insidious attack in a different method of warfare." With obvious reference to the debate over reconstruction, he urged his listeners to "make it a great and fundamental principle, to be neither evaded nor set aside by any specious sophistry, that traitors shall be purged of their treason by works meet for repentance, before they shall be suffered to enjoy the privileges and immunities of loyal men." [23]

Crapo was well satisfied with his oratorical efforts on the occasion, as were Republicans generally, although he did tell his son that he thought his speech of "little merit" compared with those of Governors Curtin of Pennsylvania and Fairfield of Wisconsin on the same day.* They, he reminded William, "are men of marked ability and high culture, whereas I came from the hard, rocky and sterile fields of old Dartmouth, without the aid and polish derived from either education or good society." [24]

A year and a half later, in February, 1868, when the struggle between Congress and the President was reaching its climax in the impeachment proceedings against Johnson, Crapo struck his final blow in support of the radical program. From a sickbed in Washington, where he had suffered another serious bladder attack, he wrote an open letter to the Michigan delegation in Congress in which he expressed his hope that

> in this hour of peril to the cause of human liberty and free institutions . . . you will not, for a single moment, falter in the great work of maintaining this liberty and these institutions, as well against Executive usurpation of every kind, as against all those who still continue to sympathize with treason and disloyalty.[25]

---

* In view of the way Crapo had taken over the occasion from the Democrats, it is perhaps little wonder that the *Detroit Free Press* of July 6, 1866, called the speech "a prosy harangue . . . tasteless and decidedly unacceptable to the tired soldiers and others who had been on their feet for hours, and not at all desirous of being read to sleep."

ten

RAILS AND LUMBER
(1864 - 1865)

I

Superficially, the dominant fact of Crapo's life in 1864 had been his nomination and then election as governor of Michigan. Actually, however, the continuing progress of his business enterprises was of more than equal importance to him. The special session of the legislature had kept him at Lansing for part of January and February, but, as we have seen, he was unwilling to let his friends' enthusiasm for his candidacy interfere with the demands of his affairs at Flint. After his nomination in July, he had felt obligated by his position as the Republican standard-bearer to devote a large part of his time and energy to the campaign, but even then he could not escape his responsibilities at home. His major concern was the Flint and Holly Rail Road, on which construction had begun the previous fall; to a very considerable extent the operation of the lumber business was entrusted to the young men whom he had trained as his lieutenants.[1]

The actual construction work was in the hands of the contractors, Walton and Wright of Detroit, but this was only a small part of the task of establishing a railroad where none had been before. The right of way had to be secured and land damages settled, railroad iron, rolling stock, and other materials and equipment purchased, accounts audited and bills paid, stock assessments collected, "and ten thousand other things." Crapo found it necessary to keep a close eye on everything that was being done, even if responsibility had been delegated to others, and he was constantly besieged with questions to which he alone could give the answer. No detail was too small to require his attention; "I necessarily have to be familiar with everything even to the size and length of spikes, the location and size of holes on the rails . . . etc." In reading his letters, one cannot but wonder how he found time to keep up with his work. Indeed, he could not. During the early stages of construction he wrote that "about one night in a week I do not go to bed at all," and, a little later, "the bare business of the office requires 14 or 15 hours each day of my time; and I have sufficient work outside for more than all my time." [2]

In these labors, it is true, Crapo had the help of Captain Humphrey Seabury, one of the New Bedford directors, but his assistance was of dubious value. Seabury, Crapo wrote his son, was "a well meaning man," but "better adapted to command a whale-ship and govern a whale-crew than he is to regulate all the complicated details consequent upon the construction of a railroad." [3] The New Bedford investors felt more at ease with one of their own men on the scene, however, and he was obliged to humor them and make what use he could of Seabury.

On other matters, too, he continued to have trouble in his relations with the eastern directors. On several occasions major purchases were made in the East without his knowledge and at the very time he was negotiating for the same items in Michigan, even though it had been agreed earlier that he would be responsible for procuring the material in question. These experiences quite naturally irritated him and made him wonder if he was safe in making any contracts, for fear that the purchases would be duplicated. He was even more upset by the haste with which the New Bedford men moved when purchasing, letting suppliers take advantage of their obvious eagerness.

> My whole life, since I left New Bedford [he wrote], has been spent in one continuous round of buying and selling and trading and bargaining, day in and day out, from morning until night; and I think that I have learned something in regard to men's minds and how they are influenced.

If nothing else, this experience had taught him not to accept first offers, and to take with a grain of salt a seller's protestations that the price quoted was one which would barely allow any profit at all. The correctness of this judgment was amply illustrated when he attempted to call off negotiations for certain items which had already been bought in the East. The prospective suppliers, who earlier had pretended reluctance to sell at the prices which had been discussed, now were more than anxious for the job even at a reduced figure.[4]

Similarly, he was greatly perturbed when the New Bedford directors talked of hiring a superintendent and treasurer for the railroad at a salary of $2,000 or $2,500 per annum. For such a sum, he assured them, *two* good men could be employed, one for each office, with the superintendent receiving $1,000 or $1,200 and the treasurer $600 or $800. The task of running a seventeen-mile railroad, on which the superintendent could "almost see the whole length of the road," was, he pointed out, hardly to be compared with the duties of such a post on a more important line.

Despite all that Crapo could do, the work proceeded slowly. The contractors were plagued by the wartime shortage of labor, and in June, 1864, the men on the job all struck for higher wages. While no details of the strike are known, the men apparently gained their point, for by July Crapo reported the common labor rate as $1.75 a day, in contrast to the $1.50 paid the preceding winter. Meanwhile, too, the costs of construction were rising well beyond the original estimates. It was, nevertheless, a proud day for Crapo when he was able to write from Detroit on November 1, 1864:

> I have come all the way from Flint this afternoon on the cars, an epoch in the history of Flint. Our road is barely passable for the passenger trains, but we shall soon have it in order.[5]

From the very beginning the line was an unqualified success. Six months after it had opened it was carrying an average of 400 passengers a day, almost double the estimate in Crapo's original prospectus, and it did not have cars enough to handle the freight traffic which was offered.[*] The first dividend, of 6 per cent, was paid seven months after the first train had been run, and from that point on dividends were paid regularly at an annual rate of 8 per cent. In 1867 a 25 per cent stock dividend was voted as well, to cover earnings which had been employed in completing the line.

---

[*] One reason for the shortage of rolling stock was that the government had requisitioned twelve of the company's thirty flatcars the day after the line had been opened for traffic. Crapo had attempted to get the order revoked, no doubt using his influence as governor-elect, but without success. "Our cars are two feet longer than on the other roads," he wrote, "and hence they are taken." Even without loss of these cars, however, it is probable that the road would still have been short of rolling stock.—HHC, Detroit to WWC, NB, Nov. 1, 1864.

Henry Howland Crapo

The Crapo Saw Mill

Skidding

The Crapo Lumber Company Camp

Prize Logs

Waiting for Spring
Flood Up the River

In 1868, when the company was consolidated with the Flint and Pere Marquette, the stockholders received dividends totaling 27.38 per cent from accumulated undistributed profits.[6]

The very success of the railroad, however, brought with it new difficulties. The superintendent, a man named Burns, had come out from the East in the summer of 1864 in time to take over some of the railroad responsibilities during Crapo's campaign. Once the road was put into operation, it became evident that the job was more than he could handle. The result was that just as Crapo was taking over his new duties as governor, he was forced to cope with all manner of petty problems connected with the running of the railroad. Burns himself found life in the West not at all to his liking, and soon began to talk of leaving. Desperately, Crapo sought a replacement for him, "an intelligent, practical R.R. man, one possessed of energy and resolution, and one who knows how to run a road." More than a month passed before a satisfactory superintendent could be found, but a good man was finally secured, and from that point on Crapo appears to have been freed from concern over the day-to-day operations of the line.[7]

Nevertheless, he still had to deal with the New Bedford directors on matters of policy, and this relationship was productive of quite enough friction to keep his position as president of the Flint and Holly Rail Road a troublesome one. He, his son, two of his sons-in-law, and Prescott together held more than $40,000 worth of stock in the railroad, and could hardly be accused of lacking an interest in its profitable operation. Nevertheless, several of the New Bedford men—and Seabury in particular—acted as though their most important function was to frustrate what they imagined to be Crapo's attempts to pervert the company's policy so as to serve the needs and interests of his lumber concern.

The first such issue of importance had been the question of locating the southern terminus of the road at Holly instead of Fentonville as he had recommended. Seabury and Knowles had gotten the idea, Crapo wrote, "that if the road was located at Fentonville it would benefit me; and a fear of this made them perfectly blind to the great interests of the road." Although Crapo had acquiesced in the decision for the sake of harmony, by the time the road was completed he was convinced that, directly and indirectly, the Holly route would cost the company $75,000 more, with "not a single benefit arising from it." The cost of construction to Holly had been higher, the road had taken at least three months longer to build, the cost of operating it would be greater, and the connections with eastbound passenger trains of the Detroit and Milwaukee were necessarily most awkward compared with what they might have been at Fentonville.

> If the New Bedford directors involve themselves in loss and difficulty by having their own way and disregarding my views I shall of course be sorry, but can't help it. They must not lay the consequences of such mistakes to me.[8]

Another incident, much less important but symptomatic of the tension which continued to exist, occurred when Crapo sought to have the company build a sidetrack for his Flint yard so that lumber could be loaded directly onto the cars. Although the Detroit and Milwaukee had earlier and without any question put in a track at Crapo's Fentonville yard twice as long as the one now desired at Flint, Seabury took the position that any siding would have to be paid for by Crapo himself even though he was the promoter and president of the road, would furnish a large share of its traffic, and had without charge permitted the main line of track to run through his yard, cutting up the property badly and spoiling a potential mill site on the river. The issue was eventually resolved to Crapo's satisfaction, but not until he had lost the use of his own railroad during the winter season of 1864–65 when his lumber could have brought higher prices by reaching market before the opening of lake navigation from Saginaw.[9]

Seabury had even gone so far as to express disapproval of Crapo's election as governor, and the memory of this was not far from Crapo's mind when in March, 1865, he reported to his son that he had secured passage of a law allowing the Flint and Holly to charge passengers four cents a mile instead of three.* "It was hard work," he wrote, "and was done mainly as a favor to me."

> [The increase] will give our road at least $15,000 per annum now with much more hereafter. This the company owe me for, and I hope it will stop Capt. Seabury's attacks upon me for being Governor of Michigan. . . . I really feel proud of my success in securing passage of the law . . . for it will be *clear gain* to our net earnings.[10]

Neither this, however, nor the obvious fact that Crapo's own shipments were a major source of revenue for the rail-

---

* Crapo justified the discriminatory law on the basis that "we have built our road with clean cash," whereas most other lines had been built with the aid of land grants. The law allowed the higher rate to roads under twenty-five miles in length; in practice this meant that it applied only to the Flint and Holly and to the Three Rivers branch of the Southern Road.—*Detroit Advertiser & Tribune,* Mar. 7, 1865.

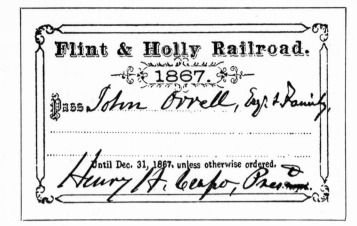

Flint and Holly
R.R. Pass

Flint and Holly
R.R. Time Table

FLINT AND HOLLY

Rail Road.

WINTER ARRANGEMENTS FOR 1864-5,

On and after Tuesday, November 1st, 1864,

Trains will run daily (Sundays excepted) as follows :

DEPARTING.

Leave **FLINT** for Holly and Detroit at **8.45 A. M.** and **2.00 P M**

Leave **GRAND BLANC** for Holly and Detroit at **9.17 A. M.** and **2.25 P M.**

RETURNING

First train over Flint and Holly Railroad

Leave **DETROIT** (from Detroit & Milwaukee Station) for Grand Blanc and Flint......	at 10.30 A. M. and 5.30 P. M.
Leave **HOLLY** for Grand Blanc, Flint, and East Saginaw	at 1.00 P. M. and 8.00 P. M.
Leave **GRAND BLANC** for Flint and East Saginaw.................	at 1.35 P. M. and 8.43 P. M.

R. B. BURNS, *Superintendent.*

Flint, October 29, 1864.

road stilled the carping and nagging. Once a competent superintendent had been secured and the operating routine had become somewhat settled, the problems which arose were less urgent and Crapo rarely found time to discuss them in his letters. Nevertheless, the animosity of Seabury and also of Knowles (another New Bedford director who spent a good deal of time in Michigan) continued to manifest itself. After the annual meeting of the board in November, 1865, Crapo felt that he had had all he could stand.* He had just been re-elected president of the company, but he wrote William:

> I have deliberately and calmly resolved that if those are the only men whom the New Bedford stockholders can send here, I shall not, after the present year, permit myself to be one of the Directors. . . . The road is already a success, far beyond what you or I ever claimed for it, and I can therefore claim some little exemption from an annoyance and absolute wrong, which my friends in New Bedford, if I have any among the stockholders, would never desire to impose upon me.[11]

The directors' meeting the following year came and went without the threat being carried out, Crapo informing his son that he had "made the sacrifice at this election on account of my New Bedford friends and for peace," but Seabury's conduct towards him was "so insulting and over-

* Crapo was also embittered by the action of the directors in voting him, "as a matter of *great favor*," the sum of $1,000 as compensation for all his services as promoter and president of the railroad. Less than $400 a year, he felt, was hardly a suitable remuneration for "all the responsibility and care and hard work, not only of myself, but all my clerks, and of disbursing and settling all the accounts and money here, as well as all the annoyance and work of drawing contracts, etc. with the contractors, and all the labor etc. of all the rights of way, etc. etc."—HHC, Holly to WWC, NB, Nov. 29, 1865.

bearing" that he determined anew that he would not "suffer a repetition of it, even if I have to sell all my stock." [12]

As the time for the 1867 meeting approached, Crapo gave vent to his irritation again, writing William that "although I have had the honor of being Prest. of the F. & H. R.R. Co. thus far in its history, yet through the conduct and management of Capt. Seabury I am only permitted to be nominally so."

> I have been berated by him, even on the Board, when in session, as though I were a school boy, and have been obliged to submit, time and again, to what I regard as the grossest insults. . . . [He], under a plea that *he* represents the N. B. stockholders, seeks to manage everything by himself, or by those whom *he* selects, without any reference to the fact that I am the Prest. of the Co. and as such, entitled to some little consideration. But this is not all. He labors in every conceivable way—without the use of direct language to that effect—to establish the idea *here* that no particular confidence is placed in me by the people of New Bedford, in regard to their interest in the road.

"What," he asked, "have I done to incur the displeasure of Capt. Seabury, and perhaps of Mr. Knowles?" His own "candid opinion" was that the two New Bedford men had always resented the fact that he had been elected president of the company and his son its first treasurer, and cherished the idea that as a result the company would "in some way be defrauded, or at least that its funds were to be used by me for my own private purposes." In actuality, he had never owed the company one dollar, "whilst on the other hand the company has been indebted to me in sums exceeding $30,-000 at a time." As he had done before, he announced that "my own self-respect forbids that I should continue to occupy so equivocal a position." Within two weeks, however, he decided that making an issue of Seabury's removal from the board would not be worth the trouble that it would cause, and the situation continued unchanged.[13]

Towards the end of 1867 a new factor entered into the railroad picture when the Flint and Pere Marquette (the line running from Saginaw to Flint) made an offer to purchase the Flint and Holly for $500,000, payment to be made in a new issue of 10 per cent bonds of the Flint and Pere Marquette. The long talked of Port Huron to Owosso line had just undergone another financial reorganization, giving renewed promise of its early completion, and this, Crapo felt, together with the Owosso and Saginaw road which was already open to Bay City, "will cut into the earnings of our road terribly." The prospective end of the Flint and Holly's monopoly position as an outlet for the Saginaw Valley, along with the wear and tear on the road which would soon make necessary "large annual outlays," would, Crapo feared, "reduce us to very moderate dividends." Many of the Flint and Holly stockholders professed to believe that the Port Huron road held no threat to their own interest, but Crapo saw it differently:

> When that road is open, the D. & M. and the Flint & P. M. roads will *use us up*. The F. & P. M. road would have no scruples to use the Port Huron road to our disadvantage.

At the same time, the Flint and Pere Marquette management would benefit greatly if it could add the link from Flint to Holly to its own line, and Crapo believed that the situation offered an opportunity to the Flint and Holly stockholders which should not be lost. "By careful negotiation," he thought it possible to make a deal for the bonds of the Flint and Pere Marquette by which the owners of the Flint and Holly would have 12 per cent on their original investment.[14]

The consolidation was effected the following year, with the Flint and Pere Marquette taking over operation of the Flint and Holly on April 1, 1868. While the details of the financial settlement are not fully known, the price agreed upon seems to have been $550,000 in Flint and Pere Marquette bonds. Another result of the merger appears to have been the election of William W. Crapo, as president of the enlarged Flint and Pere Marquette, a move no doubt calculated to ease the fears of the New Bedford investors who looked askance at that line's earlier financial history.[15]

II

During 1864 and 1865, Crapo's involvement in political affairs, on the one hand, and railroad construction, on the other, kept him from giving more than "occasional supervision and oversight" to his lumber business. For this same reason, his correspondence during these years gives little detailed information as to the operations of the concern. At intervals he would assure William in New Bedford that everything was going along smoothly, following in the pattern which he had labored so hard to establish. Soon after his inauguration as governor, he wrote from the state capital that his business was "immense," that it would be "the largest . . . this year . . . which I have ever done," and that "everything in regard to it looks flattering at the present time."[16]

Despite his other responsibilities, however, he did manage to initiate several new developments in the lumber enterprise. The completion of the Flint and Holly Rail Road late in 1864 was a major step forward for the business. In anticipation of the new route, he established a retail outlet in Detroit soon after the beginning of that year by taking over an old established lumber yard (on Atwater Street between Hastings and Rivard) and putting his son-in-law, Humphrey Henry Howland Crapo Smith, in charge.* The property consisted of a lot and wharf which he leased for five years at $500 per annum, and buildings and machinery belonging to the former occupant for which he paid $4,000, and was so located that lumber loaded on the cars on a sidetrack at his mills in Flint could be run right into the yard without any further handling. The facilities included "two planing machines, a machine for splitting inch lumber into siding, and a pony saw for splitting up all sorts of lumber," all run by steam. "Repairs and fixing up" added some $2,000 to his investment, but he was confident that it was "the best thing I have ever done." "It will pay 'big,'" he wrote, "and is what I have always wanted, as it places me above the contingencies of a demand and sale of lumber here." [17]

Even before the Flint and Holly road was finished, Crapo did what he could to get the Detroit yard under way, sending lumber over the planks to Fentonville and thence by rail. He found it impossible to get enough teams to keep

* The obvious question as to the origin of this rather unusual name is answered as follows in George W. Hotchkiss, *History of the Lumber and Forest Industry of the Northwest* (Chicago, 1898), p. 93: Humphrey Smith had been Crapo's assistant in the city offices of New Bedford for about fifteen years. "As confusion arose through there being several others of his name at New Bedford, Mr. Smith obtained an order . . . permitting the elongated cognomen by which he is now known." After a period of years in which he attempted a number of business ventures on his own, Smith returned to Crapo's employ in 1858 when the latter moved to Michigan to take better care of his struggling lumber business. In December of that year Smith married Lucy Crapo and became one of her father's most trusted assistants.

the yard stocked, however, and he looked forward eagerly to the time when he could utilize this new outlet to the full. Yet in one way, the delay in completion of the railroad served him well. The Detroit yard had only been open for some four months when it was severely damaged by fire, the first occasion on which Crapo was to suffer from this terror of the nineteenth century lumberman. Besides the destruction of buildings and machinery, some $10,000 worth of lumber and $5,000 worth of shingles were lost, making the total damage well over $20,000, of which but $5,000 was covered by insurance. Had he been able to ship lumber there as fast as he would have liked, however, his loss would have been greater yet.[18]

Because Smith was needed at the Flint mills during the rest of the campaign year, nothing was done to reestablish the Detroit yard until the spring of 1865. Between March 15, 1865, and January 1, 1866, however, Smith sold over 2 million feet of lumber as well as considerable quantities of shingles, lath and pickets, and could have handled still more had the Flint and Holly road had sufficient rolling stock to get lumber off fast enough. For "a yard 100 feet on the street by 300 feet deep . . . no mill connected," Smith felt this was quite a creditable achievement.[19]

In another expansion of his operations, in 1864 Crapo built a planing mill at Flint to enable him to supply the steadily increasing demand for dressed lumber. In the new factory he installed two of "the largest and best planing machines" available, a ripping table, and a machine for making bevel siding. With a work force of from seven to ten men, the planing mill was soon kept running steadily to capacity, and Crapo still found it impossible to meet the calls for dressed lumber and siding. A little later, he established a sash, door, and blind factory in the upper story of the same building. In it he was able to use up much lumber which would otherwise have been of little value, getting in return highly saleable merchandise to add to the stock in his retail yards. The purchase of the so-called Busenbark mill during 1865 added still another facility to the Flint establishment. Although it was acquired primarily for the purpose of extending Crapo's control of the riverfront, it added some 2 million feet a year to the capacity of his two other mills.[20]

With his steadily increasing trade, Crapo was hard put to keep his mills supplied with logs. The wartime shortage of labor made it difficult for contractors to complete their logging jobs, and after both the 1863–64 and the 1864–65 logging seasons Crapo was forced to resort to the purchase of additional lots of logs to eke out his own supply. The labor shortage also affected his mill operations, and he found it advantageous whenever possible to buy up lots of lumber from other manufacturers. "My facilities are now so great for selling lumber," he wrote in the summer of 1865, "that I can't make enough to meet my custom." [21]

Between 1862 and 1864 the prices he was receiving more than doubled, and they continued to advance well into 1865, until the end of the war and the assassination of Lincoln in April brought a sudden downward turn. "We have sustained an irreparable national loss, in the death of Abm. Lincoln," he wrote his son.

> This great and terrible calamity has cast universal sadness and sorrow and gloom over our entire state, and every one seems paralyzed by it. All business seems to be prostrated and men are everywhere waiting to see what is to follow.
> Lumber has fallen from $4 on common to $7 on

uppers, per M; but as my lumber is seasoned I am able to maintain, as yet, old prices, although sales are dull.

The nation was soon launched on a postwar boom, however, and by August he was able to report that the price of lumber was again advancing.[22]

The only jarring note in this picture was the steady increase in the costs of logging and manufacturing. "Supplies for the woods," Crapo noted in the winter of 1863–64, "can hardly be got at any price."

> Farmers are now forehanded, and with the market of Saginaw they can get just what they ask. The market here is about equal to N.Y. Why don't some of the young beginners—sons of New England farmers—come out here and get rich farming?

A year later, in the spring of 1865, he commented that it required "a mint of money, at present prices," to carry on the business.[23] The major factor in the increased cost of operations was of course the price of labor. The first mention of this in Crapo's correspondence had come when he was starting up his mills in the spring of 1862. "I had some little trouble to hire men at old prices," he reported, "but think I shall get all I want by paying a moderate advance." The following year he faced the same situation with his mill men, and when the logging season arrived he complained that wages in that field, too, were "enormous," that even "common labor is now $1.50 per day." Starting up his mills in the spring of 1864, he faced the prospect of paying the same $1.50 rate for common labor, while his sawyers were demanding $3.00 a day. "Wages are terrible," he wrote, and added that "even at these prices it will be very doubtful if I can procure men to man both mills." [24]

From the workers' standpoint, however, there was ample justification for these increases and more. In March, 1864, the *Detroit Free Press* devoted an article to the rising cost of living, pointing out that almost everything had at least doubled in price in the preceding year and a half.[25] During the spring and summer of that year, shoemakers, tailors, bricklayers, coopers, iron miners, and men of many other trades struck for higher wages. Early in June the crews at work building the Flint and Holly Rail Road had gone out on strike, and on the twenty-ninth an exasperated entry appears in Crapo's diary: "In office—my mill men strike!!!—at 10 o'clock A.M.—and both mills then shut down, all hands quit!!!!" This was a most embarrassing time for such a development, for it was on the eve of the Republican state convention where Crapo was to be a leading contender for the gubernatorial nomination. The strike lasted a week, and brought results. In the same letter in which he reported his nomination, he told his son that his common labor rate was now $1.75 a day.[26]

The incident gave the *Free Press* a perfect opening for a sharp partisan attack:

> Time was when the republican party claimed to be the friend of the laboring man; but now that it has become corrupted and demoralized by shoddy, it hardly has the impudence to lay claim to this distinction. In proof of the fact that the republican party has a total disregard of the rights of the laboring man, we may cite the fact that only the week before Mr. Crapo was nominated as the republican candidate for Governor, he refused to pay his laborers $1.75 per [day for] their work, which, with gold at $2.80, is less than

sixty-five cents per day; choosing rather to let his lumber mills lie idle, than to pay a fair remuneration for labor.

Other Democratic papers took up the charge, and a month later the *Free Press* quoted from the columns of the *Niles Republican*:

Keep it Before the People . . . That the large lumbering mills of the abolition candidate for Governor were all idle the week before his nomination, because he would not pay his men $1.75 per day, while the farmers were paying from $2 to $2.50 for help.[27]

There is no evidence that Crapo's labor troubles had much influence in the campaign, but undoubtedly the episode was an awkward one for him.

Hard as he thought it to pay this increase, the end was not yet reached. Engaging his "old hands" for the 1865 sawing season, he found it necessary to pay from $2.00 to $4.00 per day and could only say in justification that "others are paying much higher." His transient common labor he hoped to be able to get for the same $1.75 rate won after the strike, but "my best common help—men who have been with me from 4 to 7 years" were signed on at $2.00 a day.[28]

III

Crapo's resistance to paying higher wage rates was not the only noteworthy feature of his personnel policy. He had early discovered that in Michigan, in contrast to New Bedford or other older communities, "the men that can be hired to do anything *cannot* be trusted; the men of *trust* have work of *their own*." This, he told his son, "explains why I have been compelled to be such a perfect slave to my business ever since we started here." He compared the management of his mill gangs to governing "a large school of unruly boys."

> They can't be left with assistants—the principal must be there; and what he says and wants they must be taught to do at all times. I have *good men,* as good as can be found, but they are men, and require . . . a firm, steady hand. . . . When I am around they expect to study nothing but my wishes, and as they know that I do everything myself and know what every man does, and that I fear no man among them, and pay well, and *will* have my own way, and work like a dog myself, and hire them to work, they just quietly settle down to their business and do the best they can.[29]

This close personal supervision made it possible for Crapo to set and maintain the quality standards on which he relied so heavily for competitive advantage, though very likely these same quality standards led to his passing harsher judgment on his workers than was actually warranted.

Yet try as he might, he could not be in more than one place at a time, and as the business expanded he could not escape the need for responsible help in carrying on his operations. To get such assistance he frequently turned to his son in New Bedford for aid in finding a suitable man.[30]

Describing his requirements on one occasion, he wrote that "above all things I want a man who can get up in the morning and who is not afraid to work. If he is quick, and intelligent, and honest, and ambitious, and industrious, I can soon learn him, if he knows very little about lumber." The business, he felt, "would in fact be a good school for a young man, and there are many East if we only knew where to find them who would be very glad of the chance." In another letter he declared that "I need to have boys coming along all the time; and I prefer to have 'boys,' and let them come up, to hiring old men." Bringing out young men from the East did not, of course, always work out satisfactorily. Announcing the return home of one such youth, Crapo wrote that "there is not sufficient force in him for my business, and then his idea as to wages, compared with the labor I require, is better adapted to the East than to the West."

Such experiences and his own observations of what was involved in building a new career in a new country led Crapo to offer this definition of "a man for the West": "one who will leave behind him *old notions,* old peculiarities, old conceits, and old prejudices, and will come out here with his N. England habits and character, but otherwise as a *new man,* in a *new place.*" If such a man will "take things here as he finds them, and at once 'strip off,' and 'go in' for the race . . . he will be sure to win." Those, he warned, "who will bring New England with them, and who will forever discourage themselves by instituting comparisons to the prejudice of the West, had better keep away."

Merely finding new employees who fitted in well with the western environment did not solve Crapo's problems. "I have learned so many about my mills," he complained to William, "who leave me as soon as they are of real benefit, and then let their services to someone else," that he felt obliged in recruiting help "to know the probabilities of a person staying with me." It was flattering for him to recognize that "my system is so different from most concerns here that men who have been with me for a length of time are considered a little extra," but it was certainly annoying to see these men being lured away by other opportunities.[31]

There was a strong moralistic flavor in Crapo's attitude towards the men in his employ. In New Bedford he had been a leading temperance man, and in his business in Michigan he sought to apply the rule that any worker "guilty of intoxication, or other immoral act" was to be "immediately paid off and discharged." Such a policy in itself does not seem unduly harsh, although it was probably somewhat unusual in an industry such as lumbering; but Crapo's understanding of "high moral tone and character" covered considerably wider ground as well. Work was for him all there was to life, and this is reflected in his indictment of one of his eastern "boys" whom he was about to discharge. Not only did the man in question "have occasional drunken sprees," but he was known to have attended "dances and oyster suppers." [32]

Despite his strict work discipline and his puritanical views, Crapo seems to have inspired a strong allegiance among his men. He ran his mills on a twelve-hour shift, two hours longer than the other mills at Flint, but he paid his men promptly and in cash, a distinct contrast with many mills in the area which paid their workers "only in dicker and [store] orders that are not worth to them 75¢ on the dollar." * As a result, the turnover in his work force was very low; in 1862 he was able to write that "most" of the men in his mills had been with him five years, ever since the start of his operations at Flint.[33]

* For a short time during the extremely difficult period after the Panic of 1857, Crapo had resorted to payment of his men in store orders whether they wanted it that way or not. Generally, however, he paid his men "cash when they ask for it unless I have something they want which is as good to them as cash." This might include produce taken in exchange for lumber, or Crapo's own store orders which "in this community are considered as cash by everyone, or as having a cash value."—HHC, Flint to WWC, NB, Nov. 27, 1860. He boasted that his ability to pay cash "gives me a power over my men that nothing else would."—HHC, Flint to WWC, NB, June 3, 1860.

eleven

YEAR OF DECISION: II
(1866)

I

The year 1860, it will be recalled, was an important turning point in Crapo's business affairs. The reorganization of the lumber concern in that year freed him from the impossible financial burden of the Driggs pine land purchase, but it left him saddled with the task of making the sawmills pay off in the face of continuing economic stagnation. He escaped from a situation which threatened his personal bankruptcy, but only at the price of taking on new obligations which would strain his energies and resources to the utmost.

In 1866, Crapo found himself once again at a crossroads, but his situation was far different from what it had been six years before. Then his only thought had been to "stay afloat" long enough to find a buyer for the mills. But during the difficult years no advantageous opportunity for sale presented itself, and from 1863 onwards the business had been progressing so well that the very idea of closing up the enterprise was pushed to the back of his mind.

During his first year as governor of Michigan, however, the pressure of his added duties forced him to take a new look at where he stood. The lumber business was running along smoothly, with his young assistants carrying the burden of day-to-day management, but the ultimate responsibility for its profitable operation still fell on his shoulders. Since becoming involved in the broader sphere of politics, too, he was no doubt able to see his business affairs with more perspective than had been possible when he had been immersed in them to the exclusion of everything else. In any case, it was while he was in Washington, D. C., on official business in July, 1865, that he first began again to talk of winding up his lumber enterprise.

> The manufacture of lumber [he reflected] is a very uncertain business, and in the long run I fear a profit-less one. When the amount of capital required to carry it on is taken into account it is, with all its hazards, the poorest business which can be pursued.[1]

These gloomy sentiments, seemingly so out of keeping with his business experience in the past few years, were provoked not only by the memory of his earlier struggles for economic survival, but also by his acute awareness of the dangers which might still beset him. The ever-present threat of fire was one such worry; he cited a $90,000 loss which had occurred the week before in Saginaw, and commented that he too was "liable to be burnt out at any moment." Another unvoiced but very real cause for concern was the way in which the lumberman was each year at the mercy of the weather, almost to the extent of the business being an annual lottery. Favorable conditions in the woods during the winter might permit a large cut of logs, but a dry spring could make it impossible to get the logs run down to the mills, with the result that the lumberman would be faced with a heavy logging bill and no means of getting the money to pay it. If, on the other hand, all the logs should come down, the resultant glut might depress the market to the point that no profit at all could be made on the ensuing season's sawing. Crapo had been fortunate in the past in that he frequently had been able to get in his stock of logs when others had suffered from adverse conditions in either logging or running, but every year the problem was one to be faced anew.

Recognizing these facts of life in the lumber business, Crapo faced most reluctantly the prospect of putting "the proceeds of this season's cut into another stock of logs to go the rounds again of all the risks and hazards incident to the business." By continuing on, he wrote, "I may possibly make something . . . yet I may lose all." His age and health also gave him pause, for he was sixty-one and he was feeling the effects of his years of unremitted labor, indoors and out, in all kinds of weather. "Every year I continue, the chances are increased that others may have to settle up my affairs when serious loss to what little I might possibly have will be sure to follow." [2]

For all his strong feelings on the subject, he found himself unable to come to any definite decision before the start of the 1865–66 logging season. As a result, he felt impelled to prepare for keeping his mills busy through one more season, which he did by undertaking again a heavy program of logging which would cost him at least $50,000. The prospect of this expenditure was most unpleasant, however, and called forth the bitter comment:

> This lumbering is a simple turning over of money;
> for what you get out you have to put in again, just
> like whaling voyages . . . there is no stopping place.

Having missed one chance to close up, he determined at all events to make 1866 his final year in the business, and in January he wrote his son-in-law and manager of his Detroit yard, Humphrey Smith, to advertise the mill properties for sale "in your best style." [3]

It was not without regret that he had come to this conclusion, for the business was "enormous" and had "never looked so well before." The completion of the Flint and Holly Rail Road, Crapo wrote, "has made my lumber interest one of the greatest and best in the whole country." In another letter he expressed the opinion that "were I in the prime of life, I could soon make a fortune." Yet on the other side of the picture, his mills were old—"about 'used up' "—and in need of constant repairs to keep them in running order. He was firmly resolved not to sell out "for a trifle" just at the time his sawmill properties had been made valuable by his "years of hard work and severe toil," but he was equally determined to sell.[4]

Despite his strictures on the lumber business, there can be no doubt that his outlook would have been less pessimistic and his desire to sell less intense had he been able to feel that he was building up an enterprise which could continue on in the family after his death. Unfortunately, nothing like this appeared possible. Crapo and his wife had been blessed with an abundant family—it consisted of nine girls and but one boy. The son, William, whom we have seen in these pages as his father's confidant in business matters, nevertheless found little attraction in the prospect of following in his father's footsteps in Michigan. He was of an entirely different temperament, cautious where Crapo was inclined to be plunging and rash, and quite unresponsive to the challenge of the raw western country. As a rising young lawyer in New Bedford, William had already found his place in life and was of no mind to exchange it for the uncertainties which had been described to him over and over in his father's letters. Although Crapo had known this for a long time, he nevertheless could not refrain from suggesting time and again to his son that a far better solution than selling out would be for William to join him in Flint and take over active management of the concern. "So far as mere money is concerned," he wrote on one occasion, "I feel quite certain that you could make more here than there, and work infinitely less." His son could not see it that way, however, and Crapo was forced to make his plans accordingly.[5]

II

While he was canvassing the possibility of closing up the concern, he also had to take another matter into account. His silent partner, Oliver Prescott, still owned a half interest in the business. As the active partner, Crapo had the authority to take whatever actions he deemed necessary, but he felt that he would have greater flexibility in making arrangements to sell out if he were the sole owner. Accordingly, he approached Prescott with the proposition that he buy out Prescott's share. After the exchange of many letters and a stopover in New Bedford on one of his official trips to Washington, Crapo made the deal in the spring of 1866. For the sum of $58,000, he acquired both Prescott's half interest in the lumber business and his two-elevenths interest in the Driggs pine tract.[6]

The share in the lands Crapo valued at only $10,000, but according to his books the manufacturing concern was worth $199,588.* The payment to Prescott was thus considerably less than half the value of the business, but Crapo believed it an equitable settlement in view of the fact that his partner had had "no care or labor" in connection with

* This sum included both the mills and the firm's stock of logs and lumber. The mill property itself Crapo valued at $60,000 "if the present favorable condition of the lumber business continues."—HHC, Flint to WWC, NB, Mar. 6, 1866.

his investment and that "what I have made is the result more of extra labor and effort than of ordinary and regular business toil."

> I have worked very hard for years to produce this re-
> sult, and have done an amount of mental and other
> labor sufficient to break down any ordinary man, and
> for the last 4 or 5 years especially my labors Sundays
> and during the "dead" hours of night, when I should
> have been resting both mind and body by sleep, have
> been more than most men are willing to perform—
> to say nothing of what I have done during the regular
> business hours of weekdays.

Prescott himself had asked only that he get back the money he had put into the concern, together with interest, and the $58,000, when added to the amounts already divided between the partners as profits, gave him that. Indeed, in one of his letters to Crapo, Prescott on his own initiative had written that "if money has been made, or is to be made as a result of your labors at Flint, I am entirely willing that you should have the benefit of it." Deducting $48,000 from $199,588 ($10,000 being credited towards Prescott's share of the pine lands), it can be seen that Crapo emerged from the negotiations as sole owner of a business worth more than $150,000. But, as he reminded his son, "all this is not money, and after all Prescott may come out better with his $58,000, than I shall with the balance."

> If the judge gets his money and interest now he will
> get out of it infinitely better than I once supposed he
> would. As for myself I shall have all the traps and if
> lucky and have no fires or other losses I may come out
> better than he will; and then I may not.[7]

"Confidentially," he wrote William in March, 1866, "I will say now . . . that I am worth more than my debts." It was a heartening announcement, and one which Crapo could not have made before at any time since he had come to Michigan. Quite apart from the lumber business, he added, "I have very many times more property here than debts. My debts are in New Bedford."

> With this condition of my affairs here you naturally ask what my present intentions are for the future. I answer at once—drive everything I can this season and next fall shut down and put in no more logs but close up as fast as possible. If ordinarily successful this summer and prices of lumber keep something like where they now are, I can then either sell the mill property or keep it. This will depend upon the financial aspect of things there, and also upon the wishes of Smith and some of the other boys whom I must aid somewhat. Perhaps I may form some sort of a copartnership with them and let them do the work—I furnishing the mills etc. placing capital against their services, etc. But this is for the future; only, I shall wind up, however flattering things may look.

With no more than "ordinary good luck," he expected to be able to make $50,000 in the coming year and thus "close up the business with a net balance of $200,000." Even if he should fall short of the mark,

> suppose I can only make it $100,000, my children I know will be content with that, and more than willing for "Father" and "Mother" to have a respite from further hard work. I have never in the past dared to cherish the thought of "stopping" or closing because I could not see the means to pay my immense debts,

and have anything left for my children. But the point is now in a fair way of being reached, and like every other object of my life the purpose will not be relinquished, so far at least as my own will and purposes are concerned.[8]

The prospects for a profitable season were indeed good. His loggers had cut more than 13½ million feet of logs the preceding winter, twice the quantity put in during any previous year, and Crapo planned to run at least two of his mills night and day. The logs were of excellent quality, promising double the percentage of clear lumber yielded by his stock of the year before. Even more important, never since Crapo had been in Michigan had the spring been so dry and the rivers so low. The result was that as late as May, most of the logs cut in the state remained "hung up" where only an unlikely freshet would make it possible to get them down to the mills. On the other hand, he had been able to get almost all of his logs run safely, securing them, as he wrote, "upon the same principle that Grant took Vicksburg —by constant pounding." Lacking logs to saw, few of the mills in the region were able to start running, and in anticipation of a small cut the price of lumber was advancing. On June 14 Crapo wrote, "I am selling my common almost as fast as it is cut," and raised his estimate of profits for the season to more than $100,000.[9]

III

Three days later, Crapo's plans were rudely upset when his upper mill was completely consumed by fire. Originally known as the Walkley mill, it had been the mainstay of his lumber concern since the very beginning of his operations at Flint. Fortunately, very little lumber was destroyed, but the loss of the mill itself was a heavy blow. It had been cutting from 40,000 to 50,000 feet of lumber every twenty-four hours, on which there was a profit of $10 a thousand. Since he would now be unable to saw out these logs without holding them over for another season, he figured that his loss from this alone—quite apart from the value of the mill property—would be more than $40,000. Furthermore, he knew that without the most valuable of his three mills he would be severely handicapped in his efforts to sell out on satisfactory terms.[10]

In these circumstances he was forced into a reconsideration of his plans, culminating in a complete reversal of his outlook. Instead of winding up the concern, he found himself forced to conclude that his best course in the face of the disaster would be to erect, on the site of the burned mill, a large new mill with a capacity nearly as great as all three of those which he had been running. He could then sell the two remaining old mills, and with the increased efficiency of new and modern equipment, he hoped that he would be able to make up in savings over three years' running the loss which he had sustained by the fire.[11]

The decision was characteristic of the man. For years he had been talking about his hopes for getting free from the responsibilities of the lumber business, holding forth the picture of an idyllic retirement managing the two farms he had built up since coming to Michigan.[12] Yet nothing could be more foreign to his temperament than a voluntary withdrawal from active business. He thrived on challenge, on adversity, and he appears to have been utterly incapable of relaxation. In following his correspondence over a period of years—his repeated statements that he wanted to close up, his repeated decisions to carry on "for a while longer, at least"—one cannot help feeling that he almost welcomed an excuse which would force him to stay in business. Only three days before the fire he had written of his regret at the idea of giving up "the best business there is in the country, after creating it myself by years of toil and self denial"; now he could continue on with it, attempt to recoup his loss from the fire, and see what further profit might be made.[13]

The final step which made 1866 truly a year of decision for Crapo was his purchase from Arnold in October of the latter's nine-elevenths interest in the Driggs pine tract. Taken together with his earlier acquisition of Prescott's two-elevenths interest in the lands and of Prescott's half interest in the lumber concern, on the one hand, and his decision after the fire to build a large new sawmill, on the other, this action laid the basis for an expansion of Crapo's lumber business on a scale which a few years before he would never have thought possible.

His immediate motivation was his desire to avoid the haggling with Arnold's heirs which would, in the event of the elderly Arnold's death, be sure to ensue in trying to arrange an equitable division. More basically, though, he was concerned with the increasing scarcity of pine timber upriver from Flint and the probable difficulty he would soon face in stocking his mills. In his first overture on the subject, nevertheless, he carefully avoided any suggestion that the property was of any great value to him. Instead, he wrote that the tract "ought not to lay much longer in its present condition" and that Arnold would be better off "to sell me the land at a low figure than to keep it."

> The annual fires are making terrible inroads upon it, and there are large quantities every year going to decay which I could save if I owned it; . . . a large quantity of the land has now no pine on it, and the land itself is of no value. Much of it will not justify

paying taxes on; and if it belonged to me I would sell
these lots with no pine on them at 10¢ or 50¢ an acre,
or any price I could get and stop the taxes.[14]

His first offer of $40,000 met with a sharp rebuff. Wil-
liam Rotch, Arnold's agent, wrote that at this valuation
they would rather buy Crapo's two-elevenths than sell their
nine-elevenths interest. Rotch countered with a price of
$6.00 an acre, or approximately $59,500, and suggested that
if that was not satisfactory that the tract should be placed on
the market for sale. This was exactly what Crapo did not
want, and the prospect caused him quickly to raise his offer
to $45,000, at the same time telling his son that he would
go as high as $50,000 if it should be necessary. Only three
days after making this "final" offer, however, he wrote a
frantic letter to his son from Marathon:

> I am prospecting up here among the pine, and the
> result is that you must purchase that Driggs land at
> once without a moment's delay, even if you pay them
> all they ask—$6 per acre. I find it will be almost im-
> possible for me to stock my mills after the present
> year without this Driggs tract and *I must have it.* Pine
> is getting scarce, and the present high price of lumber
> causes such a rapid consumption that the Pine Tim-
> ber disappears like magic and very soon it will be
> worth $50 per acre. I fear somebody will be down
> there to purchase it if I don't close the trade immedi-
> ately. You must purchase it at once and without a
> moment's delay, even if you pay their price. Go to Mr.
> Arnold direct. . . . I want 15,000,000 [feet of] logs
> a year to run my mills.[15]

Under such prompting, William acted swiftly, and a week
later his father had a telegram reporting that the purchase

had been made.* How far he had had to yield on the price is not recorded, but in any event Crapo considered it "a good purchase, and . . . also a necessity." [16]

During the late summer and fall of 1866 Crapo pushed his two remaining mills as hard as he could, running them both on double shifts, in an attempt to minimize the amount of logs which would have to lay over until the following year. His main effort, however, was focussed on the construction of his new mill. Work on it had begun little more than a month after the fire. Crapo was determined to make it large enough to handle all the lumber he would want to saw, and assured his son that with its completion he would then have "the best lumbering establishment in America to make money with." His first thought had been a mill with a capacity of 40 to 50,000 feet in twelve hours, costing "at least $25,000." As he worked over the plans his estimate rose to $50,000, and by the time the mill was finished the following spring its cost had grown to nearly $70,000, its capacity to 75 or 80,000 feet of lumber a day. Such an expenditure was large indeed for a man whose intention was to close up his business within a few years, but he had seen no satisfactory alternative. He had paid for it in cash, however, and when it was completed he was gratified to be able to report to his son that it "was said to be the best in the state." [17]

---

* Since Crapo had considered Prescott's two-elevenths share worth $10,000, he had acquired the entire 12,107 acres of the Driggs tract for between $60,000 and $70,000. This sum—less than half the original cost of the tract in 1855—is in striking contrast to the glowing statements he had made as to the potential value of the lands in 1860, when he had succeeded in getting the two New Bedford men to relieve him of his own obligations in connection with the original purchase. The absence of any comment in Crapo's letters on this aspect of the transaction is certainly noteworthy.

twelve

GOVERNOR OF MICHIGAN: SECOND TERM

I

Eighteen sixty-six, the year which had seen so many important developments for Crapo's lumber business, also marked the end of his first term as governor of Michigan. The year before he had written that he would never accept renomination—"I want rest, a spot where there is not that constant demand for thought and labor"—but by May, 1866, he had begun to reconsider. "I think there will be a very general public sentiment in my favor, and perhaps little opposition, . . . so that perhaps I had better try to endure the burden another term." He took no active steps to seek the nomination, but resolved to "let things take their course."

> The office I do not want, and would be glad to be freed from its immense cares and labors; but I do want to know whether my policy—wholly my own in many important particulars—is sustained by the people of the state.[1]

There was some talk in Republican ranks that a soldier should receive the nomination, but the actual contest, just as in 1864, was between Crapo and H. P. Baldwin of Detroit. Baldwin, Crapo wrote his son, "wants to wipe out the memory of his old defeat . . . but I shall be sadly disappointed if I am not sustained by the substantial men of the state."

He need have had no fear, for when the party convention met at the end of August he was renominated on the first ballot, receiving 138 out of 208 votes against Baldwin's 52.[2]

The Republican radicals in Congress looked to the 1866 elections for a popular mandate in support of their policy on southern reconstruction, and this issue dominated the campaign. Crapo took his stand firmly behind the Congressional program, and in a series of speeches across the state did his best to spread their arguments. His confidence in his ability as an orator was considerably greater than it had been two years before. "I have come to be ranked as among the better class of stump speakers," he assured his son, "and you hear no more said about the 'lumberman.' " [3]

When they went to the polls the people of Michigan showed conclusively that they supported the radical Republican point of view; Crapo received 96,746 votes to 67,-708 for his Democratic opponent, the largest majority ever received by a gubernatorial candidate.[4]

Two days after Crapo arrived at Lansing in January, 1867, for the meeting of the legislature, he was prostrated by another attack of his bladder ailment, even more severe than the one which had halted his Upper Peninsula tour of a year and a half before. The bladder muscle had been damaged by the delay in treatment at Marquette, so that even after his recovery from the acute phase of the attack his condition had remained serious enough to require regular medical care and frequent catheterization. At that time he had recognized that the illness had been brought on by constant and prolonged overexertion, and he had resolved to take better care of himself in the future. These good intentions had proved no match for the challenge of his private and official duties, however, and he soon had resumed a schedule hardly less exhausting than ever.

Because of the way he had neglected his health, this new attack was so serious that for a time it was even feared that he might not live. He suffered several internal hemorrhages, was in acute pain for days at a time, and was confined to his sickroom for almost three months. Yet even in these circumstances he persisted in working as hard as many a healthy man. Whether flat on his back, sitting up in bed, or perhaps in a chair for a few hours, he wrote countless letters, consulted with members of the legislature, and received other visitors on matters connected with state business. It was characteristic of the man that on one occasion, when he had been free from pain for several days and was experiencing no bad symptoms, he insisted that the doctor (who was also his son-in-law) telegraph his son in New Bedford that his condition was greatly improved, even though the doctor himself could see no basic signs of improvement.[5]

II

The critical nature of his illness which kept him an invalid for virtually the entire session of the legislature did not, however, prevent him from entering into the most important political fight of his life. When the legislature convened in January, 1867, the vast majority of its members were committed to the support of schemes to enable local governments to use their credit to aid the construction of railroads. The idea was not new. In 1863 two bills authorizing the issuance of municipal bonds for this purpose were passed. During the special session the following year, twelve such measures were approved, and as we have seen earlier Crapo had waged a vigorous and successful battle from his seat in the Senate to incorporate certain safeguards which had been lacking in the measures as originally proposed. In

Lumberjacks of
Crapo's Time

Felling the
Trees

Sharpening
Axes and Saws

Flint and Holly RR

Sawing

The H. H. Crapo Family

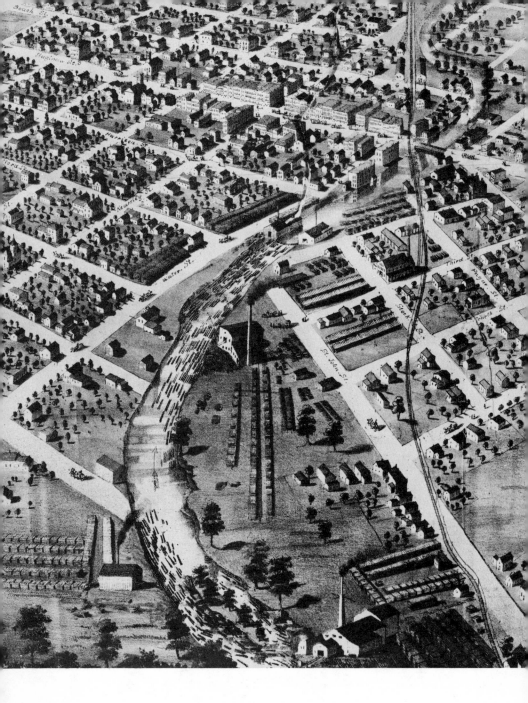

Downtown Flint, 1867

1865, Crapo's first year as governor, ten more bills received legislative approval.[6]

What made the session of 1867 different was the tremendous number of such schemes which were proposed, and the active involvement of nearly every member of the legislature in a combination to secure their passage. "We are in the midst of an era of railroads," wrote the Lansing correspondent of the *Detroit Daily Post*, "and the Legislature may fairly be said to be afloat on a sea of railroad bills." The paper listed twenty routes to which aid was proposed by local bond issues, and a month later reported that a number more had been added, "probably with the intention of increasing the strength of the railroad interest in both Houses by furnishing every member a local reason for supporting the bond issuing scheme." [7]

The railroad partisans picked for the first test the measure which appeared to offer the strongest ground. The year before, the townships of Kalamazoo and Portage had issued $63,000 worth of bonds for the benefit of the Kalamazoo and Schoolcraft Railroad. The aid was similar in every respect to that authorized for other projects by the various enactments of 1865, but in this instance the localities involved had acted without any specific authorization from the legislature, in the belief that the matter was too urgent to wait for the next biennial session. Considering such approval as a mere formality which might as well come after the act as before, the railroad lobby put forward a bill to legalize the bonds which had already been put on the market and sold. It passed the Senate by a vote of 18 to 9, and the House by 72 to 3.[8]

Ill as he was, Crapo had been watching the progress of the railroad bills carefully and with mounting alarm. He had his veto message ready even before the Kalamazoo bill reached him, and on February 5 he returned it to the legislature with a vigorous denunciation of the notion that an illegal action could be justified merely because it had already been taken. Legislative sanction to "unauthorized and invalid municipal grants," he wrote, would immeasurably weaken "the binding force of and the reverence due to the laws enacted by the State." The precedent which would be established

> cannot fail hereafter to be used by interested parties, and by unwarrantable combinations, to legalize acts, not only of the most objectionable character, but such, also, as may be opposed to reason, and in violation of all law. No matter how desirable the end may be regarded which is sought to be secured by this legislation, nothing can compensate for the mischief and for the long catalogue of evils which . . . is sure to result from it in the future.

In answer to the argument that a majority of the voters in the two townships had "deliberately signified their desire to be taxed" to pay the railroad aid bonds, he pointed out that the minority had certain rights as well and that if they were to be asked to share the "burden of this heavy taxation," the least they could expect would be the faithful compliance with "all the forms of law" in the course of its imposition. Going further, however, he thought it "fair to presume that many of the electors, conscious of the illegality of the proposed action, believing that the votes adopted could have no binding force, or fearful lest their participation in the same might prejudice their rights, purposely abstained from voting." He recognized that a failure to legalize the bonds

may occasion loss to capitalists who have invested in
them; yet it must be remembered that the persons
who thus purchased [them] did so with knowledge,
actual and implied, of the very invalidity and worth-
lessness of the bonds, in consequence of having been
issued without authority of law. There was no decep-
tion or misapprehension about the character of these
bonds; and the class of persons investing in such securities had undoubtedly the ability and disposition
thoroughly to investigate their merits, and calculate
the chance of their ultimate payment.[9]

The veto hit the legislature like a "bombshell," Crapo
wrote. "No one supposed that a man could be found with
sufficient courage to dare venture on so bold a measure as to
act independent of two such Legislative bodies." Senator
Curtenius from Kalamazoo, the author of the bill, arose and
stated, "The only object for which I came here having been
defeated, I resign my seat in the Senate." Crapo was well
aware that in exercising the "one man power" he would
bring down on his head the fury of one of the most powerful
combinations ever seen in the Michigan legislature, but he
could take no other course. "I am acting," he assured his son,
"with the most honest convictions, and believe I am right,
and I am strong in the faith that I shall come out, in the
end, 'all right.'"

I am one branch of the Govt. and have my responsibilities and duties, and the Legislature are another
branch occupying the same position with respect to
the people; and both of us must go to the people for
support. There is this difference, however. The members of the Leg. are acting in the interest of certain
R.R. cliques, and are laboring almost exclusively to

promote their interest, whereas I stand upon the question as the guardian of the public interest.[10]

The Kalamazoo senator had spoken too hastily, however, when he assumed that Crapo's veto would doom his project. Within a few days both houses of the legislature had voted to override the governor, the Senate by 24 to 7 and the House by 70 to 20.[11]

Flushed with success, the railroad lobby pushed ahead with its program. In 1865 the legislature had authorized cities and townships of St. Clair, Lapeer, Genesee, and Shiawassee counties which were on the line of the railroad being built westward from Port Huron to Lansing to pledge their credit to aid in its construction. The next bill put forward was one to amend this act by: (1) increasing the borrowing authority from 5 to 10 per cent of assessed valuation, (2) permitting the aid to take the form of a donation instead of a loan if desired, (3) extending the authorization to cities and townships in the counties named which were not actually traversed by the route of the railroad, and (4) legalizing bonds already voted by the city of Flint to the extent of 10 per cent of assessed valuation (instead of the 5 per cent actually authorized). The measure was approved by a resounding 20 to 0 vote in the Senate, a 62 to 18 vote in the House, and was sent on to the governor for his signature.[12]

Once again, Crapo refused to give his assent, and on February 25 his second veto message was delivered to the legislature. Announcing his intention to give his views on municipal railroad aid legislation in general, he began first with a specific reference to two features peculiar to this particular bill. The provision for legalizing that part of the

Flint bonds issued in excess of 5 per cent of assessed valuation he pronounced inadmissible for the same reasons which had applied in the case of the Kalamazoo bill. As for the authorization to towns not situated on the route of the railroad to lend their credit, he pointed out that in some cases "residents and owners of property" more than twenty miles from the road would "be compelled to aid in its construction . . . while in consequence of the remoteness of the road, little or no benefit can accrue to them."

His main fire, however, was directed at the general character of all the railroad bills which had been under consideration in the legislature. The bill now before him, like the rest of the proposed laws, he felt was "in conflict with the spirit and implication" of the state constitution, even if the prohibition of lending the public credit for private ends was expressly stated only with regard to the state itself.

> If it be so unwise a thing, on the part of the State at large, thus to engage in, or aid uncertain enterprises of this character, it must be vastly more unwise and perilous, for the feebler townships and cities, thus to involve themselves, and expose to serious hazards, their more limited credits.

Referring briefly to court decisions in other states on both sides of the question, he concluded this point with the statement that "the legislation proposed in this bill is, at least, of doubtful constitutionality."

On the economic aspects of the proposed legislation he took an even stronger stand. He freely admitted the benefits to be gained from the construction of new railroads, calling attention even to "the personal advantage which I should derive from the construction of the road named in this bill."

But, he warned, the bills which had been proposed "promise no realization of the end sought, but indicate disaster to the people."

> If by a rash and unconsidered legislation, in the accumulation of municipal indebtedness and enormous taxation, we destroy the value of property, and retard the settlement of our territory, then, instead of increased growth and added resources, we become, by this very process, poor in population and in wealth. The policy . . . of permitting villages and sparsely settled townships to incur the heavy indebtedness, which the enterprise and zeal of their citizens are willing to vote, in order to secure the construction of railroads to their particular localities, is fraught with disaster in the future. Its tendency will be to cripple our industrial interests, to repel capital which is tending here in consequence of our vast natural advantages and unequaled position, to discourage manufactures and agriculture, and deter the flow of immigration. These results naturally follow in any State or community overburdened by taxation.

At a time when other states were seeking to extricate themselves from the burden of wartime taxation, he wrote, "the people of Michigan, by municipal action, are competing with each other, in the creation of vast amounts of indebtedness." Taking into consideration all the various bills proposed, there were some localities in which "the different railroad projects . . . if equally treated, and aid granted as asked for, will create a bonded indebtedness of *forty* per cent upon their whole taxable property." Admitting that these situations were as yet the exception, what, he asked, would prevent their increase once the principle of municipal aid became firmly entrenched? The whole history of this legislation to date had been marked by an increase in demands, coupled with an easing of safeguards and restrictions, and an extension of the principle of aid from a few major routes to a multitude of purely local and speculative projects. Instead of requiring that the roadbed be completed and the ties paid for and delivered before aid bonds could be delivered, it was now proposed that these preliminary construction steps be financed with public money, at which point the railroad companies could then "go upon the market with their own bonds" to raise the money for buying and laying the rails, purchasing rolling stock, erecting depots, and otherwise completing the road. The companies, in other words, would be enabled to build the entire railroad without the need of putting up any money of their own! If under these circumstances private investors were hesitant about taking the company bonds, how easy it would be, Crapo suggested, to demand further public assistance in order to salvage the original investment.

He admitted that he had given his approval to similar acts in 1865, but, he declared,

> in doing so, I was governed more by a deference to the practice of my predecessors, and the views of the then Legislature, than by my own judgment. If I erred at that time, it was because I distrusted my own convictions too much to act in direct opposition to the opinions entertained by the majority of the Legislature.

Now, he warned, "the increasing demands for this legislation, both in the numbers of the applications, and in the amounts asked for . . . should excite apprehension and alarm." He estimated the aggregate length of the railroads proposed at 2,000 miles, and the amount of actual capital necessary to build them at $60,000,000.* If, as was claimed, with one-third of this cost raised by taxation "the balance can be procured of capitalists, either in stock or upon the mortgage of the roads," the question still remained: could buyers be found for $20,000,000 worth of such municipal bonds? Certainly not outside the state, at any price, and in Michigan only "at a very small per centage on their par value." Then,

> as the bonds continue to be depreciated in value, additional taxation will be called for and urged to make up the deficit . . . until in the end, the very magnitude of the indebtedness will compel, if it does not seek to justify a repudiation of the whole debt.

There are now, he reminded the legislature, "scores of towns, cities, and counties in the neighboring states, which have refused or neglected to pay, not the principal alone, but the interest of bonds issued in aid of local railroad schemes." Millions of dollars of such bonds were now worth but a few cents on the dollar. "Can we reasonably expect, that the experience of Michigan, adopting the same policy, will differ materially from that of Wisconsin, Iowa, Illinois, Missouri and Canada?"

> The credit of Michigan today is second to that of no State in the Union; and upon this fact . . . we have a right to expect large accessions of wealth and population from abroad. . . . Let us pause before we . . . lay the foundation for an evil of such magnitude, as will seek a remedy by a general system of repudiation.[13]

* The *Detroit Free Press* of March 1, 1867, presented a tabulation of the completed railroads totaling 3,777 miles, nearly twice Crapo's estimate.

The veto caused tremendous excitement, not only at Lansing but throughout the state wherever railroad projects were afoot. Since it was now clear that none of the bills under discussion would ever become law unless sufficient strength could be mustered to override a veto by a two-thirds vote, the railroad men in the legislature took frantic steps to tighten their organization. A caucus was set up to plan strategy; mass meetings were held both at the state capital and in many of the aspiring railroad towns; delegations of lobbyists descended on the legislature to keep wavering members under constant pressure.[14]

Much to Crapo's disgust, his own attorney general aided the railroad lobby, giving a legal opinion in support of the constitutionality of the aid bills right on the heels of Crapo's veto. "Breathing the malaria of this R.R. atmosphere," Crapo wrote, "he thought it was all one way, and no doubt calculated that by giving opinions against me, he should make himself a great man." [15]

The caucus decided to postpone any immediate attempt to pass the bill over Crapo's veto, and devoted its attention instead to devising means of strengthening its position. To meet one of the governor's objections, it was decided to insert in all bills the provision that in voting railroad aid, municipalities should be limited to a total of 10 per cent of their assessed valuation, no matter how many different lines might be involved. More important, however, it was decided to agree on a list of projects to be passed, and then to stand together to carry them over the anticipated veto. In a single day the House gave its approval to twenty railroad bills, passing them "as fast as the Clerk could read them and call the yeas and nays." [16]

Meanwhile, Crapo was holding firm. A group of Flint lobbyists, in Lansing to work for overriding his veto of the

Port Huron bill, found him "not a subject to be managed by coaxing" when they called on him in his sickroom. While they were pleasant enough, he wrote his son, "some of the hard heads among the number thought I was an incorrigible puritan." If so, he was not ashamed of it. He had stood for what he believed was right, and if nothing else, few men in the state would now repeat the question of two years ago: "Who is Henry H. Crapo?" [17]

His outspoken opposition to the railroad schemes was beginning to have some effect. His vetoes were circulated in pamphlet form, and the subject was being discussed intensively throughout the state. Although the railroad lobby had "done everything that could be done to coerce members and manufacture public opinion against my views . . . [and were] determined that their plans should not be defeated by *one man,*" Crapo felt by mid-March that "the sentiment of the people is changing very rapidly . . . even in many of the towns most interested in some of the roads." "It is not to be doubted," wrote the *Advertiser and Tribune,* "that the great majority of our cool and clear-headed businessmen . . . look with very great apprehension upon the railroad building furore that is now so widely prevalent." All three of the Detroit papers supported the governor's stand, as did many, perhaps a majority, of the local papers throughout the state.[18]

After repeated postponements, the strength of the railroad forces was finally put to the test when the veto of the Port Huron bill was brought to a vote in the Senate on March 20. "We had quite an exciting time," wrote Crapo's private secretary:

> Senator Howell made a big speech on the constitutionality and used the Atty. Genl. completely up. He

> took the same cases cited by the Atty. Genl. and
> showed that in all of them the first thing established
> by the Judge . . . was the right of the State to engage
> in these improvements; and that as the State had the
> constitutional right, it could delegate it to its agents,
> the towns, etc. Then he took our constitution and
> showed that it was forbidden and therefore we could
> not let our towns etc. do it. This was only one of his
> points but it was too strong for some of them. Sen.
> Williams tried to answer him but fell far short of the
> mark. Mr. Pringle also made a *few remarks* (time 2
> hours) but it was all of no avail.

Despite all the pressure which had been brought to bear,
the 21 to 10 vote for overriding fell one short of the necessary two-thirds.[19]

The railroad spree was over. Crapo had been holding
the bills as they had come to him, and in two omnibus
vetoes he returned a total of thirty-three railroad bills. A
half-hearted attempt to override them failed miserably, and
the issue was dead.[20]

As a sequel to this controversy, it should be noted that
two years later, after Crapo's retirement from the governorship, a general act was passed permitting indiscriminate
municipal aid to railroad corporations—the very thing Crapo
had forecast when he wrote in his veto of the Port Huron
bill:

> Once having admitted the principle, by sanctioning
> the practice, that the majorities in townships, cities,
> and counties, shall have the right to aid railroads or
> other corporations, in the prosecution of private en-
> terprises, by what rule can the Legislature discrimi-
> nate in regard to the exercise of this right?

The following year, however, the Michigan supreme court held invalid one of the municipal railroad aid acts of 1864, and in 1871, in a case arising under the 1869 general act, the court decided once and for all that the pledging of municipal credit for private ends was unconstitutional.[21]

III

The railroad agitation had overshadowed everything else during the 1867 session of the legislature. Apart from the ratification of the Fourteenth Amendment by a strict party vote, only one other policy matter of importance was dealt with. This was the provision for a constitutional convention which met during the summer of 1867. While Crapo had certain formal functions to perform in connection with it, both his illness and his preoccupation with business affairs prevented any active participation in its deliberations.

The state governorship was traditionally considered a stepping stone to the office of United States senator, and towards the middle of Crapo's last year in Lansing many of his friends urged him to declare his candidacy for the seat held by Zachariah Chandler, whose term was about to expire. In June, 1868, Crapo wrote a large number of acquaintances in various parts of the state asking their candid opinion on whether he should run. In his letters he expressed his own great respect for Chandler, but the replies showed that many Republicans were not of the same opinion, and indeed that the writers welcomed the idea of his candidacy as a means of dumping the Radical leader. J. J. Woodman of Paw Paw assured Crapo that against Chandler he would "command more strength from the Republican party throughout the *whole state* than . . . any other man." Crapo's feeble health made many of his correspondents doubt the wisdom of his running, however, both for his own sake and because they felt it would hurt his chances of making an effective bid for the seat. This consideration ultimately proved decisive, and in January, 1869, Chandler was returned to the Senate without significant opposition.[22]

Reviewing Crapo's tenure as governor of Michigan, one cannot escape noting that he had failed to accomplish many of the things which he had hoped would mark his administration. No action was taken by the legislature on his repeated recommendations for a positive program to encourage immigration. His requests for a thorough geological survey of the state were ignored, and he was unable to get anything started on the two wagon roads to Mackinac which had been projected as an aid in opening up the Upper Peninsula.[23]

With the exception of his courageous and successful stand against the railroad aid mania, Crapo's main achievements as governor were administrative in nature. When he took office the program for using the "swamp lands" for building state roads had the makings of a major scandal. Millions of acres of land had been appropriated, but little could be seen by way of results, and rumors of extensive fraud were widespread. During the 1865 session of the legislature, he secured passage of a law authorizing the appointment of a general swamp land road commissioner to work part-time on a per diem basis. He named his brother David to the post, and with his aid began to examine the maze of contracts under which the roads were supposedly being built. A bulky notebook in his own hand is preserved in the Crapo Manuscripts, detailing the record of this investigation.[24]

When the legislature met in 1867, Crapo devoted a long section of his message to a report on the situation. Calling the program an "expensive failure," he charged that instead of serving to open the unsettled parts of the state, it had been used "for the promotion of personal interests, and for the advancement of private ends."

> Many of these roads have been laid out in such a manner, that contractors have acquired their lands at a trifling cost, by merely brushing up and patching old roads through settled parts of the country, or by expending a small amount of labor over those portions having but little timber to be removed; whilst sections of the same roads leading through an entire unsettled timbered district have been left untouched.

He urged that if further appropriations were to be made, safeguards should be adopted to secure "the construction of really traversable highways, instead of mere imaginary lines," and pointed to the need for a full-time state official charged with the supervision of the program. In accordance with his recommendation the legislature created the permanent post of state swamp land road commissioner, and he promptly named Lorenzo B. Curtis for the job. Although an attempt was made at this session to pass a large number of swamp land road bills by combining forces with the members interested in railroad bills, the coalition broke down when the Senate decided to postpone action on any of the requests until the new commissioner had been able to report at the next session of the legislature.[25]

Crapo also gave considerable personal attention to the management of the various state institutions. In his valedictory address in 1869, he told how he had spent several days at the Asylum for the Insane, "residing as an inmate of the Superintendent's family, with a view to satisfy myself in regard to the mode of keeping the books and accounts, and of disbursing the public moneys, as well as in respect to the general management of the Institution, the treatment of the patients, etc." Reassuringly, he added that he had been "exceedingly gratified" with the results of the inspection.[26]

It was Crapo's course on matters such as these which led a contemporary, writing seven years after his death, to credit his "careful supervision" with having "saved the State from mismanagement in some of the multitudinous contracts which required almost the eyes of Argus to watch":

> His great business experience and strict economy and integrity induced him to give a degree of personal supervision to the details of road building and other outlays, which was more than one man could devote to such work without injury to himself.[27]

In his inaugural message, it will be recalled, Crapo had announced his opposition to the lenient policy of pardoning convicts practiced by earlier governors. In January, 1866, he addressed a long letter, subsequently published in the *Detroit Advertiser and Tribune,* to a prominent Republican lawyer who had written him in behalf of a convict in the state prison. In it he explained that, in general, his exercise of executive clemency would be limited to those cases in which new facts had come to light to prove either innocence or at least a lesser offense than that on which the original sentence had been based. He specifically rejected the idea which had become generally accepted that pardons should automatically be extended when requested by the prosecuting attorney and judge who had presided at the original trial. The results of this policy showed a sharp contrast with the record of previous administrations. Of his immediate predecessors, Governor Blair had granted 143 pardons in four years, Governor Wisner 72 in two years, and Governor Bingham 100 in four years. During Crapo's four years in office, executive clemency was extended on only 13 occasions.[28]

In this, as in other matters, he had acted solely with reference to his own views as to what was right, and the fact of his continued popularity in the face of his independence of policy bears abundant testimony to the respect accorded him by the people of Michigan. It was no small tribute when the Democratic *Detroit Free Press* conceded not only that "his official conduct was such as to command the confidence of his own party" but also "in many instances the commendation of his most vigilant political opponents." [29]

thirteen

CLIMAX OF A CAREER
(1867 - 1869)

I

Crapo's decision in 1866 to erect a large new sawmill on the fire-blackened ruins of his original mill, coupled with his acquisition in that same year of sole ownership of both the lumber concern and the Driggs pine tract, set the stage for the climactic period of his business career and of his life. From 1867 until his death in July, 1869, his lumber operations were on a larger scale than ever before, as he carried on a successful battle to discharge his long-standing New Bedford indebtedness while at the same time waging a losing fight against the illness which ultimately cost him his life.

When he returned to Flint in April, 1867, after his successful battle with the legislature over the railroad bills, he was exhausted. It was not long, however, before he was back in harness. During his absence, he wrote, the business "had become demoralized . . . and everything has dragged."

> Since my return I have been compelled to see things creep along, zig zag, helter skelter, without system or force, until I have felt the absolute necessity of going into the concern and reducing disorder to some kind of system and order, as well as to get on "more steam." My life may be the sacrifice, but I don't feel as though I could see things move as they did when I first got out; and yet I know that my strength and

health is not equal to the task. Many of my trusted
men are not aware how I am now suffering in consequence of an easy slack way of letting things take care
of themselves. They mean well, but they get indifferent. I shall however change this mode of operations,
or there will be some noise about the premises.

As a check on the way the mills were running, he had a
watch privately kept on the production of one of the saws
in the lower mill, and on finding that an average day's total
was only a little over 3,000 feet of lumber he determined to
go into the mills himself, show the men what they were doing
wrong, and insist that they *"double* that amount hereafter,
and more, or shut down and leave."

The "Boys" think that I am not only cross, but rather
uneasy for a sick man; and that I scold a great deal.
But, my scolding and lecturing will cease when my
business moves off again with the proper amount of
speed, and not before.[1]

He was even more concerned with the failure to get his
large new mill into production. "I find a thousand things
around the mill not yet touched . . . and as I dig them out
and inquire what has or is to be done the answer is—'don't
know—no orders.'" He complained that many of the details
which had not been attended to would now cost double the
amount for which they could have been done during the
winter, "to say nothing of a loss of $100 to $200 per day,
every day the mill is delayed." After having "scolded and
drove up until the men begin to think that I have some voice
in what is going on here," he was able to get the new mill
under way at last by the beginning of May, though at the
price of two days' confinement in bed from his labors.[2]

230

Crapo's family was greatly alarmed at the way he was plunging into his work without any regard for his health. He himself was quite aware of what was happening, admitting to his son that when he enjoyed "a favorable turn of a few days my exertions, during that period, throw me back again for a week." Yet both "the necessity and temptation" of work were more than he could resist. Humphrey Smith received a steady stream of long letters from him, "seemingly one every day," telling of his troubles at Flint and urging along the Detroit end of the business. One of these, quoted at length above, Smith passed along to William in New Bedford as a sample, warning that "this is not going to do at all." "I can't do everything," he complained, adding that "even if I do more it may not be satisfactory," for he had many times experienced Crapo's meticulous insistence on things being done just as he himself thought they should be done. Dr. Willson, another son-in-law, was even more worried, and went so far as to write William that if he could not come out to Michigan and take charge of the business, that he should come out for the sole purpose of persuading his father to close up the business at once, resign as governor, and do nothing but rest.[3]

II

Despite all this, Crapo did not slack his pace. His loggers had put in 15 million feet of logs the previous winter. Late in the spring of 1867 he bought an additional lot of 3½ million feet for $35,000, making a total of 18½ million feet of logs, nearly half again the size of his stock the season before and not far from three times that of any earlier season. Even he was frightened by the prospect—"you can hardly imagine the labor of manufacturing this quantity with the additional labor of selling it and getting it off;

and especially by only one principal, and a sick man at that"
—but he looked forward to a profitable year. "To form
some idea of the extent of my business," he wrote William,
"you have only to compute the quantity which I saw at $20
per M. ft. (which is about the average sales per M. at present prices) in order to get at my gross amount of sales." He
estimated the gross receipts from the lumber this stock of
logs would produce at $370,000, and if the wear and tear
on the mills were not to be taken into account he figured
that he would be able to clear more than $140,000 from
the season's work. He could not resist congratulating himself
that "at present prices of lumber that purchase of the Driggs
land was really a 'big thing.' " [4]

To get this tremendous quantity of logs sawed he struggled hard to get the new mill running at peak efficiency, as
well as his two older mills, neither of which had been sold.
By the end of July he was able to report that they were
"doing very finely indeed; . . . in fact coming fully up to
my expectations, which is saying not a little for them." In
three months of sawing, close to 9 million feet of lumber
had been turned out, and barring accidents, he hoped to
continue at the 3 million feet a month pace through the end
of November. The daily output of all three mills was about
120,000 feet of lumber, with around 80,000 feet of this being
cut by the new mill alone. Although Crapo was pleased, he
was still not satisfied; "the new mill . . . can and must saw
100 M. feet per day = 20,000,000 ft. in a season of 200 days."
By September considerable progress towards this goal had
been made, with the total daily cut of the three mills sometimes reaching over 137,000 feet, and Crapo felt that he was
safe in selling the Busenbark mill, to be delivered to the
buyer after the end of the sawing season. He had given it
four years' work in the three he had owned it (having run

it night and day during 1866), and he thought the $15,000 he received a good price since "the mill was sham built, and the terrible 'drive' that I have subjected it to has taken the best wear out of it." He decided to keep the other old mill, however, and to continue to run it in conjunction with his large new mill.[5]

With the great increase in his mill capacity over previous years, Crapo had to make new efforts to find buyers for the lumber which was streaming from his saws. In the early stages of the business, it will be recalled, he had been successful in opening up a market among Ohio lumber yards and industrial consumers of lumber, but in the intervening years the growth of other markets closer at hand had made it unnecessary to devote much effort to holding or expanding the trade in that direction. Now he felt the necessity of moving again to open a wider outlet for his lumber, and he sent Chase, his chief clerk, down into Ohio as a traveling salesman. On his first trip he sold $4,000 worth of lumber, $6,000 on his second, $11,000 on his third, and $16,000 on his fourth tour, all within the space of a few months. With continued effort, Chase reported, it would be possible to "lay the foundation for a big semi-wholesale business down there . . . at good prices," indeed that almost any amount could be disposed of "by going from yard to yard, and selling a carload here and a carload there." [6]

Aside from these orders, however, sales were slow. Crapo had hoped for a single "big wholesale trade of uppers" which would take him "out of the woods," but no such opportunity had presented itself by the end of the 1867 sawing season. The large scale of his operations during the year had left him short of money, but even so, his resources were more ample than those of most Michigan lumbermen, and he was confident that if he could manage until the coming spring "my immense stock of dry lumber will give me the inside track of all competitors, for they can't interfere with me then with green lumber, and they are now selling off all their this year's cut for what they can get." [7]

Chase's sales work in Ohio continued to pay off in orders, but by the spring of 1868 when the lumber trade generally had improved, Crapo found himself up against a new problem: he could not get anything like enough railroad cars to ship out what he was able to sell. The difficulty was aggravated by the fact that shipments to Ohio had to be made on "compromise" cars whose wheels could be adjusted to the different gauges over which they would have to pass. In April, 1868, Crapo wrote Smith in Detroit with extreme annoyance that he was "disgusted with the whole Rail Road system." Although he had one of the largest businesses in Michigan, was governor of the state, and even a former railroad man himself, he complained that despite "all the power and influence and begging and fretting and importunity" he was unable to get off "much over 50 M. feet per day, on an average, whereas I am now—every day—manufacturing more than twice that amount."

Unless he could break the bottleneck, he feared that he would have to stop manufacturing for lack of room to pile up the new lumber as it came from his saws. When compromise cars were sent up towards Flint, he wrote his son, "I can only get a small share of them." Even Kimball, who had been superintendent of the Flint and Holly and was now with the Flint and Pere Marquette after the consolidation of the two lines, "does not seem to realize . . . that as I have five times as much lumber to ship off as all the rest of the manufacturers, I should have five times as many of those compromise cars when they come up, as all the others." Instead, they were divided "so as to let all hands have a portion, and some days a person with only 500,000 ft. to ship will get one car, whilst I with 8,000,000 ft. to ship will get only two cars . . . this they call favoring me." Only after several anxious weeks during which he devoted nearly all his time to "writing all the R.R. agents and employees about cars" did he feel confident that he would be able to get enough for his needs.[8]

III

Crapo never fully recovered from his illness after the attack in January, 1867, and throughout that year his condition continued to trouble him. In July he reported to his son that "for several days at a time I have been comparatively free from pain, followed by several days of severe suffering." While he kept at work in his office and around the mills as much as he could, frequently his pain was so severe "that I cannot even read, much less concentrate my mind on mental labor." A little later, he wrote William asking that he purchase and send on to Michigan "a good, second hand chaise, with a good leather top and good clean lining."

> I want it to ride in constantly about the village and lumber yards, so that I can get out and in 50 times a day, vastly more easily than I can creep over the wheels of a 4 wheeled buggy. My health is so poor, and especially my limbs so enfeebled, that I want some sort of a carriage which I can more easily get in and out of almost every 20 minutes, when I am not in my office; and I could not think of anything better than a chaise. I suppose they are somewhat out of date; but I want one for comfort.

For several weeks during the fall his left eye was almost completely blinded by a blood clot, and while this of course had no connection with his other difficulty, he wrote somewhat despairingly that "I am now, physically, little better than a 'wrack,' and am paying the penalty of overtaxing myself." Luckily the clot in his eye was soon absorbed without any permanent damage to his sight. But when he announced this to his son, and then added that "my health also has very much improved of late . . . so as to enable me to endure quite an amount of physical labor," it was clear that more trouble would soon be forthcoming.[9]

In Washington on official business the following February, he was stricken once again with an acute bladder attack, involving a near-fatal hemorrhage, and it was only at the expense of great pain that he was able to return to Flint. There, he remained bedridden for almost two months. Resting his body, he still could not relax his mind, but at least things were proceeding more smoothly than they had been on his return from Lansing the year before. "I am within the sound of the whistle," he wrote, "and know everything that is going on. The 'Boys' are all very good, and faithful, and do just what I want to have done, and report everything that takes place in all the different departments." Even while he was flat on his back, he worked an average of twelve hours a day, dictating letters and going over accounts. It was a great day for him when, late in April, he was able to ride out in his chaise "all over the lumber yards . . . through the piles and all about the premises," and confirm with his own eyes the reports he had been receiving in his sickroom.[10]

During this long convalescence his mind very naturally turned again to the idea of closing up the business, coming, he wrote William, to the "deliberate conclusion" that after sawing out the large stock of logs which had been put in during the past winter, he would then put no more money into logs but would "sell out all my lumber as soon as it can be possibly done, and apply the proceeds to the payment of my debts." He had intended to run the mills a few years longer, at least, but he felt that his precarious health made a settlement of his financial affairs more urgent than ever.

> If I were on my feet and in perfect health, and could be everywhere, and keep the control of everything, myself, it might be prudent to carry on my business, as it now is. But it is too vast, and has too many parts, and is spread out too much, and has to be entrusted to too many, who do not and will not exercise that care and judgment which I do, and who are no doubt studying their own interest as well as mine, to be carried on by an old man, flat on his back.

Although he had been doing well compared with his early years as a lumberman, he recognized nevertheless that "the business is now very hard and competition among sellers forces the prices far below what there is any necessity." It was his same old complaint, about the "one-horse men who are now killing the market," and who were frequently forced to sell at any price to avoid bankruptcy.

> It costs me double to sell lumber than it did previously at Fentonville and Holly, and the yard at Detroit costs me a great deal more than it should and 3 times as much per M. as at any other of my yards; and to sell what I manufacture, instead of being able to close any of the yards, I must establish more, or sell my lumber here at Flint, at wholesale, at just what I can get, which will be some $2 or $3 less than Saginaw prices.

Even if he should live, he felt that he had nothing to lose by shutting down, "for I do not think that I have made anything this last year that begins to compensate for the working up of my timber, for the great risk I run, for my taxes, interest, etc. and for the vast amount which I pay for salesmen, foremen, laborers, etc." [11]

By early in July, sales had brought in enough extra money to enable him "to make one step forward" at last. He sent William a draft for $11,446.35 to be applied on his debts in the East and reported that he had paid almost all that he owed in Michigan and had in addition in cash and notes nearly $40,000. "You see by this statement," he continued, "that I shall now begin to have a small stream turned upon your wheel; and if nothing happens before next January, I wish to make a sensible reduction of my large indebtedness there." During the next several months further remittances were made, and by the end of October the amounts forwarded totaled $88,000. At this point he could not help commenting proudly that there were "few men in any business" who could withdraw so much money from their operating funds over such a short period "without seriously feeling it," and suggested to his son that he drop a hint of the amounts sent to several of his New Bedford friends who had "felt doubtful of the propriety of my removal to Michigan." [12]

Among the first of the debts which he wanted canceled were the balances still due Prescott for his half of the business and Arnold for the Driggs pine lands. He had other older obligations to be taken care of as well, but he felt it was particularly urgent to get the Michigan lumber property free of encumbrance before anything should happen to him.[13]

IV

Crapo's mill operations during 1868 had gone along well. He had started the season with close to 18 million feet of logs, nearly as many as he had had the year before, and when he shut down the mills in the fall he had sawed out all but a few million feet. In May he wrote his son that

> there is probably no man making lumber in this state any cheaper per M. than I am. Several large Eastern manufacturers have recently been into my new mill and they say that they have seen nearly all the principal mills in the state, and that my mill—in its arrangements for convenience of being operated—in its arrangements to prevent lost time, etc. for thoroughness of work as well as for rapid and orderly despatch, is decidedly *unrivalled.*

He had decided in the spring that the logs already on hand would be the last he would ever put in, but—probably encouraged by the amount of money he had been able to put aside for the payment of debts—towards the end of the summer his resolution had begun to weaken, and by December he was writing that "if I am able to carry on the business I had better put in my own logs and clear from it $10 per M. than to purchase them and clear $2." Accordingly, he had his loggers at work to get in a stock sufficient to run the new mill throughout the season and the lower mill at least "until hot weather thins out the men and I want mowers." In April, 1869, he reported that he had more than 16 million feet of logs, including those that were held over, and assured his son that "that is none too many as the business looks very fair for the coming season." [14]

All this activity did not mean that his health had improved. Indeed, if anything it was gradually growing worse, but the constant attention he gave to the business, even from his bed, made his suffering more bearable because it kept his mind and his spirit occupied. Much to his disgust, he was forced to rely on regular doses of morphine to enable him to bear the constant pain, though on several occasions he made unsuccessful attempts to free himself from dependence on it. In the fall of 1868 after a particularly sharp attack, the presence of a large calculus or stone in the bladder was finally established. Dr. Willson had long suspected that this was the root of his patient's difficulties, but he had deferred to the judgment of consulting physicians who had repeatedly said there was no stone.[15]

The only possible cure would be through surgical removal of the calculus which was causing the irritation, but the time was long past when such an operation could be performed with any degree of safety. In Crapo's greatly weakened condition it was feared that the shock of the operation itself might prove fatal, and that in any case his powers of recuperation would not prove sufficient to bring him through. Finally, however, his prolonged sufferings made the risks seem worth taking, and in the summer of 1869 he underwent a lithotomy at the hands of a famous New York surgeon.[16]

At first the results seemed magical. In a letter to William, Crapo wrote exultantly that he had begun "to feel once more like a man. . . . I shall be moving about soon as though this terrible thing had never occurred." Proudly he declared that "I am rapidly accumulating a stock of lumber never before equalled in my yard," and he looked forward eagerly to a visit from his son so that he could show him the progress which had been made. He even dared think that he might be able to return with William to New Bedford for a short stay in his old home town. Only a few weeks later, however, he suffered a fatal relapse, and on July 23, 1869, he died at the age of sixty-five, the victim of "indulgence in that energetic industry which has marked his entire career." [17]

He left behind an estate variously estimated at between five hundred thousand and one million dollars, comprising not only the mills at Flint and the pine lands up the river from which he had drawn his logs, but also securities of various kinds, several well stocked and profitable farms in the vicinity of Flint, and pine tracts and farm lands in other parts of the state which had been bought for speculative holding.* Under the terms of his will, the business continued for many years after his death to be operated for the benefit of his widow and children under the direction of his son. William, who had never taken kindly to life in Michigan, maintained his residence in New Bedford but spent a good portion of his time each year in Flint, while the more immediate management of the business was in the hands of Crapo's two sons-in-law, Humphrey H. H. C. Smith and H. P. Christy.[18]

* Even during the final years of his life, when his thoughts had been concentrated on getting his business affairs in shape to close up, Crapo had continued to buy lands whenever a good opportunity appeared. During the fall of 1866 he had his brother David at work for three months hunting up scattered tracts of pine in the Saginaw region, resulting in the acquisition of about 10,000 acres at a cost averaging 80 cents an acre; similar purchases were made in 1867, 1868, and 1869, securing the pine at low prices because of his ability to pay cash.—HHC, Flint to WWC, NB, Jan. 1, 1864, Nov. 21, 1866, Dec. 17, 1867, Nov. 2, 3, 1868, Apr. 17, May 11, 1869.

fourteen

RETROSPECT

Henry Crapo's fourteen-year career in Michigan was dominated by his struggle to bring a new economic enterprise into life and to make it successful. The demands which this effort made on his time and energy shaped his entire existence, forcing him to subordinate all else to the needs of his business. In a very real sense, the man became the business, the business a reflection of the man. No one can read Crapo's letters in the early years of the enterprise without marveling at how completely he had immersed himself in the task of making his lumber business pay. Later he allowed himself the luxury of broadened interests, but even then his ventures into other fields were colored by the dominating fact of his lumber business.

His ill-fated experiment at boring for salt was an attempt to escape the burdensome realities of lumbering and find an easier way to make money. His successful railroad promotion was conceived as an important aid to the prosecution of the lumber enterprise, and was important as much for this reason as for the fact that it proved a sound and profitable investment. His speculative land interests, which in other circumstances might have received a major share of his attention, were permitted to lie neglected except insofar as holdings could be sold off to provide working capital for lumbering.

At least in the beginning, Crapo even sought to justify

his excursions into politics by their potential utility to his lumber concern (if we may take at face value his statements in letters to his son). His sense of civic responsibility came to outweigh personal considerations, but we should not forget that in even his most active years in public office he continued to devote much of his time to his business.

His one hobby, if it may be called that, was agriculture and stockbreeding. From the time he moved permanently to Flint, he had carried on some small-scale farming as a side-line to the lumber business, raising crops which could be used to supply his loggers and sawmill gangs. In the early sixties, he undertook drainage operations on two large farms which had formerly been considered worthless swamp, and was soon raising fine crops on both. In addition to his practical farming, he engaged in much experimentation with both crops and livestock breeding, reflecting his deep interest in scientific agriculture.[1] He served a term as president of the Genesee County Agricultural Society, and when he gave the annual address he wrote that "the farmers were highly delighted with it and say it is by far the best address they have ever had since the formation of the society." As always keeping an eye to the business advantages which might be gained, he noted that "I shall . . . be amply paid for it."

> These farmers are a curious set; they are all for you or all against you; and perhaps it was rather hazardous for me to undertake so important a task as a failure would have been a defeat; but I wanted to give the finishing stroke to McFarlin [his competitor in the Flint retail lumber trade], by getting on the side of the farmers, and I have fully succeeded. They call me a great farmer here now, which answers every purpose of really being such.

Since he took three first prizes and one second prize for his livestock exhibits, his appraisal of his own efforts seems unduly modest.[2]

During his tenure as governor, he gave unstinting support to the struggling Agricultural College (now Michigan State University) which was under attack as a waste of public funds. Suggesting in his inaugural address that it be given time to prove its value, he wrote that

> agriculture is no longer what it was once regarded by the majority of other professions of men, and partially admitted by the farmer himself to be—a low, menial employment, a mere drudgery . . . in which no thought, or mind, or study, was necessary, but is becoming recognized as a noble science.

In 1866 he addressed the Sheep-Shearing Exhibition of the Central Michigan Agricultural Society, praising the work of the agricultural societies and giving a practical discussion of wool growing both in terms of breeds and of commercial practices. Only a few months before his death, he had an article published in *The Cultivator and Country Gentleman* on "Wheat Culture in Michigan," detailing methods by which he was raising from eighteen to twenty-five bushels of wheat per acre while the average crop in the state was rarely more than twelve bushels, and often less.[3]

II

From the standpoint of business history, the significance of Crapo's business career lies not in any spectacular exploits or unusual achievements. There were many men who amassed greater wealth, who brought into being economic enterprises of vastly wider import. His story is of interest precisely because he was representative of the rising business class of mid-nineteenth century America. To say that he was representative of this new group does not, of course, mean that he was typical. But granting all the unique elements in his experience, the fact remains that the pattern of his life falls within a framework common to hundreds or thousands of other men in every state.

The place of Crapo's enterprise in the overall picture of the lumber industry in Michigan merits some comment. His was one of the largest firms in the field, perhaps the largest under individual ownership, though the great number of small operators meant that his annual output of lumber was somewhat less than 1 per cent of the total sawed in the state. Apart from mere size, his enterprise was noteworthy for the way he combined in one concern all of the steps of the lumbering process, from the purchase of pine lands and the cutting of logs to the wholesale and retail marketing of lumber. Such vertical integration was not unknown in this early period of Michigan lumbering, but the general pattern was for each of the several steps to be in the hands of distinct and separate groups of men. The scope of Crapo's enterprise committed him to expenses and involved him in problems which at times he undoubtedly wished he could avoid, yet the fact remains that it gave him a measure of control over his operations which he would not otherwise have had.

He also pioneered in his approach to marketing, taking pains to provide finished lumber in such forms as would best meet the needs of various classes of customers and making strong efforts to reach directly to the ultimate consumer, or at least to the retail yard dealer, without the intervention of middlemen. By way of contrast, marketing at Saginaw consisted largely of piling up green lumber on the docks where it could be purchased in cargo lots by traveling buyers from such large lumber centers as Chicago and Albany. Many of the mill owners there were dependent for operating funds on advances from such brokers, and both for this reason and because they lacked a home market of any importance, Saginaw lumbermen were generally much more at the mercy of prevailing economic conditions than was Crapo. As late as 1874 it was commented that one of Saginaw's most urgent needs was to pay more attention to the buyer of a few carloads of lumber and to spend more time in preparing their product for the ultimate consumer by seasoning and planing it.[4]

When Crapo came to Michigan, the lumber industry in the state had only recently risen to major commercial significance. It had never undergone any serious setbacks in its growth, and the result was a prevailing air of boundless optimism. On all sides he received assurances that the current prosperity was bound to continue. Considering these circumstances, it is easy to understand his original expectations of a large and rapid profit from the purchase of the Driggs tract, even though in practice these expectations proved to be little short of ridiculous. What led him astray in his calculations were, on the one hand, his illusions as to the speed with which the lands could be exploited, and on the other, the radical change in the economic picture caused by the Panic of 1857, which brought an abrupt fall in prices and a drastic curtailment of the market for lumber just when he was beginning to get his operations fully under way.

Had it not been for this turn of events, his story might well have been just another example of an eastern businessman reaping a quick harvest from the resources of the West. As it was, his struggle for survival in the face of a prolonged period of depression forced him to adopt a long-range perspective, keeping his mills running steadily but holding over his lumber for the day when he could secure better prices. Here again he struck out on his own, pursuing a course directly opposite to that of most lumbermen in the region, who were shutting down their mills and selling lumber at any price they could get.

Among the consequences of this enforced change in the outlook of the concern was Crapo's realization that he would have to move permanently to Flint so that he could devote his entire energies to the management of the concern. Although he came to this conclusion reluctantly, once the decision was made he accepted it wholeheartedly, and his personal identification with his adopted state was so complete that only six years after making Michigan his home he could be elected as its chief executive despite his brief period of residence.

His determination to avoid selling at sacrifice prices made it necessary for him to find other means of financing his continued manufacturing operations. Even in the most difficult times he received some revenue from lumber sales, but it was far from sufficient to enable him to meet his mill payroll and loggers' bills as they came due. "I have got over another Saturday night with my men," he wrote on one occasion in 1858, "but it is an ordeal to pass through." [5] In order to keep going, he could not avoid making further calls on his New Bedford partners, who had already provided almost the entire initial investment for lands, mills, and working capital. In addition, he was forced to sink in the business nearly every cent he himself could raise from sales of his speculative landholdings. Since most of these lands had been bought in company with various eastern investors, only a part of the money he was receiving belonged to him, and by using it in the lumber business he was of course gambling that he would be able to pay it back when the day should come for a settlement with his co-owners. By the time of the 1860 reorganization which took Arnold out of the picture, income from lumber sales was generally sufficient to cover the annual round of operating expenses, but what little was left had to be applied towards meeting payments on the mills. Indeed, it was not until 1863 that Crapo felt safe in making any distribution of profits, and this was after the value of his large and well-seasoned stock of lumber, manufactured at low cost during the depression years, had appreciated sharply with the general rise in lumber prices. Nevertheless, his ability to hold over lumber from season to season during the hard times from 1858 to 1862 testified to the fact that his enterprise was more adequately capitalized than most in the field.

The absence of facilities for short-term credit complicated his financing problems by compelling him to keep sizable amounts of cash on hand. Discounts on commercial paper were available only at ruinous rates of 2 or 3 per cent a month, causing him to adopt a strict rule of holding all notes until maturity. As late as the spring of 1862, he commented to his son that "having no bank accommodations to fall back on, nor any friends of whom to borrow money . . . it sometimes will happen that my cash runs almost out." [6]

In view of these difficulties it is hardly surprising that his initial enthusiasm for the lumber business dimmed rapidly. In the early years it was his running complaint that "prices have continued to keep down to a point that is death to the very hope of a profit. Everything goes for labor, taxes, repairs, etc." [7] Long after lumber prices had improved, however, he continued to feel that the rate of profit was far too low in view of the risks involved and the amount of capital employed.

Somewhat wistfully, he wrote his son in 1865 that "I very often feel that if I had the capital in a bank here which I now have in lumbering it would be the most desirable business that could be pursued, and infinitely more profitable than lumbering." Largely because of state legislation severely restricting the establishment and operation of banks, Flint prior to that time had had only, as Crapo put it, "three Broker's offices . . . that let their money at from 10 to 25%, or who rather *buy* paper to run on very short time at their own figures." A new situation had arisen, however, with the National Banking Act of 1863, and Crapo wrote that "Eastern people" had been taking charters under the Act at many "desirable points" in Michigan. In his letter to William he wondered whether the opening for a bank at Flint might not "be secured to ourselves or some of our friends East."

> The National banks in this state are declaring dividends from 15 to 20%. The stock being in government securities upon which we should receive interest, in addition to interest received on our issues, and for Exchange, etc., a bank would pay in Flint a large dividend. . . . I have not had in my business here on an average for years less than $120,000 including real estate, mills, etc. subject to all the hazards and wear and tear connected with such business. This, under our present National Banking System, would have, at one-tenth the care and labor, afforded abundantly greater profits than I have ever been able to reach; and at infinitely less risk.

Even as he wrote he knew that the idea was wishful think-ing. Nevertheless it was with some regret that he announced, a month and a half later, the chartering of a bank with $100,000 capital by a group of Flint businessmen.[8]

III

Quite apart from his zeal in advancing his own enter-prise, he was active both as governor and as a private citizen in promoting the development of his adopted state. The *Detroit Free Press* wrote in its obituary that as chief execu-tive of Michigan, he had

> fostered and encouraged any scheme that seemed likely to prove beneficial to the growth and welfare of the commonwealth, or to portions of it, being particu-larly zealous in the movements for opening up to market the great pine interest of Northern Michigan, the protection of our mining industries, the encour-agement of immigration, and such acts as might the better develop and increase the salt wealth of the Great Saginaw Valley.

He had been the means of securing the investment of nearly a million dollars of eastern capital in Michigan railroads, in addition to promoting his own Flint and Holly line. His choice of Flint as the site for his sawmill operations had an important influence on the growth of that city, and shortly before his death one of its citizens, though opposed to him in politics, is said to have remarked that "for three years of life to Governor Crapo, Flint could well afford to burn one-third of the city to ashes." [9]

Despite the incessant labor, the anxiety, the many dis-appointments that Crapo had had to endure from the very beginning of his lumber venture, he had soon become an enthusiast for the West in general and for Michigan in particular. In the midst of the depression in 1858, he wrote William that

> this country has decided advantages to the real work-
> ing, business man over New England. . . . Whilst
> New England, or perhaps I should say some of its
> older cities—New Bedford for instance—may at the
> present time very justly be likened to an infirm old
> man, who during a life of toil has enriched himself
> and is now under the decrepitude of old age, sitting
> quietly—almost helplessly—down with his pockets and
> coffers full of gold, Michigan, or "the West," may be
> as justly compared to a young, robust man, the owner
> of almost unnumbered acres of the richest and unre-
> claimed lands, with a physical organization perfectly
> developed and whose thews and sinews give evidence
> of almost unlimited powers of endurance, but who for
> the time being, in consequence of a too rapid growth
> as well as of a sudden and violent derangement of the
> physical system, induced by the mere surfeiting of
> food . . . is equally as helpless as the "old man" with
> his money bags.[10]

"When I say 'the west,'" Crapo had written on another occasion, "I do not mean fast men nor railroad speculators in Chicago and other cities of the west, but I mean the farmers who are the muscle—the bone and sinew—'the west' in fact."

> Although a great many of them are in debt to their
> neighbors, still these debts have been made to enable
> them to hurry forward the clearing of their land and
> they have their farms to show for it; and although the
> East says a great deal about the debts of the west, yet

at the same time there are single firms in the East who perhaps owe enough to pay all the debts of every farmer in Michigan. . . . The difference is here a farmer will not make a new debt to pay an old one for he is independent in one sense, whereas East it is necessary for the debtor to do this to keep his credit good, at any sacrifice of means.[11]

Capitalist though he was himself, he was not overly impressed with the power of money alone. "Thirty years since," he wrote in 1860, Michigan "was a wilderness, and almost exclusively the home of the savage; now she has every improvement of the most flourishing and prosperous state in the union, with as many thriving and populous villages as the same extent of purely agricultural country can exhibit anywhere."

I may venture the assertion with safety that the monied wealth of all the hardy adventurers and settlers who have made her what she is in that short space, and who have reclaimed and subdued . . . wild and uncultivated lands, would not in the outset average $400 each, and I presume it would almost be safe to say $200. Look at what she has done with her limited means, and what she is even now doing without money or capital of any sort, and I say her business men will compare favorably with even New England. . . .

All that Michigan wants is a little time to pay all her debts, and the use of a little capital, a small amount compared with what Massachusetts requires, to set in motion a thousand branches of industry and enterprise, that would at once not only free her from debt, but make her prosperous and rich.[12]

Crapo spent little time declaiming the virtues of "progress," but he was himself an active agent in bringing it about. As a participant in the building of the great Middle West, he decried the failure of eastern men to appreciate or even see what was going on in the rest of the nation. "How very few men there are East," he protested in 1862, "who do or can understand the gigantic power and strength, the unlimited wealth and resources and the extent of the political power which the 'West' is destined to possess in a very few years."

> If its future history could be now written, it would be regarded as the wildest, the most improbable fiction. Its resources are immense, and although it has already reached a point of no small importance, these resources have hardly yet begun to be developed. . . . The time will very soon come when the whole South whether with us, or opposed to us, will be a matter of very little consequence; and even New England must soon learn that her glory can only be reflected from the "West." [13]

When Crapo penned these words he had barely reached the midpoint of his Michigan career, but they provide a most fitting conclusion to this story of his life in the West.

Appendix A

THE LUMBER INDUSTRY IN NINETEENTH CENTURY AMERICA

TABLE 1 *
The Six Most Important Manufacturing Industries, 1860 and 1870

	Capital		Value of Product	
	1860	1870	1860	1870
Flour milling	$84,585,004	$151,565,376	$248,580,365	$444,985,143
Lumber (sawed and planed)	76,642,890	161,500,273	104,928,342	252,339,029
Iron (pig, cast, forged and rolled)	72,384,140	163,009,661	94,045,452	274,156,678
Cotton goods	93,143,759	140,621,092	107,337,783	177,183,570
Boots and shoes	23,357,627	48,994,366	91,889,298	181,644,090
Clothing	28,707,243	53,653,598	88,095,363	140,621,092

* Compiled from U. S., Census Office, *Manufactures of the United States in 1860* (Washington, 1865), *Ninth Census of the United States: 1870,* Vol. III, *Industry and Wealth* (Washington, 1872).

TABLE 2 *

Relative Importance of Lumber-Producing States, 1840–1900

Census Year	United States	States in Order of Importance by Value of Product (1840–1870) and Lumber Sawed (1870–1900)				
1840	$12,943,507	New York $3,891,302	Maine $1,808,683	Pennsylvania $1,150,220	Virginia $538,092	South Carolina $537,684
1850	$58,521,976	New York $13,126,759	Pennsylvania $7,729,058	Maine $5,872,573	Ohio $3,864,452	Michigan $2,464,329
1860	$93,338,606	Pennsylvania $10,743,752	New York $9,710,945	Michigan $7,040,190	Maine $6,598,565	Ohio $5,158,076
1870	$209,852,527	Michigan $31,946,396	Pennsylvania $28,938,985	New York $21,238,228	Wisconsin $15,130,719	Indiana $12,324,755
	12,755,543 M ft.	2,251,613 M ft.	1,629,631 M ft.	1,310,066 M ft.	1,098,199 M ft.	656,400 M ft.
1880	18,125,432 M ft.	Michigan 4,178,610 M ft.	Pennsylvania 1,734,170 M ft.	Wisconsin 1,542,021 M ft.	New York 1,185,223 M ft.	Indiana 717,900 M ft.
1890	27,038,734 M ft.	Michigan 5,478,358 M ft.	Wisconsin 3,182,029 M ft.	Pennsylvania 2,439,993 M ft.	Minnesota 1,309,887 M ft.	Washington 1,160,023 M ft.
1900	35,077,595 M ft.	Wisconsin 3,389,166 M ft.	Michigan 3,018,338 M ft.	Minnesota 2,342,338 M ft.	Pennsylvania 2,333,278 M ft.	Arkansas 1,680,536 M ft.

* Compiled from Henry B. Steer, *Lumber Production in the United States, 1799–1946*, U.S. Dept. of Agriculture Misc. Pub. No. 669 (Washington, 1948), p. 11. Value of product figures for 1870 have been added from U.S., Census Office, *Ninth Census of the United States: 1870*, Vol. III, *Industry and Wealth*. Figures on physical output are not available for the years prior to 1870, but since this is a more reliable indicator it has been employed as the basis for ranking the states from 1870 through 1900. To facilitate comparisons between the first three census years and the last four, both dollar value of product and physical output are shown for the year 1870.

A Note on Lumber Industry Historiography

Considering the importance of lumbering in nineteenth-century America, remarkably little work has been done on the history of the industry. Aside from such popularizations as Stewart Holbrook's *Holy Old Mackinaw* (New York, 1938), the only attempt to survey the national picture is James E. Defebaugh's two-volume *History of the Lumber Industry in America* (Chicago, 1906–1907). Written by the editor of *The American Lumberman* (an industry periodical), it fails to satisfy many of the requirements of modern scholarship, and carries the story of the industry's westward expansion no further than Pennsylvania. It may be supplemented by George W. Hotchkiss, *History of the Lumber and Forest Industry in the Northwest* (Chicago, 1898), but this, too, is an example of amateur historiography, and is indeed little more than a bulky collection of notes on individual lumbermen and particular localities.

The number of monographs on the industry has grown steadily in recent years, however, and should in time make possible a comprehensive history of lumbering meeting the needs of the student of economic history. Three state studies head the list: Richard G. Wood, *A History of Lumbering in Maine, 1820–1861* (Orono, Maine, 1935); Robert F. Fries, *Empire in Pine: The Story of Lumbering in Wisconsin* (Madison, 1951); Agnes M. Larson, *A History of the White Pine Industry in Minnesota* (Minneapolis, 1949). Three other volumes give more information on the Wisconsin picture: Paul W. Gates, *The Wisconsin Pine Lands of Cornell University* (Ithaca, 1943), Richard N. Current, *Pine Logs and Politics: A Life of Philetus Sawyer, 1816–1900* (Madison, 1950), A. R. Reynolds, *The Daniel Shaw Lumber Co.* (New York, 1957). William G. Rector, *Log Transportation in the Lake States Lumber Industry, 1840–1918* (Glendale, California, 1953) is a detailed study of one aspect of the industry, but provides much general information and contains an excellent bibliography.

The Michigan story, however, remains untold. Perhaps the best of the brief discussions on lumbering in general histories of the state is in George N. Fuller, editor, *Michigan: A Centennial History of the State and Its People* (Chicago, 1939), Vol. I, chap. 27. Ormund S. Danford, "The Social and Economic Effects of Lumbering on Michigan, 1835–1890," *Michigan History*, XXVI (Summer, 1942), 346–59, is interesting, but disappointingly general. As usual, local histories offer sketches of individual lumbermen and lumber concerns, but they should only be used with extreme caution, if we may judge by the number of inaccuracies in their accounts of Crapo's career. An article by Walter Buell, "The Michigan Lumber Industry as Told in Sketches of Some of Its Leading Men," *Magazine of Western History*, IV (September, 1886), 712–17, V (November, 1886), 126–39, is of a similar nature. Two unpublished Master's theses at Wayne State University, Charles J. Wolfe, "Hannah, Lay and Company, a Study in Michigan's Lumber Industry" (1938) and Lloyd M. Atwood, "Cheboygan as a Nineteenth-Century Lumber Area" (1947), appear to be the only detailed treatments of aspects of Michigan lumbering apart from the present study.

Appendix B

THE CRAPO MANUSCRIPTS

1. Description and Evaluation

The principal source for this study has been the Crapo Manuscripts in the Michigan Historical Collections at the University of Michigan. The materials comprise thirty-five boxes of letters, notes, clippings, receipts, and other papers, together with a large number of letter press books, diaries, and memorandum books. Chronologically, they range from the 1820's through the end of the century. Although they center on Crapo's Michigan career as a lumberman and politician between 1855 and 1869, they also include fragmentary records of his earlier years in Massachusetts, correspondence relating to his activities as a land speculator and land dealer in the early 1850's, and papers pertaining to certain western business affairs of his son William in the years after the elder Crapo's death in 1869.

The heart of the collection is the series of nearly one thousand letters from Crapo in Michigan to his son in New Bedford.

There are a few letters written between 1853 and 1855 during his western trips to look after his land interests, but the correspondence begins in earnest in December, 1855, when he arrived in Michigan to take charge of the newly-purchased Driggs pine land tract. At first he made frequent trips back East and could report in person to his son and his partners on the progress of the lumber venture; during this period, therefore, the story told in the letters has many gaps. From March, 1858, on, however, when he moved permanently to Flint, the correspondence provides a running account of his experiences and problems as a lumberman. The letters continue virtually without interruption until his death, although after 1863 details of the lumber business receive less attention, due to his increasing involvement in railroading and politics. The letters to William are supplemented by his correspondence between 1865 and 1868 with his son-in-law, H. H. H. C. Smith, who was the manager of his Detroit lumber yard.

The letter press books, containing copies of letters written by Crapo from New Bedford between July, 1853 and March, 1858 provide some of the background to the pine land purchase and details of the early years of the lumber enterprise but deal in the main with his western landholdings. The value of the diaries is generally limited to tracing his travels, but the memorandum books which he kept after his arrival in Michigan contain a wide variety of miscellaneous information about the lumber business.

If the collection has a weakness as the record of a business enterprise, it is in the lack of systematic financial records, with the exception of summary accounts covering operations between 1857 and 1860. This shortcoming, however, is more than compensated for by the vivid and detailed descriptive material in the letters, which affords an insight into the lumberman's problems far greater than could ever be derived from the most complete set of account books.

The value of the Crapo Manuscripts is not limited to telling Crapo's own story. Much interesting and significant material which was not germane to the present study has necessarily been omitted here. The collection is a primary source of considerable importance for the history of economic and even social conditions in Michigan in the 1850's and 1860's, and it is hoped that much use will be made of it in the future.

Whittemore Lake, 10 miles N. of Ann Arbor
In a "one horse" Whiskey tavern, with a stub of a tallow
candle & the accompaniment of such a place — with the
Bar-room counter for a desk — 9 O'clock in the
Evening, Jany. 4th 1859

Wm. W. Crapo,

My Dr. son, I have just arrived here & just
finished my supper, on a general tour of observation, &c
Left home last Friday since which I have canvassed a
large territory. Have driven my horse nearly 50 miles
to day & have left my cards & hand bills at every suitable
place. Find every one wants lumber but none can buy
for want of means. But the time will come when
all the Mills at Flint will be unable to supply the
demand here. As I shall not reach home in several
days I write this that you may not think
my long silence is occasioned by indolence.
Tell ___ now that I am not idle. In fact what with
getting in logs — looking after the yard at Flint —
keeping things straight at Fentonville — seeing to
some 20 teams hauling lumber to the R.R. to go E.
in the spring — trying to sell lumber in this region
— attending to my correspondence — financiering
to get money to keep along — & now making
an effort to haul lumber to Ann Arbor, — you
must make allowances if your letters are not
answered by return of mail. My own team went
past here at 2 O'clock this p. m., with lumber for
Ann Arbor, & to morrow I expect to move lumber for

Facsimile Letter of H. H. Crapo, January 4, 1859

2. Selected Documents from the Manuscripts

a. ESTIMATE OF THE VALUE OF THE PINE LANDS OF WM. S. DRIGGS ON FLINT RIVER IN LAPEER COUNTY, MICH.

[This statement was an enclosure to a letter written to Crapo in New Bedford by William S. Driggs of Detroit, December 15, 1854, and may be found in Box 16.]

Supposing the quantity to be but 200 millions of feet. The following is the value of 1,000 feet as the average product of the Land.

1st Clear	25 pct	average price at Chicago			$29	$7.25
2nd do	20 "	do	do	do	22	5.50
Select Box	5 "	do	do	do	20	1.00
Common	40 "	do	do	do	15.50	6.20
Culls	10 "	do	do	do	11	1.10

Average value of 1,000 feet in Chicago $21.05

From the above deduct as follows:

Cost of cutting & running Logs to Saginaw	$2.00	
Cost of manufacturing into lumber including Interest on investment, wear of mill, labor, insurance, etc.	2.00	
Transportation to Chicago	3.50	
Comˢ· on sale & other incidental expenses	1.50	9.00

Nett product or profit of each 1000 feet $12.05

From this deduct for other possible contingencies such as fluctuation in market value, other costs and waste not foreseen 25 per cent   say per thousand   3.05

Nett profit over all contingencies $9.00

This on an estimate of 200 million amounts to $1,800,000 as the present value of the pine timber as it stands. The above estimate is made from the Published reports of the Chicago lumber market as per the newspapers of that city of April last. And the same prices have been maintained until the present time.

b. SUMMARY BY H. H. CRAPO OF PROBABLE RECEIPTS AND EXPENDITURES AND OF THE FINAL PROFITS

[This document, in Crapo's own hand, was prepared during the negotiations which led to the purchase of the Driggs tract in December, 1855, and may be found in Box 15, "Lapeer Pine Lands folder 1." The schedules B, D, and E referred to have apparently not been preserved.]

By Schedule B it is shown that the quantity of
   Pine on the Wm. S. Driggs tract is   426,859,672 ft.
But for safety, in our estimates we say there is   300,000,000 ft.

By Schedules D and E it is shown that the net
   value of lumber on the stump is $10 per M.
But for safety in our estimates we say only one-
   half this sum $5 per M.

It is proposed to convert into lumber 10,000,000
   ft. per annum after the first year, which at the
   reduced estimate of $5 is $50,000

If from this we deduct:
   7% interest on the entire cost of $150,000 $10,500
   Compensation & board & traveling expenses
      of H. H. Crapo   6,000
   Taxes, say   1,000
   And all other possible contingencies   2,500   20,000

And we have for net profits per annum $30,000

This clear annual profit of $30,000 would in 5 yrs. repay the
   original investment of $150,000, with Int. thereon at 7%:

10,000,000 ft. of lumber per year for 5 years, taken
   from the lot would make   50,000,000

This would leave upon the land at the end of that
period 250,000,000 ft. of lumber, and the land itself, which 250,000,000 ft. at $5 per M. is $1,250,000

The land, viz., 12,107-78/100 acres, at $5 per acre, a
fair price exclusive of the Pine Timber upon it, is   60,535

Net profits over all costs $1,310,535

NOTE: As the present season for lumbering will be somewhat
advanced, the receipts for the first year must necessarily fall
below the foregoing estimate of annual receipts, although it is
hoped that five million feet of logs may be taken off and landed
upon the banks of the river in time for being floated down in the
spring.

This deficit in the present winter's operation will render it
necessary that the first payment of semi-annual interest and also
a part of the interest and the payment of $75,000 due in Janu-
ary, 1857, will have to be raised from some other source than
from the receipts of lumber for the present year.

It will also be necessary to advance a small sum—say $2000
—with which to pay for cutting and logging this winter.

NOTE: The sum of $3000 at 6% commission, say $3000 more,
equal $6000, is certainly no more than a fair compensation for
services, board, traveling expenses, risk of health in a new and
unsettled country, and of accidents in traveling, etc., etc. The
expenses of traveling will comprise RR and other fare to and
from Michigan some four or five times in the course of the year,
also from the land to and from Saginaw a great number of times
to make contracts for sawing, selling logs, selling lumber, shipping lumber to Chicago, and other places, and engaging freight
for lumber; and also from the land and from here to Chicago
and to other places to sell lumber, engage freight, make collections, etc., etc., and also in riding about the country to hire men,
etc., etc.

C. SALES OF LUMBER FROM FEBRUARY 26, 1857, TO DECEMBER 1, 1859

[This is a condensation of Statement B, Accounts, 1857–1859, "Recapitulation of Sales of Lumber from February 26, 1857, to December 1, 1859." The totals differ from those appearing in the text, Chapter V, in that this statement does not include sales of lumber at Crapo's Fentonville yard and certain other minor items. The average prices received are either the prices at Flint or the net prices at Flint after deducting charges for transportation on lumber sold for delivery elsewhere.]

Quantity (Board Feet)	Grade	Average Price Per M Feet	Amount
293,586	Clear Lumber	$ 18.77	$ 5,512.85
388,440	2d Rate	13.02	5,057.21
85,535	Box	10.61	908.02
2,158,848	Common	6.46	14,948.93
255,991	Cull	4.58	1,171.59
375,266	Clear Siding	11.42	4,285.37
104,589	2d Rate	9.89	1,035.29
75,728	Common	7.31	553.81
16,334	Cull	4.42	72.29
266,606	Fencing	7.84	2,091.16
18,702	Clear Dressed Lumber	19.35	361.99
108,689	2d Rate	15.03	1,633.86
277,706	Common	10.62	2,951.05
14,794	Clear Dressed Siding	15.36	227.27
19,179	2d Rate	11.45	222.01
3,036	Common	9.38	28.48
20,611	Pickets	14.25	293.76
14,763	Oak	10.19	150.41
4,498,403	TOTAL		$41,506.35
273,387	Lath		1,268.37
1,136½ M	Shingles		1,948.53

NOTES

Unless otherwise stated, all manuscript material cited is located in the Crapo Manuscripts at the Michigan Historical Collections, Ann Arbor, Michigan. It is quoted with a minimum of changes in the spelling, punctuation and capitalization.

ABBREVIATIONS: HHC – Henry H. Crapo
WWC – William W. Crapo
NB   – New Bedford
LPB   – Letter Press Book

INTRODUCTION

1 *The Pine Lands and Lumber Trade of Michigan, Exhibiting the Extent, Quality and Advantages, Compiled from Official Sources, By an Old Resident of the State* (Detroit, 1856), pp. 9–10. This interesting pamphlet is in the University of Michigan Library.

2 *Detroit Daily Tribune,* Sept. 30, 1857.

CHAPTER ONE

1 The account of Crapo's years in Massachusetts is based on Henry Howland Crapo [II], *The Story of Henry Howland Crapo, 1804–1869* (Boston, 1933). This privately-published work by Crapo's grandson (cited hereafter as Crapo, *Crapo*) offers an unusually vivid and stimulating account of his life, although it is largely in the form of a family reminiscence.

2 HHC to WWC, Mar. 22, 1849, quoted in Crapo, *Crapo,* pp. 88–89.

3 HHC, Flint to WWC, NB, Oct. 3, 1865; Crapo, *Crapo,* pp. 61–64, gives the story of this purchase, but is in error as to the amount of the profit.

4 HHC, NB to William S. Driggs, Detroit, Feb. 23, 1854, in LPB 1.

5 HHC, NB to William S. Driggs, Detroit, Nov. 29, 1854, in LPB 3.

6 HHC, NB to William S. Driggs, Detroit, Dec. 11, 1854, in LPB 3.

7 William W. Crapo's own account of the trip is given in Crapo, *Crapo,* pp. 118–21.

8 For the account of Edson's visit, see HHC, NB to William S. Driggs, Detroit, Nov. 26, 1855, in LPB 4. Unfortunately, nothing more is known about Mr. Edson.

9 HHC, NB to William S. Driggs, Detroit, Nov. 26, 1855, in LPB 4. This version of Crapo's involvement in the Driggs purchase differs in several important particulars from that given in Crapo, *Crapo,* p. 122, which is based on the recollections of his son William. Though William said his father participated at the urging of Arnold, it appears clear from the letters that the initiative came from Crapo himself and that he persuaded Arnold to back the venture.

10 HHC, NB to William S. Driggs, Detroit, Dec. 12, 1855, in LPB 4. The actual terms of payment were modified slightly by both sides, and the final arrangement was accepted by Crapo in his letter to Driggs of Dec. 21, 1855, in LPB 4.

11 Crapo, *Crapo,* p. 122.

12 William S. Driggs, Detroit to HHC, NB, Dec. 15, 18, 1855.

13 HHC, Detroit to WWC, NB, Dec. 29, 1855.

14 HHC, Lapeer to WWC, NB, Dec. 31, 1855.

15 HHC, Pierson's Mills, Mich., to WWC, NB, Jan. 3, 1856.

16 Pencil draft of letter, HHC, East Saginaw to William S. Driggs, Detroit, Jan. 5, 1856, Box 15, Crapo MSS. (The actual date appearing on this draft is July 5, 1855. However, Crapo was prone to misdate letters written early in the new year, and it is clear from other evidence, including Driggs' reply, that this letter was actually written on the date given here.) The $7,000 note was one of several falling due on Jan. 1, 1858; at Driggs' request the payments due were in several cases divided into separate smaller notes for his convenience should he find it necessary to discount them in advance of maturity.

17 William S. Driggs, Detroit to HHC, Lapeer, Jan. 10, 1856.

18 HHC, Marathon to WWC, NB, Jan. 11, 1856.

CHAPTER TWO

1 LPB 4, 5, 6, *passim.*

2 The three separate purchases which accounted for this total are detailed in Crapo's Memorandum Book, 1855–1856, p. 57, and letters, HHC, NB to William S. Driggs, Detroit, Mar. 11, 19, 22, Apr. 19, 1856, in LPB 5.

3 HHC, NB to William S. Driggs, Detroit, Mar. 19, 1856, in LPB 5.

4 Notes on the conversations appear in his Memorandum Book, 1855–1856.

5 Notes on conversation with William Final, Jan. 5, 1856, in Memorandum Book, 1855–1856, p. 34.

6 E. H. Thompson, "The City of Flint," *Michigan Pioneer and Historical Collections*, III (1881), 435, 456; pamphlet, *Saginaw Weekly Enterprise—Extra: The Saginaw Valley: Its Salt, Lumber and Other Resources* (Saginaw, 1863), p. 15.

7 Memorandum Book, 1855–1856, *passim*.

8 HHC, NB to William M. Fenton, Flint, Aug. 20, 1856; HHC, NB to Noah T. Hart, Lapeer, Aug. 25, 1856; HHC, NB to James Arnold, Crawford House, N.H., Sept. 4, 1856, in LPB 6.

9 HHC, NB to Durfee & Atwater, Buffalo, N.Y., Apr. 4, 1856; HHC, NB to G. G. Dorr, East Saginaw, Apr. 4, 1856, in LPB 5. A month later another offer was turned down in similar terms. HHC, NB to James Seymour, Flushing, Mich., May 2, 1856, in LPB 5.

10 Memorandum Book, 1855–1856.

11 HHC, NB to William M. Fenton, Flint, July 9, 21, 1856, in LPB 5, Aug. 20, 1856, in LPB 6.

12 HHC, NB to Titus Merritt, Ionia, Mich., July 22, 1856, in LPB 5.

13 HHC, NB to James Arnold, Crawford House, N.H., Sept. 4, 1856, in LPB 6; Diary, 1854–1858.

14 Agreement, Jan. 14, 1856, with James Robertson, Marathon, to build "a store building"; letters, James Robertson, Marathon, to HHC, NB, July 5, Aug. 5, 1856; six letters, HHC, NB to various Michigan men regarding logging contracts, July 22, 23, 1856, in LPB 5; HHC, NB to William Final, East Saginaw, Sept. 6, 1856; HHC, NB to Charles E. Colburn, East Dixfield, Maine, Nov. 25, 1856, in LPB 6.

15 HHC, NB to Eddy, Murphy & Co., Bangor, Maine, Sept. 16, 1856, in LPB 6.

16 Accounts, 1857–1859, Statement F. The Accounts are found in Boxes 15 and 28, Crapo MSS.

17 HHC, NB to Charles E. Colburn, East Dixfield, Maine, Nov. 25, 1856, in LPB 6; Memorandum Book, 1856–1857.

18 HHC, NB to W. L. Gee, Flint, Apr. 21, 30, May 13, 1857, in LPB 6.

19 HHC, NB to McQuigg, Turner & Co., Flint, Jan. 22, 1857, in LPB 6.

20 HHC, NB to Charles Harthan, Nearic, Maine, July 1, 1857; HHC, NB to W. L. Gee, Flint, July 1, 1857, in LPB 6; Accounts, 1857–1859, Statement M, "Mill Property Account."

CHAPTER THREE

1 Memorandum Book, 1855–1856, *passim*.

2 HHC, NB to W. L. Gee, Flint, May 13, 1857, in LPB 6.

3 HHC, NB to Charles Harthan, Marathon, Dec. 5, 1857, in LPB 6.

4 HHC, Flint to WWC, NB, Nov. 5, Dec. 21, 1857, Mar. 31, 1858.

5 HHC, NB to George W. Burrell, Flint, Aug. 25, 1857, in LPB 6.

6 HHC, Flint to WWC, NB, Sept. 13, 1857.

7 HHC, Detroit, proposal "To the Pres't. and Directors of the Detroit & Milwaukee R. Road," Sept. 19, 1857.

8 HHC, Flint to WWC, NB, Nov. 5, Dec. 30, 1857, Jan. 4, 1858.

9 HHC, Flint to WWC, NB, Dec. 24, 1857.

10 Accounts, 1857–1859, Statements N, O, W; HHC, Flint to WWC, NB, Sept. 13, 1857.

11 HHC, NB to W. L. Gee, Flint, Nov. 25, 27, 1857, in LPB 6.

12 HHC, Flint to WWC, NB, Dec. 26, 1857, Jan. 11, 1858.

13 HHC, Flint to WWC, NB, Dec. 21, 1857.

14 HHC, Flint to WWC, NB, Dec. 22, 26, 1857, Jan. 11, 1858.

15 HHC, Flint to WWC, NB, Jan. 4, 28, 1858; Accounts, 1857–1859, Statements N, O, W.

16 HHC, NB to David Crapo, Odessa, Mich., Feb. 6, 1856, in LPB 4.

17 HHC, Flint to WWC, NB, Jan. 11, 15, 26, 1858.

18 HHC, Flint to WWC, NB, Jan. 15, 1858.

19 HHC, Flint to WWC, NB, Dec. 22, 24, 26, 30, 1857, Jan. 28, Mar. 28, 1858.

CHAPTER FOUR

1 HHC, Flint to WWC, NB, Mar. 28, 31, 1858.

2 HHC, Flint to WWC, NB, Apr. 12, 1858.

3 HHC, en route Fentonville to Detroit to WWC, NB, Apr. 22, 1858; HHC, Flint to WWC, NB, Apr. 30, 1858.

4 HHC, Flint to WWC, NB, Apr. 11, 14, 1858; HHC, en route Fentonville to Detroit to WWC, NB, Apr. 22, 1858; HHC, en route Detroit to Fentonville to WWC, NB, Apr. 22, 1858.

5 HHC, Flint to WWC, NB, Apr. 19, July 18, 1858.

6 HHC, Flint to WWC, NB, May 25, 1858.

7 HHC, Flint to WWC, NB, Apr. 14, May 17, 20, Aug. 9, Nov. 12, 29, 1858.

8 HHC, Detroit to WWC, NB, June 14, 1858; HHC, Flint to WWC, NB, Dec. 26, 1858, Mar. 27, 1859; Accounts, 1857–1859, Statement F.

9 HHC, Flint to WWC, NB, Jan. 16, Apr. 5, 17, May 29, 1859.

10 Accounts, 1857–1859, Statement B.

11 HHC, Flint to WWC, NB, Dec. 21, 1857, Jan. 25, 1858.

12 HHC, Flint to WWC, NB, Feb. 6, 10, 13, 16, Oct. 10, 1858.

13 HHC, Flint to WWC, NB, Oct. 14, 1858, Jan. 14, 27, Feb. 2, 1859.

[14] HHC, Flint to WWC, NB, Apr. 3, 5, 1858.

[15] HHC, Flint to WWC, NB, May 25, 1858.

[16] HHC, Flint to WWC, NB, July 23, 29, 1858.

[17] HHC, Flint to WWC, NB, May 9, July 19, Oct. 14, Nov. 4, 1858.

[18] HHC, Flint to WWC, NB, Oct. 10, Nov. 4, 1858, Jan. 14, 27, May 29, 1859.

[19] HHC, Flint to WWC, NB, Feb. 26, May 15, 1859.

[20] HHC, Flint to WWC, NB, Apr. 26, June 10, 1859.

[21] HHC, Flint to WWC, NB, Jan. 14, Feb. 26, 1859; HHC, Albany to WWC, NB, June 26, 1859.

[22] HHC, Flint to WWC, NB, May 29, 30, 1859; HHC, Detroit to WWC, NB, June 20, 1859; HHC, Chicago to WWC, NB, June 21, 1859; HHC, Cincinnati to WWC, NB, June 22, 23, 1859.

[23] HHC, Albany to WWC, NB, June 26, 1859.

[24] HHC, Flint to WWC, NB, July 3, 24, Aug. 13, 1859.

[25] HHC, Flint to WWC, NB, July 24, 26, Aug. 13, 16, 25, 1859.

[26] HHC, Flint to WWC, NB, Jan. 14, July 24, Aug. 13, 1859.

[27] HHC, Flint to WWC, NB, Mar. 20, 27, Apr. 12, May 1, Aug. 14, Sept. 21, 1859.

[28] HHC, Flint to WWC, NB, May 21, 1859.

[29] HHC, Flint to WWC, NB, July 26, Aug. 13, 25, Sept. 21, Oct. 7, 1859.

[30] HHC, Flint to WWC, NB, Oct. 7, 1859.

[31] HHC, Flint to WWC, NB, Oct. 5, 7, Dec. 13, 17, 1859, Jan. 7, 1860.

CHAPTER FIVE

[1] HHC, Flint to WWC, NB, May 17, July 3, 1859.

[2] HHC, Flint to WWC, NB, May 29, June 10, July 24, 1859.

[3] HHC, Flint to WWC, NB, Nov. 8, 1859, transmitting letter to Arnold and Prescott.

[4] HHC, Flint to James Arnold and Oliver Prescott, NB, Feb. 25, 1860.

[5] HHC, Flint to James Arnold and Oliver Prescott, NB, Mar. 3, 1860.

[6] HHC, Flint to WWC, NB, Dec. 17, 1859.

[7] HHC, Flint to WWC, NB, Dec. 26, 1859, Jan. 12, 25, 29, 31, Feb. 6, 12, 1860; HHC, Fentonville to WWC, NB, Jan. 3, 1860; Accounts, 1857–1859.

[8] HHC, Flint to James Arnold and Oliver Prescott, NB, Mar. 3, 1860; Accounts, 1857–1859. Because of the involved character of Crapo's accounts, it is not feasible to make specific citations for the details of this summary of the firm's operations. In some cases it has been neces-

sary to make estimates for figures not specifically given in the manuscript accounts.

9 Accounts of the Driggs Land Purchase, Box 28, Crapo MSS. The 1860 figure given in the text does not appear in these accounts, but is an extension of the figures given in them with interest compounded semi-annually. For no apparent reason the interest for 1857 was figured on an annual rather than a semi-annual basis, as was the case for 1856 and 1858. On $50,000 of the cost of the lands, the rate of interest was 10 per cent instead of 7, since the former figure had been the rate payable on the $50,000 loan to Driggs which Arnold had assumed as part of the purchase price.

10 HHC, Flint to WWC, NB, Mar. 14, 1860. Various alternative settlements are discussed in this letter and in HHC, Flint to Oliver Prescott, NB, Mar. 25, 1860.

11 WWC, NB to HHC, Flint, Mar. 28, 1860; HHC, Flint to WWC, NB, Apr. 1, 1860.

12 WWC, NB to HHC, Flint, Mar. 28, 1860.

13 HHC, Flint to WWC, NB, May 18, 25, July 1, 1860.

14 For comment on the value of the Driggs tract, see HHC, Flint to WWC, NB, July 1, 1860, and HHC, Flint to James Arnold, NB, July 16, 1860. Other letters pertaining to the negotiations are HHC, Flint to WWC, NB, May 27, July 7, 17, 31, Aug. 3, 4, 5, 9, 11, 17, 28, 1860, and WWC, NB to HHC, Flint, Aug. 1, 5, 1860. The supplementary agreement between Arnold, Prescott, and Crapo, dated Aug. 22, 1860, is also found in the Crapo MSS.

15 WWC, NB to HHC, Flint, Aug. 5, 1860.

CHAPTER SIX

1 HHC, Flint to WWC, NB, May 27, Sept. 9, Dec. 23, 1860.

2 HHC, Flint to WWC, NB, Jan. 12, 15, Apr. 26, May 27, 1860.

3 HHC, Flint to James Arnold, NB, July 16, 1860.

4 HHC, Flint to WWC, NB, Apr. 29, May 6, 13, 27, 29, June 7, 1860.

5 HHC, Flint to WWC, NB, June 3, July 1, Aug. 3, 5, 20, 23, Sept. 5, 9, 1860.

6 HHC, Flint to WWC, NB, Oct. 5, 16, 25, Nov. 13, 1860.

7 E. D. Fite, *Social and Industrial Conditions in the North During the Civil War* (New York, 1910), pp. 107–11. The *Tribune* quotation is from the issue of Mar. 23, 1861.

8 HHC, Flint to WWC, NB, Nov. 25, Dec. 23, 1860.

9 HHC, NB to WWC, Jackson, Mich., Sept. 19, Oct. 2, 1855; HHC, NB to Joseph R. Williams, Toledo, Ohio, Oct. 27, 1855, in LPB 4; HHC, NB to P. W. Norris, Pioneer, Ohio, Sept. 13, 1856, in LPB 6.

[10] HHC, Flint to WWC, NB, Apr. 5, 26, May 6, 1860.

[11] HHC, Flint to WWC, NB, Dec. 14, 23, 1860.

[12] HHC, Flint to WWC, NB, Feb. 19, 1861.

[13] HHC, Flint to WWC, NB, Apr. 9, 25, May 23, 1861.

[14] HHC, Flint to WWC, NB, Dec. 23, 1860.

[15] HHC, Flint to WWC, NB, Apr. 9, 14, 1861.

[16] HHC, Flint to WWC, NB, Nov. 25, 1860; Fite, *op. cit.,* pp. 110–17.

[17] HHC, Flint to WWC, NB, May 12, 1861; HHC, Flint to Oliver Prescott, NB, Nov. 23, 1861.

[18] HHC, Flint to WWC, NB, May 6, 12, June 26, 1861.

[19] HHC, Flint to WWC, NB, June 30, 1861.

[20] HHC, Flint to WWC, NB, Feb. 2, 1861.

[21] HHC, Flint to WWC, NB, June 30, 1858, Feb. 1, 1862; HHC, Detroit to WWC, NB, Feb. 12, 1861; HHC, Lansing to WWC, NB, Feb. 4, 1863.

[22] HHC, Flint to WWC, NB, Feb. 8, 1861. We may also note Crapo's comment a year later: "I lose some teams to McFarlin" because of the price difference, "although many go there and examine, and then come back and take my lumber, on account of its superior manufacture, being smooth and of uniform thickness."—HHC, Flint to WWC, NB, Feb. 1, 1862.

[23] HHC, Detroit to WWC, NB, Feb. 19, 1861; HHC, Flint to WWC, NB, Mar. 24, May 12, June 26, 30, Aug. 12, 24, Oct. 21, Nov. 20, 1861, Jan. 19, 1862; HHC, Flint to Oliver Prescott, NB, Nov. 23, 1861.

[24] HHC, Flint to Oliver Prescott, NB, Nov. 23, 1861.

CHAPTER SEVEN

[1] Fite, *op. cit.,* p. 106; George W. Hotchkiss, *History of the Lumber and Forest Industry in the Northwest* (Chicago, 1898), pp. 678–79.

[2] HHC, Flint to WWC, NB, June 29, Nov. 23, 1862.

[3] Hotchkiss, *op. cit.,* p. 684.

[4] [Michael A. Leeson], *History of Saginaw County, Michigan* (Chicago, 1881), p. 412; *Detroit Free Press,* Feb. 14, 1864.

[5] HHC, Flint to WWC, NB, Nov. 9, 1862.

[6] HHC, Flint to WWC, NB, Nov. 17, 23, 1862; HHC, Lansing to WWC, NB, Jan. 25, 1863.

[7] HHC, Lansing to WWC, NB, Feb. 24, 1863; HHC, Flint to WWC, NB, Mar. 20, Apr. 16, May 3, 1863.

[8] HHC, Lansing to WWC, NB, Jan. 15, 1863; HHC, Flint to WWC, NB, Mar. 20, Apr. 8, May 21, June 17, 25, 30, Aug. 13, 1863.

9 HHC, Lansing to WWC, NB, Jan. 25, 1863; HHC, Flint to WWC, NB, Dec. 28, 1862, Feb. 4, Mar. 20, Apr. 6, 16, May 3, June 28, 1863.

10 HHC, Flint to WWC, NB, Apr. 6, June 28, Aug. 13, Sept. 11, 1863.

11 HHC, Flint to WWC, NB, Nov. 22, 1863.

12 HHC, Flint to WWC, NB, June 30, 1861.

13 HHC, Flint to WWC, NB, June 28, July 2, Sept. 28, Oct. 7, 1863.

14 HHC, Flint to WWC, NB, Sept. 11, Oct. 19, Nov. 9, 17, 1862.

15 HHC, Lansing to WWC, NB, Mar. 15, 1863; HHC, Flint to WWC, NB, Apr. 23, May 17, 24, June 24, 1863.

16 *Wolverine Citizen* (Flint), Dec. 13, 1862.

17 HHC, Flint to WWC, NB, Nov. 9, 1862, Feb. 4, 1863.

18 HHC, Flint to WWC, NB, Nov. 9, 1862.

19 HHC, Flint to WWC, NB, Dec. 17, 1862.

20 *Wolverine Citizen,* Feb. 15, 1862; HHC, Flint to WWC, NB, May 13, 1863.

21 *Wolverine Citizen,* Jan. 10, 1863; HHC, Flint to WWC, NB, Dec. 17, 1862, Jan. 4, 1863; HHC, Lansing to WWC, NB, Jan. 9, 1863.

22 Prospectus, printed letter signed Henry H. Crapo, Flint, Mich., Mar. 10, 1863, in the Crapo MSS.

23 HHC, Flint to W. C. Durant, Boston, Apr. 22, 1863; HHC, Flint to WWC, NB, Apr. 20, May 3, 7, 17, 1863.

24 *Wolverine Citizen,* June 6, 1863; HHC, Flint to WWC, NB, Apr. 23, 29, May 13, 16, June 8, 20, 1863.

25 HHC, Flint to WWC, NB, May 8, 26, June 20, 27, 28, 1863.

26 HHC, Flint to WWC, NB, June 17, 19, July 2, Aug. 17, 1863.

27 HHC, Flint to WWC, NB, July 2, Aug. 18, 22, Sept. 9, 1863.

28 HHC, Flint to WWC, NB, July 18, Sept. 11, 1862.

29 HHC, Flint to WWC, NB, Oct. 19, 1862.

30 HHC, Flint to WWC, NB, Nov. 10, 1862.

31 HHC, Flint to WWC, NB, Nov. 23, 1862.

32 HHC, Lansing to WWC, NB, Jan. 9, 13, 1863.

CHAPTER EIGHT

1 HHC, Lansing to WWC, NB, Jan. 13, 1863, Feb. 28, 1864.

2 HHC, Lansing to WWC, NB, Mar. 15, 1863.

3 George N. Fuller, ed., *Messages of the Governors of Michigan* (Lansing, 1926), II, 479–90: message of Jan. 19, 1864.

4 HHC, Flint to WWC, NB, Feb. 28, 1864; Michigan, *Acts, 1864.* Eleven new laws were passed and one from the 1863 session amended.

It is not known why Crapo referred in the passage quoted to nine railroads.

5 HHC, Flint to WWC, NB, Feb. 28, 1864.

6 Excerpt from a letter, J. E. Tenney to HHC, in HHC, Flint to WWC, NB, Feb. 28, 1864. Tenney, in addition to holding the librarianship (a patronage office), was editor of the *Marshall Statesman,* the paper with the largest circulation in central Michigan. In a later letter Crapo described him as the man "who has probably travelled more, and written more letters, and spent more time for me than any other man."—HHC, Flint to WWC, NB, June 26, 1864.

7 HHC, Flint to WWC, NB, Feb. 28, 1864.

8 *Ibid.*

9 HHC, Flint to WWC, NB, Mar. 13, 1864; *Saginaw Republican,* Mar. 17, 1864, clipping in the Crapo MSS.

10 Copy of letter, J. E. Tenney to HHC, Apr. 12, 1864, in HHC, Flint to WWC, NB, Apr. 25, 1864.

11 *Wolverine Citizen,* June 18, 1864.

12 HHC, Flint to WWC, NB, Apr. 25, May 5, June 26, 1864.

13 HHC, Detroit to WWC, NB, July 9, 1864; *Detroit Advertiser & Tribune,* July 8, 1864. Two ballots too many were recorded, but it was ruled that Crapo was properly elected, since, even had the two fraudulent votes been his, he would have had a majority of one.

14 HHC, Detroit to WWC, NB, July 9, 1864.

15 *Detroit Advertiser & Tribune,* July 8, 1864.

16 *Ibid.*

17 Charles S. May to Austin Blair, July 13, 1864, in Blair MSS, Burton Historical Collection, Detroit Public Library.

18 *Detroit Free Press,* July 8, 1864.

19 *Detroit Free Press,* July 10, 13, 1864.

20 Wilmer C. Harris, *The Public Life of Zachariah Chandler, 1851–1875* (Lansing, 1917), pp. 65–66.

21 HHC, Flint to WWC, NB, Oct. 19, 1862; Crapo, *Crapo,* p. 193.

22 *Detroit Advertiser & Tribune,* July 8, 22, 1864.

23 HHC, Adrian, Mich. to WWC, NB, Aug. 7, 1864.

24 HHC, Adrian to WWC, NB, Aug. 7, 1864; HHC, Flint to WWC, NB, Aug. 26, 1864.

25 *Detroit Free Press,* Sept. 28, 1864; HHC, Flint to WWC, NB, Sept. 8, 19, Nov. 20, 1864.

26 HHC, St. Johns, Mich. to WWC, NB, Sept. 30, 1864; manuscript draft of 1864 campaign speech, in Box 12, Crapo MSS.

27 HHC, Coldwater, Mich. to WWC, NB, Oct. 22, 1864; *Wolverine Citizen,* Oct., 1864, clipping in the Crapo MSS.

28 *Lansing State Republican,* Oct. 5, 1864, clipping in the Crapo MSS.

29 HHC, Flint to WWC, NB, Nov. 12, 20, 1864; *Detroit Advertiser & Tribune,* Dec. 22, 1864.

CHAPTER NINE

1 HHC, Lansing to WWC, NB, Jan. 13, 1865.

2 *Sturgis Journal,* Jan. 12, 1865, clipping in the Crapo MSS.

3 HHC, Flint to WWC, NB, Jan. 1, 8, 1865; HHC, Lansing to WWC, NB, Jan. 13, 1865. The letter of Jan. 8 bears the date of July 8, but internal evidence shows it to have been misdated by the writer.

4 Fuller, *op, cit.,* II, 523–45, message of Jan. 4, 1865.

5 *Detroit Free Press,* Jan. 7, 1865.

6 Michigan, *House Journal, 1865,* II, 1434–35; *Detroit Advertiser & Tribune,* Mar. 10, 1865. The veto, dated Mar. 7, 1865, is unaccountably missing from the compilation of governor's messages.

7 HHC, Lansing to WWC, NB, Feb. 5, 1865. The message referred to urged the enactment of conservation laws comparable with those of Canada protecting the fisheries in waters between the two nations.

8 HHC, Lansing to WWC, NB, Mar. 2, 1865.

9 HHC, Lansing to WWC, NB, Mar. 19, 1865.

10 *Detroit Advertiser & Tribune,* Mar. 24, 1865; H. H. H. C. Smith, Detroit to WWC, NB, Apr. 14, 1865.

11 HHC, Washington, D. C. to WWC, NB, July 2, 1865. Crapo's earlier visit to Washington is mentioned in HHC, Lansing to WWC, NB, Mar. 19, 1865; HHC, Flint to WWC, NB, Apr. 27, May 7, 1865. In October, discussing the claim again with McCulloch, Crapo reported that while he had not achieved everything he had wanted, he had nevertheless made enough progress to feel satisfied. HHC, Washington to WWC, NB, Oct. 19, 1865.

Crapo's efforts to secure the release from service of Michigan troops are revealed in HHC, Lansing to Edwin M. Stanton, Secretary of War, Washington, Aug. 17, Oct. 3, Dec. 8, 1865, May 11, 1866, and HHC, Lansing to Maj. Gen. P. H. Sheridan, Commanding Military Division of the Gulf, New Orleans, La., Jan. 23, 1866, in the Executive Journal in the Crapo MSS.

12 HHC, Flint to WWC, NB, Aug. 16, 1865.

13 HHC, Marquette, Mich. to WWC, NB, July 26, 28, 29, 1865; HHC, Flint to WWC, NB, Aug. 11, 16, 1865.

14 HHC, Flint to WWC, NB, Feb. 21, 1866.

15 *Detroit Advertiser & Tribune,* Feb. 2, 3, 8, 1865.

[16] HHC, Flint to WWC, NB, Apr. 8, 1866.

[17] *Detroit Free Press,* Apr. 6, 1866.

[18] *Ibid.*

[19] HHC, Flint to WWC, NB, Apr. 8, 1866.

[20] *Detroit Advertiser & Tribune,* Apr. 7, 1866; *Detroit Daily Post,* Apr. 6, 10, 1866.

[21] *Detroit Daily Post,* Apr. 9, 10, 1866.

[22] HHC, Flint to WWC, NB, June 7, 1866.

[23] *Detroit Advertiser & Tribune,* July 5, 1866.

[24] HHC, Flint to WWC, NB, July 7, 1866.

[25] *Detroit Advertiser & Tribune,* Feb. 29, 1868; *Detroit Daily Post,* Feb. 29, 1868; HHC, Flint to WWC, NB, Mar. 15, 1868.

CHAPTER TEN

[1] HHC, Flint to WWC, NB, July 9, 1864; HHC, Adrian to WWC, NB, Aug. 7, 1864.

[2] HHC, Flint to WWC, NB, Sept. 7, Nov. 14, Dec. 7, 12, 1863, Mar. 22, May 8, Nov. 12, 30, 1864. The letters preserved in the Crapo MSS include but a small portion of the correspondence which passed back and forth between Flint and New Bedford while the railroad was under construction. Crapo's grandson has written: "Acting under my father's direction, I destroyed a barrel of these letters about the railroad. It seems to me that those destroyed documents told the history of every meeting held, every shovelful of earth turned, every rail bought, every spike driven, and the application of every dollar subscribed for the stock."—Crapo, *Crapo,* p. 164.

[3] HHC, Flint to WWC, NB, Aug. 26, 1864.

[4] HHC, Flint to WWC, NB, Jan. 10, 13, 1864.

[5] HHC, Flint to WWC, NB, Oct. 14, 1863, June 10, 20, July 9, 1864; HHC, Detroit to WWC, NB, Nov. 1, 1864.

[6] HHC, Flint to WWC, NB, Apr. 1, 21, 1865; Flint & Holly Railroad Co., *Second Annual Report to the Stockholders, for the year ending Sept. 29, 1866* (Flint, 1866); annual report of the F. & H. R.R. to the State of Michigan, for the year ending Jan. 1, 1865, in Michigan, *Senate Journal, 1867,* I, 926–27; Michigan, Auditor General's Office, "Compilation of the Annual Reports of the Railroad Corporations in the State of Michigan for the year 1867," in Michigan, *Joint Documents, 1868,* pp. 57–60; "Compilation . . . 1868," in Michigan, *Joint Documents, 1869,* pp. 39–40. These compilations, although required under the General Railroad Act of 1859, do not appear to have been published prior to 1867.

[7] HHC, Lansing to WWC, NB, Jan. 7, 11, 13, 16, 22, 29, Feb. 18, 1865.

8 HHC, Flint to WWC, NB, Nov. 30, Dec. 12, 1864.

9 HHC, Flint to WWC, NB, Dec. 3, 12, 1864.

10 HHC, Lansing to WWC, NB, Mar. 18, 1865.

11 HHC, Holly to WWC, NB, Nov. 29, 1865.

12 HHC, Flint to WWC, NB, Nov. 7, 1866.

13 HHC, Flint to WWC, NB, Sept. 14, 26, 1867.

14 George C. Kimball, Supt. F. & H. R.R., Flint to WWC, NB, Sept. 6, 1867; HHC, Flint to WWC, NB, Nov. 12, Dec. 22, 1867, Jan. 12, 1868. Crapo was careful to specify that in the event of sale he should have secured to him "the privileges, etc. which I have earned and now enjoy on the F. & H. as some small compensation for my services and labor in building our road . . . the right of pass for myself and family, and to give them to particular persons under circumstances as I do now, also special rates for my lumber, etc. with any other little accommodations which I now enjoy as Prest. of our road. . . . I have given too much labor and too much land, etc. for Depots, etc. to give it all up, to pass into the hands of another concern, who will deprive me of all I have earned in aiding the construction of the F. & H. R.R."—HHC, Flint to WWC, NB, Jan. 12, 1868.

15 Crapo, *Crapo*, p. 166; Michigan, Auditor General's Office, "Compilation of the Annual Reports of the Railroad Corporations in the State of Michigan for the year 1868," in Michigan, *Joint Documents, 1869,* pp. 39–40; Michigan, Railroad Commission, *Aids, Gifts, Grants and Donations to Railroads, including Outline of Development and Successions in Titles to Railroads in Michigan* (Lansing, 1919), pp. 40–41.

16 HHC, Adrian to WWC, NB, Aug. 7, 1864; HHC, Coldwater to WWC, NB, Oct. 22, 1864; HHC, Lansing to WWC, NB, Mar. 2, 1865.

17 HHC, Flint to WWC, NB, Sept. 28, 1863, Feb. 6, 22, 1864.

18 *Detroit Advertiser & Tribune,* May 23, 1864; HHC, Buffalo, N.Y. to WWC, NB, June 20, 1864.

19 H. H. H. C. Smith, Flint to WWC, NB, Feb. 4, 1865; HHC, Lansing to WWC, NB, Mar. 19, 1865; H. H. H. C. Smith, Detroit to WWC, NB, Jan. 16, 1866.

20 HHC, Adrian to WWC, NB, Aug. 7, 1864; HHC, Lansing to WWC, NB, Mar. 18, 20, 1865; HHC, Flint to WWC, NB, Aug. 16, Sept. 5, Nov. 1, 1865, Sept. 17, 1867; HHC, Flint to H. H. H. C. Smith, Detroit, Jan. 22, July 18, 25, 1866, Apr. 20, 1867.

21 HHC, Flint to WWC, NB, Dec. 7, 1863, Nov. 25, 1864, Aug. 16, 1865; HHC, Lansing to WWC, NB, Mar. 2, 1865.

22 HHC, Flint to WWC, NB, Apr. 27, Aug. 10, 1865; H. H. H. C. Smith, Detroit to WWC, NB, Jan. 16, 1866.

23 HHC, Flint to WWC, NB, Dec. 19, 1863; HHC, Lansing to WWC, NB, Mar. 2, 1865.

24 HHC, Flint to WWC, NB, Mar. 18, 1862, Oct. 14, Dec. 19, 1863, Feb. 22, Mar. 18, 1864.

25 *Detroit Free Press,* Mar. 5, 1864.

26 Diary, 1864; HHC, Flint to WWC, NB, July 9, 1864.

27 *Detroit Free Press,* July 16, Aug. 25, 1864.

28 HHC, Lansing to WWC, NB, Mar. 2, 20, 1865.

29 HHC, Flint to WWC, NB, Feb. 12, 1860, July 24, 1859.

30 See for example HHC, Flint to WWC, NB, Sept. 9, 1859, Dec. 23, 1860, Jan. 11, Apr. 4, 1861, Mar. 18, 1864, Sept. 5, 19, 1865, June 20, 1866, Aug. 10, 1867.

31 HHC, Flint to WWC, NB, Oct. 25, 1860, Mar. 6, 1864, Mar. 23, 1862, Nov. 9, 1862, Nov. 27, 1860.

32 HHC, Flint to WWC, NB, Nov. 11, 1861, Feb. 5, 1863.

33 HHC, Flint to WWC, NB, Nov. 27, 1860, Nov. 10, 1862.

CHAPTER ELEVEN

1 HHC, Washington to WWC, NB, July 2, 1865.

2 *Ibid.*

3 HHC, Flint to WWC, NB, Jan. 21, 1866; HHC, Flint to H. H. H. C. Smith, Detroit, Jan. 8, 1866; H. H. H. C. Smith, Detroit to WWC, NB, Jan. 16, 1866.

4 HHC, Flint to WWC, NB, Aug. 16, 1865; HHC, Holly to WWC, NB, Nov. 29, 1865.

5 HHC, Flint to WWC, NB, Mar. 6, May 7, 15, June 14, 18, 1866.

6 HHC, Holly to WWC, NB, Nov. 29, 1865; HHC, Flint to WWC, NB, Feb. 21, 26, Mar. 3, 1866; HHC, Flint to H. H. H. C. Smith, Detroit, Jan. 8, 22, 1866.

7 HHC, Flint to WWC, NB, Mar. 3, 6, 1866.

8 HHC, Flint to WWC, NB, Mar. 6, 21, 1866.

9 HHC, Flint to WWC, NB, May 8, 15, June 14, 1866.

10 HHC, Flint to WWC, NB, June 18, 1866.

11 HHC, Flint to WWC, NB, June 26, July 20, 1866.

12 HHC, Flint to WWC, NB, Aug. 21, 1864, Mar. 29, May 7, 1866.

13 HHC, Flint to WWC, NB, June 14, 1866.

14 HHC, Holly to WWC, NB, July 9, 1866.

15 HHC, Flint to WWC, NB, Oct. 13, 1866; HHC, Marathon to WWC, NB, Oct. 16, 1866.

16 HHC, Pontiac to WWC, NB, Oct. 25, 1866; HHC, Ionia to WWC, NB, Oct. 26, 1866.

17 HHC, Flint to WWC, NB, June 20, 26, July 20, 1866, Apr. 14, 1867; HHC, Lansing to WWC, NB, Mar. 19, 1867; HHC, Flint to H. H.. H. C. Smith, Detroit, July 21, 1866.

CHAPTER TWELVE

1 HHC, Flint to WWC, NB, Sept. 17, 1865, May 15, July 7, 1866.

2 *Lansing State Republican,* July 4, 1866, clipping in the Crapo MSS; *Detroit Advertiser & Tribune,* July 21, 1866; HHC, Flint to WWC, NB, July 7, 1866; *Detroit Daily Post,* Aug. 31, 1866.

3 HHC, Flint to WWC, NB, Oct. 13, 1866; *Jackson Daily Citizen,* Oct. 4, 1866, clipping in the Crapo MSS.

4 HHC, Flint to WWC, NB, Nov. 7, Dec. 7, 1866; *Detroit Free Press,* Dec. 6, 1866.

5 *Detroit Daily Post,* Jan. 5, 10, 1867; HHC, Lansing to WWC, NB, Jan. 7, 22, 23, 27, 30, Feb. 11, Mar. 17, 1867; Dr. J. C. Willson, Lansing to WWC, NB, Jan. 31, Feb. 1, Mar. 17, 1867.

6 Michigan, *Acts, 1863, 1864, 1865.* The term "municipal" is here used to include county, city, township, and village governmental units.

7 *Detroit Daily Post,* Jan. 16, Feb. 13, 1867.

8 *Detroit Daily Post,* Jan. 22, Feb. 5, 1867; Michigan, *Senate Journal, 1867,* p. 189, *House Journal, 1867,* p. 406.

9 Fuller, *op. cit.,* II, 592–95: message of Feb. 5, 1867.

10 HHC, Lansing to WWC, NB, Feb. 5, 11, 1867; T. J. Cobb, Lansing to WWC, NB, Feb. 5, 1867.

11 Michigan, *Senate Journal, 1867,* p. 447, *House Journal, 1867,* p. 703. A review of the debates preceding the votes appears in the *Detroit Advertiser & Tribune,* Feb. 11, 13, 1867, and the *Detroit Daily Post,* Feb. 11, 12, 1867.

12 Michigan, *Senate Journal, 1867,* p. 507, *House Journal, 1867,* p. 1105.

13 Fuller, *op. cit.,* II, 597–608: message of Feb. 25, 1867.

14 T. J. Cobb, Lansing to WWC, NB, Feb. 27, 1867; *Detroit Advertiser & Tribune,* Feb. 28, Mar. 8, 1867; *Detroit Daily Post,* Mar. 1, 2, 1867.

15 HHC, Lansing to WWC, NB, Mar. 17, 1867. The attorney general's opinion, in Michigan, *Senate Documents, 1867,* No. 8, argued that the legislature, in the absence of any express prohibition in the state constitution, was omnipotent.

16 T. J. Cobb, Lansing to WWC, NB, Mar. 1, 1867; *Detroit Advertiser & Tribune,* Mar. 1, 2, 9, 12, 1867.

17 HHC, Lansing to WWC, NB, Feb. 28, 1867.

18 HHC, Lansing to WWC, NB, Mar. 17, 1867; Dr. J. C. Willson, Lansing to WWC, NB, Mar. 17, 1867.

19 T. J. Cobb, Lansing to WWC, NB, Mar. 21, 1867; Michigan, *Senate Journal, 1867,* p. 1488. One element in the failure of the attempt to override was the breakdown of a coalition between the railroad forces and those legislators interested in the passage of a large number of bills granting "swamp lands" to contractors who would undertake to build roads with the proceeds.—T. J. Cobb, Lansing to WWC, NB, Mar. 18, 1867.

20 *Detroit Daily Post,* Mar. 23, 1867; Fuller, *op. cit.,* II, 609–14: messages of Mar. 21 and 22, 1867.

21 Michigan, *Acts, 1869,* I, 89–96, Act No. 45; Fuller, *op. cit.,* II, 602; Michigan, Railroad Commission, *Aids, Gifts, Grants and Donations to Railroads, including Outline of Development and Successions in Titles to Railroads in Michigan,* p. 11; *The People v. Salem,* 20 Michigan 452 (Apr. Term, 1870); *Bay City v. State Treasurer,* 23 Michigan 499 (Oct. Term, 1871).

22 J. J. Woodman, Paw Paw, Mich. to HHC, Flint, June 22, 1868, and other letters to Crapo on the senatorial question in Box 23, Crapo MSS.

23 Fuller, *op. cit.,* II, 553–87, 617–38: messages of Jan. 2, 1867 and Jan. 6, 1869.

24 *Detroit Advertiser & Tribune,* Mar. 20, 25, 1865.

25 The commissioner's report, published in Michigan, *Joint Documents, 1868,* is important for any study of the swamp land state road question.

26 Fuller, *op. cit.,* II, 628.

27 James V. Campbell, *Outlines of the Political History of Michigan* (Detroit, 1876), p. 568.

28 HHC, Flint to WWC, NB, Jan. 23, 1866; *Detroit Advertiser & Tribune,* Jan. 10, 1867; Fuller, *op. cit.,* II, 631.

29 *Detroit Free Press,* July 24, 1869.

CHAPTER THIRTEEN

1 HHC, Flint to WWC, NB, Apr. 14, 1867; HHC, Flint to H. H. C. Smith, Detroit, Apr. 21, 1867.

2 HHC, Flint to H. H. C. Smith, Detroit, Apr. 15, 27, 1867.

3 HHC, Flint to WWC, NB, May 3, 1867; H. H. C. Smith, Detroit to WWC, NB, pencilled comment at end of HHC, Flint to H. H. C. Smith, Detroit, Apr. 21, 1867; Dr. J. C. Willson, Flint to WWC, NB, May 30, 1867.

4 HHC, Flint to WWC, NB, May 3, 1867.

5 HHC, Flint to WWC, NB, July 14, Aug. 4, 28, Sept. 9, 10, 17, 1867.

6 HHC, Flint to WWC, NB, Sept. 26, Nov. 16, Dec. 17, 22, 1867.

7 HHC, Flint to WWC, NB, Dec. 17, 1867.

8 HHC, Flint to H. H. H. C. Smith, Detroit, Apr. 21, 24, 25, 1868; HHC, Flint to WWC, NB, Apr. 23, 29, May 1, 14, 1868.

9 HHC, Flint to WWC, NB, July 14, Aug. 18, Sept. 9, 26, 1867.

10 HHC, Flint to WWC, NB, Mar. 5, 15, 29, Apr. 19, 29, 1868.

11 HHC, Flint to WWC, NB, Mar. 17, 1868.

12 HHC, Flint to WWC, NB, July 9, Oct. 23, 1868.

13 HHC, Flint to WWC, NB, Oct. 16, 21, Dec. 15, 1868.

14 HHC, Flint to WWC, NB, Mar. 15, May 10, Aug. 5, Oct. 11, Dec. 11, 1868, Apr. 1, 1869; HHC, Flint to H. H. H. C. Smith, Detroit, Dec. 23, 1868.

15 HHC, Flint to WWC, NB, June 21, July 31, Sept. 25, Dec. 8, 1868; Dr. J. C. Willson, "Synopsis of the Case of the Late Henry H. Crapo, Esq., Governor of Michigan," in the Crapo MSS.

16 *Detroit Advertiser & Tribune,* July 24, 1869.

17 HHC, Flint to WWC, NB, July 9, 1869; *Detroit Daily Post,* July 24, 1869.

18 *Lansing State Republican,* July 29, 1869; *The Mercury* (New Bedford, Mass.), Aug. 3, 1869, clippings in the Crapo MSS; HHC, Flint to WWC, NB, Aug. 18, 1868; Henry Howland Crapo [II], *The Story of William Wallace Crapo, 1830–1926* (Boston, 1942), p. 87; Franklin Ellis, *History of Genesee County, Michigan* (Philadelphia, 1879), p. 134; Hotchkiss, *op. cit.,* p. 93.

CHAPTER FOURTEEN

1 HHC, Flint to WWC, NB, May 3, 1859, Nov. 25, 1860, Nov. 22, 1863, May 10, 1868; *Lansing State Republican,* Aug. 20, 1868, July 29, 1869, clippings in the Crapo MSS.

2 HHC, Flint to WWC, NB, Oct. 13, 1861.

3 Fuller, *op. cit.,* II, 536; *Address Delivered by Hon. Henry H. Crapo, Governor of Michigan, Before the Central Michigan Agricultural Society, at their Sheep-Shearing Exhibition, held at the Agricultural College Farm, on Thursday, May 24th, 1866* (Lansing, 1866); *The Cultivator & Country Gentleman* (Albany), Mar. 4, 1869, clipping in the Crapo MSS.

4 James C. Mills, *History of Saginaw County, Michigan* (Saginaw, 1918), p. 413.

5 HHC, Flint to WWC, NB, May 23, 1858.

6 HHC, Flint to James Arnold and Oliver Prescott, NB, Feb. 25, 1860; HHC, Flint to WWC, NB, Apr. 8, 1862.

7 HHC, Flint to WWC, NB, Mar. 31, 1862.

8 HHC, Washington, D.C. to WWC, NB, July 2, 1865; HHC, Flint to WWC, NB, Aug. 16, 1865.

9 *Detroit Free Press,* July 24, 1869; *Lansing State Republican,* July 29, 1869, clipping in the Crapo MSS.

10 HHC, Flint to WWC, NB, Nov. 29, 1858.

11 HHC, Flint to WWC, NB, May 21, 1859.

12 HHC, Flint to James Arnold and Oliver Prescott, NB, Feb. 25, 1860.

13 HHC, Flint to WWC, NB, June 29, 1862.

INDEX

Albany, N.Y., 75–78, 83

Arnold, James: provides capital, 19, 20, 23, 50, 53, 63, 88; wants accounting, 85; sells interest in mills, 95–98; sells interest in lands, 97, 207–209

Baldwin, H. P., 146–147, 149, 151, 153, 210–211

Banking: wildcat, 105, 112–113; Crapo's views on, 249

Barter, 52, 63

Blair, Austin, 142, 146, 151, 162, 164

Burrell, George W., mill foreman, 40, 41, 56–57

Chandler, Zachariah, 146, 153, 224–225

Chase, Zachariah, clerk, 56–57, 85, 233

Christy, H. P., 241

Commercial Mutual Marine Insurance Co., 1, 17, 30

Crapo, Henry H.: in New Bedford, 1–2, 13–25; family, 14, 16, 201; real estate dealings, 15, 18–21, 97, 100–101; buys pine lands, 22, 30–31, 207–209, 241n; wealth of, 22–23, 154, 204, 238, 241; moves to Flint, 54–55;

drills for salt, 126–128; illness, 168, 211–212, 231, 236, 239–240; death, 240

Crapo, Henry H., lumber business: partnership arrangements, 22–24, 88–91, 95–98, 202–203; mode of operation, 25, 31–38, 102, 115–117; doubts wisdom of, 26–27, 55; sawmills, 36–37, 39–43, 45, 90, 93–94, 191, 205–206, 209, 232–233, 239; financing, 23–24, 30, 37, 50, 52–53, 62–64, 72, 88, 94–95, 111, 118, 247–248; general store, 62, 118; accounts, 85–86, 91–95, 260, 267; plans to sell out, 101, 125–126, 198, 200–202, 204, 206, 236–238, 239; prospers, 120–122, 188, 204–205, 232; planing mill, 190–191; value in 1866, 202. *See also* Driggs tract, Labor, Logging, Lumber, Personnel policy, Sawmill operation, Wages

Crapo, Henry H., political career: in New Bedford, 15, 16, 106; mayor of Flint, 107–108; state senator, 137–144; as campaigner, 138, 155–160, 211; proposed for governor, 144–149; elected, 160; re-elected, 211; proposed for U.S. senator, 224; opposes pardoning, 227–228

DESIGNED BY RICHARD KINNEY

SET IN BASKERVILLE AND ALTERNATE GOTHIC NO. 2

PRINTED ON WARREN'S OLDE STYLE ANTIQUE

JACKET, END PAPERS AND ILLUSTRATIONS IN OFFSET
BY CUSHING-MALLOY, INC., ANN ARBOR, MICHIGAN

BOUND IN HOLLISTON'S ROXITE CLASS C

PRINTED AND BOUND BY
H. WOLFF BOOK MANUFACTURING CO., NEW YORK

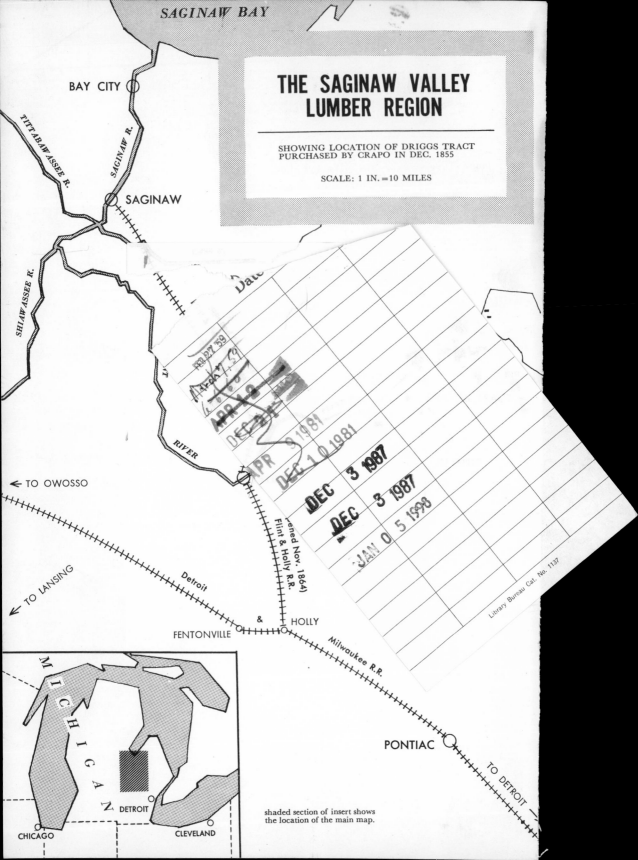

SAGINAW BAY

BAY CITY

TITTABAWASSEE R.

SAGINAW R.

SAGINAW

SHIAWASSEE R.

THE SAGINAW VALLEY LUMBER REGION

SHOWING LOCATION OF DRIGGS TRACT
PURCHASED BY CRAPO IN DEC. 1855

SCALE: 1 IN. = 10 MILES

RIVER

← TO OWOSSO

← TO LANSING

Detroit

(Opened Nov. 1864)
Flint & Holly R.R.

&   HOLLY
FENTONVILLE

Milwaukee R.R.

PONTIAC

TO DETROIT

MICHIGAN

DETROIT

CHICAGO

CLEVELAND

shaded section of insert shows
the location of the main map.